HISTORIES

I.B.TAURIS SHORT HISTORIES

I.B.Tauris Short Histories is an authoritative and elegantly written new series which puts a fresh perspective on the way history is taught and understood in the twenty-first century. Designed to have strong appeal to university students and their teachers, as well as to general readers and history enthusiasts, *I.B.Tauris Short Histories* comprises a novel attempt to bring informed interpretation, as well as factual reportage, to historical debate. Addressing key subjects and topics in the fields of history, the history of ideas, religion, classical studies, politics, philosophy and Middle East studies, the series seeks intentionally to move beyond the bland, neutral 'introduction' that so often serves as the primary undergraduate teaching tool. While always providing students and generalists with the core facts that they need to get to grips with the essentials of any particular subject, *I.B.Tauris Short Histories* goes further. It offers new insights into how a topic has been understood in the past, and what different social and cultural factors might have been at work. It brings original perspectives to bear on manner of its current interpretation. It raises questions and – in its extensive bibliographies – points to further study, even as it suggests answers. Addressing a variety of subject┄ ┄ ┄reater degree of depth than is often found in comparable series, y┄ ┄ ┄compact handbook form, *I.B.Tauris Sh┄ ┄ ┄ns with an edge'. In combining questi┄ ┄ ┄nformed history writing, it brings histo┄ ┄ ┄plex and globalized digital age.

www.short ┄┄┄

'Michael Fisher's *A Short History of the Mughal Empire* is a long overdue scholarly study of the Mughal period in early modern India. There has been no comparably cohesive study of the empire since the great John Richards brought out *The Mughal Empire* in the early 1990s. While it is described as a "Short History," Fisher's study is surprisingly comprehensive and detailed, successfully engaging much of the recent scholarship in Mughal studies and braiding it into a highly accessible and thorough narrative of imperial events. Fisher pays particular attention to creating a rich and thorough context for historical events; for example, his detailed exploration of early sixteenth century Hindustani politics and culture creates a richly contextualized setting for early Mughal raids and military conquest. Unlike earlier narrative histories of the Mughals, including that of Richards, Fisher's work is sensitive to the critical political role played by women of the dynasty. He also proves willing to engage the highly complex religious identities and performances of the Mughals. Although this is essentially a political narrative, Fisher displays consistent interest in the power of language and poetry, of art and architecture. One of the most valuable sections of the book, and a great boon to teachers and their students, is the final chapter, "Contested Meanings." Having very efficiently wrapped up the last hundred years of the disintegrating empire, Fisher halts the narrative flow to explore the meaning and debates of Mughal historiography, beginning with the writings of Mughal chroniclers and memoirists, moving to that of their contemporaries in the region and in Europe, into the period of the Raj and even engaging the treatment of the Mughals by post-independence historians, briefly tracking intellectual movements in the historiography of the modern nations of Pakistan and India. Fisher's book will become the go-to resource for scholars of the Mughals and early modern South Asia and it holds great value for historians of Empire and the pre-modern Islamic world. A natural niche for Fisher's book will be in the classroom, where the Short History will offer undergraduate and graduate students a lively yet exacting narrative of the Mughal dynasty, critically and intellectually examined. Fisher's study is nuanced and insightful, and written in an authoritative but contemporary and engaging style that powerfully enhances its readability.'

Lisa Balabanlilar, Associate Professor of History, Rice University

'Professor Fisher has done a great scholarly service by producing a comprehensive, up-to-date and insightful survey of Mughal history. It is detailed enough in its mention of sources, personalities, and concepts that serious students of the Mughal Empire can benefit from it. Yet it is also eminently readable, making it accessible to the general reader.'

A. Azfar Moin, Assistant Professor of Religious Studies, University of Texas at Austin

'This erudite and accessible book wonderfully combines Michael Fisher's decades-long experience thinking about the Mughals with the best insights of recent scholarship on the Mughal Empire. What emerges is a rich picture of a dynamic and evolving imperial state and society, shaped as much by contingency as by deliberate policies. A must-read for anyone interested in the Mughal Empire.'

Munis D. Faruqui, Associate Professor of South Asia Studies, University of California at Berkeley

A Short History of . . .

A Short History of the American Civil War   Paul Anderson (Clemson University)

A Short History of the American Revolutionary War   Stephen Conway (University College London)

A Short History of Ancient China   Edward L Shaughnessy (University of Chicago)

A Short History of Ancient Greece   P J Rhodes, FBA (Durham University)

A Short History of Ancient Rome   Andrew Wallace-Hadrill (University of Cambridge)

A Short History of the Anglo-Saxons   Henrietta Leyser (University of Oxford)

A Short History of the Byzantine Empire   Dionysios Stathakopoulos (King's College London)

A Short History of the Celts   Alex Woolf (University of St Andrews)

A Short History of Christian Spirituality   Edward Howells (Heythrop College, University of London))

A Short History of the Crimean War   Trudi Tate (University of Cambridge)

A Short History of English Renaissance Drama   Helen Hackett (University College London)

A Short History of the English Revolution and the Civil Wars   David J Appleby (University of Nottingham)

A Short History of the Etruscans   Corinna Riva (University College London)

A Short History of the Hundred Years War   Michael Prestwich (Durham University)

A Short History of Irish Independence   J J Lee (New York University)

A Short History of the Italian Renaissance   Virginia Cox (New York University)

A Short History of the Korean War   Allan R Millett (University of New Orleans)

A Short History of Medieval Christianity   G R Evans (University of Cambridge)

A Short History of Medieval English Mysticism   Vincent Gillespie (University of Oxford)

A Short History of the Minoans   John Bennet (University of Sheffield)

A Short History of the Mongols George Lane (SOAS, University of London)

A Short History of the Mughal Empire Michael H Fisher (Oberlin College)

A Short History of Muslim Spain Alex J Novikoff (Rhodes College, Memphis)

A Short History of New Kingdom Egypt Robert Morkot (University of Exeter)

A Short History of the New Testament Halvor Moxnes (University of Oslo)

A Short History of Nineteenth-Century Philosophy Joel Rasmussen (University of Oxford)

A Short History of the Normans Leonie Hicks (Canterbury Christ Church University)

A Short History of the Ottoman Empire Baki Tezcan (University of California, Davis)

A Short History of the Phoenicians Mark Woolmer (Durham University)

A Short History of the Reformation Helen Parish (University of Reading)

A Short History of the Renaissance in Northern Europe Malcolm Vale (University of Oxford)

A Short History of Revolutionary Cuba Antoni Kapcia (University of Nottingham)

A Short History of the Risorgimento Nick Carter (Australian Catholic University, Sydney)

A Short History of the Russian Revolution Geoffrey Swain (University of Glasgow)

A Short History of the Spanish Civil War Julián Casanova (University of Zaragoza)

A Short History of the Spanish Empire Felipe Fernández-Armesto (University of Notre Dame) and José Juan López-Portillo (Pembroke College, Oxford)

A Short History of Transatlantic Slavery Kenneth Morgan (Brunel University)

A Short History of Venice and the Venetian Empire Maria Fusaro (University of Exeter)

A Short History of the Vikings Clare Downham (University of Liverpool)

A Short History of the Wars of the Roses David Grummitt (University of Kent)

A Short History of the Weimar Republic Colin Storer (University of Nottingham)

A SHORT HISTORY OF THE MUGHAL EMPIRE

Michael H. Fisher

I.B. TAURIS

LONDON · NEW YORK

Published in 2016 by
I.B.Tauris & Co. Ltd
London • New York
www.ibtauris.com

Copyright © 2016 Michael H. Fisher

ISBN: 978 1 84885 872 5 (HB)
ISBN: 978 1 84885 873 2 (PB)
e ISBN: 978 0 85772 976 7

A full CIP record for this book is available from the British Library
A full CIP record is available from the Library of Congress

Library of Congress Catalog Card Number: available

Typeset by Freerange
Printed and bound in Great Britain by T.J. International, Padstow, Cornwall

Contents

List of Charts, Maps and Illustrations   ix

Note on Transliteration and Names   xiii

Introduction: The Mughal Empire's Dynamic Composition in   1
       Time and Space

Timeline   11

Part I: The Central Asian and Indian Origins of the Mughal Empire, 1526–40, 1555–6

Chapter 1: Babur until His Conquest of North India in 1526   15

Chapter 2: Indians and Emperor Babur Create the Mughal   34
       Empire, 1526–30

Chapter 3: Emperor Humayun and Indians, 1530–40,   56
       1555–6

Part II: Establishment of the Mughal Empire under Emperor Akbar, 1556–1605

Chapter 4: Emperor Akbar Makes Himself the Center of the   73
       Mughal Empire

Chapter 5: Emperor Akbar and His Core Courtiers Build the   93
       Mughal Administration and Army

Chapter 6: Emperor Akbar's Courts, Ideologies and Wars,   108
       by Main Capital

Part III: The Mughal Empire Established, 1605–1707

Chapter 7:   Emperor Jahangir and the Efflorescence of the   143
             Imperial Court, 1605–27

Chapter 8:   Emperor Shah Jahan and Building Up the Mughal   166
             Empire, 1628–58/66

Chapter 9:   Expanding the Frontiers and Facing Challenges   186
             under Emperor 'Alamgir, 1658–1707

Part IV: The Fragmentation and Memory of the Mughal Empire, 1707–the Present

Chapter 10: The Thinning of the Empire, 1707–1857   209

Chapter 11: Contested Meanings of the Mughal Empire into   226
             the Twenty-first Century

Notes   241
Bibliography   251
Index   263

List of Charts, Maps and Illustrations

(unless otherwise noted, the work of the author)

Cover: Emperor Jahangir (r. 1605–27) Shooting Poverty While Astride the Globe, attributed to Abu-al-Hasan, *c.* 1620–25 (detail). Courtesy Los Angeles County Museum of Art (M.75.4.28) www.LACMA.org

Charts

Chart 1: Mughal Emperors (with Reign) and Imperial Princes   7
(to 1707)

Chart 2: Later Mughal Emperors (with Reign)   215

Maps

Map 1:   Babur's World to 1526   16

Map 2:   South Asian Macro-regions and Main Physical Features   35

Map 3:   Major States and Regions as of 1526   46

Map 4:   Humayun's World during His Indian Reigns   60

Map 5:   Akbar's World on Accession, 1556   75

Map 6:   Fatehpur   119

Map 7:   Plan of 'Exalted Fort,' known as 'Red Fort'   177

Map 8: Major States and Regions, 'Alamgir's Reign 189

Map 9: Padshahi Mosque and Lahore Fort Palace Complex 193

Illustrations

Tomb of the Emperor Babur, Kabul, c. 1844 55

Sher Mandal, Built by Sher Shah, Site of Humayun's Library and 68
Fatal Fall

Tomb of Maham Anaga and Adham Khan, Delhi, c. 1562 74

Agra, from South West, Engraved by J. Walker from Painting by 110
W. Hodges, 1793

Humayun's Tomb, Delhi, c. 1570 110

Tomb of Salim Chishti in Fatehpur, Main Mosque, c. 1581 118

Rare Partly Surviving Fatehpur Interior Wall Fresco (detail) 121

Anup Talao with Columned Building in Background 123

Columned Building Today and Transected 123

A Square Silver Rupee of Emperor Akbar with 'Allah-o-Akbar' 126
and 'Jalal-ud-Din,' 33rd Regnal Year, 996–7 H (1587–9 CE)

Prince Salim Hunting (detail), by Muhammad Nasir al-Munshi, 145
1600–1604 (Allahabad period)

Akbar's Tomb, Sikandara, outside Delhi, c. 1890 148

Jahangir's Coins with Zodiac Images and Bust with Wineglass 150

Caravanserai Gateway, Commissioned by Nur Jahan, Punjab, 160
c. 1620

Silver Rupee with Nur Jahan and Jahangir's Names 161

Tomb of I'timad-ud-Daula and Asmat Begum and Interior, 165
Commissioned by Nur Jahan

Imperial Farman with Shah Jahan's Handprint 168

Canopied Jharoka, Lahore 169

Emperor Shah Jahan (detail), attributed to Bichitr, c. 1650 170

The 'Illuminated Tomb,' Known as the 'Taj Mahal,' Today 176
and Transection

List of Charts, Maps and Illustrations

Cascading Perfumed Water (left panel) and Glazed Tiles (right panel) Adorned Shahjahanabad Palace Complex — 178

Jami' Mosque, Shahjahanabad, *c.* 1891 — 178

The Moti Mosque, Red Fort, Shahjahanabad, 1890 — 192

Cannon from Bijapur Fort, *c.* 1688 — 200

Emperor 'Alamgir, As Remembered (detail), *c.* 1725 — 202

Prince Mu'azzam, *c.* 1675 (detail) — 210

Emperor Muhammad Shah (detail), Presiding over Spring Festival of Colors (Holi), *c.* 1725–50 — 218

A Sepoy Matchlock Infantryman, by W. Hodges, 1793 — 220

Emperor Shah 'Alam II (detail), Blinded but on Reconstructed Peacock Throne, by Khair Ullah Musawir, 1801 — 223

Shahjahanabad, Last Mughal Domain, *c.* 1857 — 223

Empty Diwan-i Khas, Shahjahanabad, *c.* 1890 — 225

Indian Prime Ministers Deliver the Independence Day Address to the Nation from the Lahore Gate of Shahjahanabad's Red Fort — 237

Note on Transliteration and Names

Adapting Persian and Indic words into English requires simplification. Except in direct quotations, this book does not use diacritical marks (since they distract most readers and experts will recognize the original word). Since the Persian letters *ayn* and *hamza* have no English alphabetical equivalents, they appear respectively as single opening (') and closing (') quotation marks. On first appearance, non-English terms are italicized. Most people who appear in this book had multiple names at different points in their lives. This book features the most prominent name, but indicates others on that person's first mention.

Introduction

THE MUGHAL EMPIRE'S DYNAMIC COMPOSITION IN TIME AND SPACE

> Mogul: An important, influential, or dominant person; an autocrat. Now chiefly ... a business or (esp. in recent use) media magnate.
>
> *Oxford English Dictionary*

THE IMPERIAL DYNASTY AND ITS SUBJECT INDIAN PEOPLE AND LANDS

The Mughal Empire consisted of the contested, cooperative and creative interactions between the imperial dynasty and people with a vast array of cultures in the various Indian lands currently under its rule. The Empire endured for three centuries. At its peak, the Empire contained 3.2 million square kilometers, extending across most of the subcontinent, and 150 million diverse people (roughly a third the size of Europe and double its total population). The Empire rose at its peak to be humanity's most powerful and richest state (perhaps excepting China's contemporary empire) with a vast military force and nearly a quarter of the global GDP.[1] During the Empire's final century-and-a-half, however, it fragmented: its administration faltered, its core supporters broke away, and Indian and European challengers dismantled it. Even as the Empire rapidly lost virtually all its territory, however, successor states and rising imperial powers—both Indian and European—continued to recognize nominal Mughal sovereignty down to 1857.

1

The consequences and significance of the Empire continue in South Asia and internationally, with multi-faceted meanings (see epigram). Original sources from that time reveal their author's understandings of the Empire, which often contrast with ours. Thus, even a short history of the Mughal Empire leads to insights about the nature of imperial processes, especially in Asia and in the Islamic world, about a key transitional period for South Asia and its many people and cultures, and about relations among Asians and the globally expanding colonial powers of Christian Europe.

Empires all share some characteristics, but every empire is unique in its specifics. If an empire means a state incorporating and ruling over more than one people, then the Mughal Empire certainly fits. But this Empire was also distinctive in many significant ways.

The Empire had improbable origins: a family of Muslim Central Asian warriors led two separate invasions (1526, 1555) and then conquered and settled in north India, extensively engaging in complex ways with Hindus, Muslims and other Indians, thus producing the Mughal Empire. This dynasty's male founders claimed imperial sovereignty, even when not ruling any territory. They invaded and ruled not their long-remembered Central Asian homeland, but rather initially alien lands and people. Revealing their self-identify as leading figures in the larger world of Islam, they continued throughout their reign to highlight (in varying degrees and ways) their Muslim identity and to honor new Sunni and Shi'i Muslim immigrants from Central Asia, Iran, Afghanistan, Ottoman Turkey and Arabia.

Over time, the ethnic identity 'Mughal' changed. Originally 'Mughal' was the Persian term for uncultured (but fierce) Mongols, but it eventually became the most widely used term for Babur's dynasty in India. While the dynasty featured its Sunni male Central Asian patrilineage, it also included, by marriage, many women with Shi'i and Hindu ancestries. Further, the imperial clan remained only a tiny proportion even of the imperial elite—the vast bulk of the Empire consisted of many other people and cultures. Over nearly two centuries, this dynasty, and other immigrants and Indians who formed the imperial elite, created a highly sophisticated court culture and a vast military and civil establishment. Both these attracted and employed many South Asians directly or indirectly and also drew acceptance and revenues from most of the rest.

The Mughal Empire was thus never an indigenous national empire with a uniform elite and a predominantly mono-ethnic army. Rather, the dynasty drew eclectically from a range of cultures and people. Hence, a continued tension remained almost throughout the dynasty's history about where sovereignty lay. For most of the Empire, all males who were closely related to the current emperor shared his sovereignty, and could potentially themselves emerge as emperor. This explicitly invoked the Mongol and Turkish models of their Central Asian world-conquering ancestors. Most Mughal emperors parceled out some of their authority to sons or brothers, and willed that their surviving sons should divide the Empire after their deaths. But in tension with these Central Asian imperial traditions were the Islamic and Indic concepts that, once enthroned, the incumbent emperor alone held semi-divine (or divine) sovereignty. Each of the first five emperors asserted, in one form or another, that he was the Islamic millennial sovereign.[2] Even thereafter, emperors claimed that they alone were destined by God to rule the entire world, or at least the Muslim or South Asian parts of it. Further, various emperors projected themselves as objects of worship, in the mode of Sufi saints and Hindu deities. When Europeans arrived, the dynasty incorporated Christian symbols of divine authority as well, particularly through art.

The Mughal Empire also remained contingent on forces and events beyond its control. Most printed maps (alas, including in this book) give the impression of the Empire as a two-dimensional static entity, with a uniform internal system of laws and with fixed and policed borders. More suggestively, we should envision the Empire as a dynamic process, with administrative, military and cultural layers, that over time varied in depth and extended and contracted in extent.[3] Continuing this metaphor, in some places and time periods, this layering was quite dense, since the imperial administration extended deeply into local society down to the level of individual fields, the military had an effective coercive dominance, and the emperor's authority prevailed with relatively few serious challenges. Such conditions largely existed, for instance, in most of the territories within the Mughal core provinces from the mid-sixteenth through the late seventeenth centuries.

But these imperial processes were always uneven. The Empire constantly faced resistance and repeated rebellions, among its core elite and also on its internal and external frontiers. There were occasional and persistent thin spots where imperial armies might overcome local opposition, but imperial administration had little control and Mughal culture had little appeal. There were also gaps, especially in heavily forested areas, even within the Mughal core or in newly conquered provinces. Similarly, the relationships between the Empire and various individuals were also lumpy, even in the Mughal heartland, with some people having thick administrative and ideological bonds to the state, while others very weak ones, or none at all.

Further, the Empire repeatedly faced fragmentation. Each emperor tried to keep the Empire intact and also protect his sons from each other by proposing ways to divide it internally. At virtually every imperial succession, some claimants sought to split the Empire apart, before the one triumphant successor pulled it together. Over the dynasty's final century, the imperial process was still widespread but very thin, extending over territories where Mughal sovereignty was recognized only nominally since the imperial center could assert no substantial administrative or military control. Thus, the Mughal Empire was more of a composite and dynamic process than a stable and static system.

In terms of South Asian history, the Mughal Empire was also distinctive, coming at a transitional time and including a complex combination of external and indigenous personnel as well as cultures. Throughout its history, South Asia has usually remained divided among regionally based states. The Mughal Empire made itself the largest and most powerful state that South Asia had yet seen. But the majority of the Empire's core officials were always either ethnically diverse immigrants, or descendants of recent immigrants, especially from Central Asia, Iran, or Afghanistan, who valued that external origin as a vital part of their identity. Nonetheless, the Empire also incorporated many local rulers into its military-administrative order. Thus, a minority of the Empire's high officials were identified, and identified themselves, as Hindus or long-settled Muslims from a particular region within South Asia. For example, for about a century, Hindu royal clans based in north India joined the core imperial cadre, supplying wives and service to successive emperors, yet always held a distinct identity and role there. But before and after that, these clans stood largely apart from the Empire. Especially over the seventeenth century, substantial numbers of men from central India entered imperial service, although most felt alienated there. Thus, the limits of the imperial domain constantly fluctuated.

While the Empire remained land-based, it became ever more integrated with the burgeoning European-based world system of trade and colonialism, with profound positive and negative consequences. From the sixteenth century onward, various Europeans went to the imperial court seeking favors, but also to attempt to convince the emperor of the superiority of Christian beliefs and European culture. The imperial center selectively adapted aspects of European culture, and employed some Europeans in its service. European imports of bullion, military technology, and new crops and diseases (particularly from the Americas) affected the imperial economy. Mughal emperors sought European protection on the seas and, during the dynasty's last century, as regents. The British Empire in India in many ways modeled itself on, as well as contrasted itself with, the Mughal Empire. The independent states of India, Pakistan and Bangladesh have all selected national symbols from the Empire. Thus, from the Mughal Empire's origins down to today, South Asians, Europeans and others have represented it in shifting ways.

Like all the Tauris *Short Histories*, this book presents crucial representative events and themes in a chronological historical narrative that incorporates the latest contributions from a range of scholars. My goal as author is to engage a wide array of readers with the Mughal Empire, intending to encourage them to explore more extensively by suggesting more focused studies in areas of their particular interest, especially through the final chapter, reference notes and Bibliography. Discussion of many of the central issues and unresolved questions that fascinate today's specialists in the field arise in the course of this book. Readers more familiar with academic studies of the Empire will recognize how I have tried to contribute to these ongoing discussions.

STRUCTURING THE BOOK

The Mughal Empire encompasses a vast topic: geographically spanning almost the entire Indian subcontinent, chronologically covering over three centuries, and internally including a vast array of people and their complex interactions. To organize all this into a short history, the book explores selected themes within its general narrative. As in the Empire's own official histories, and also in contemporary elite and popular understanding, the chapters use imperial reigns for periodization. However, the themes of long-term cultural, social and political developments and also of contested innovations and transitions integrate the book as a whole.

Chapter 1 considers the multiple origins of the Mughal Empire which combined a Central Asian dynasty with Indian people and lands. The founding emperor, Babur, particularly celebrated his status as descendant and heir to earlier Mongol and Turkman 'world-conquerors.' But Babur spent his lifetime frustrated in his efforts to recover his ancestral lands in Central Asia. Further, while Babur described India as a foreign and largely unknown land, he also claimed as his ancestral heritage the lands beyond the Khyber Pass as far as Delhi.

We turn in Chapter 2 to the complex lands, cultures and people of South Asia. Some environmental and cultural features spanned the subcontinent. But never in history had the entire ecologically, culturally and socially diverse subcontinent ever been brought under a single ruler. Instead, each region had its own ecology, main language and long traditions of political autonomy. Most people followed the various traditions that outsiders have called Hinduism. But a growing number were Muslim, including recent immigrants, their settled descendants and also local converts (by the late eighteenth century, Muslims would total about a third of India's population). However, most Indian Muslims, including settled Afghans who ruled much of north India, regarded Babur as alien, even if some pragmatically supported him in their intra-ethnic conflicts.

Thus, Babur entered a complex and highly contested world in which he was only one of many contenders for power. After Babur successfully invaded in 1526, he conquered much of north India during his four-year imperial reign. But virtually none of the people living in these lands shared the Central Asian ethnic identity of Babur or his main commanders. So, he incorporated relatively few Indians into his inner circle of advisors, even Muslim Indians. His nascent regime never established very deep or enduring bonds with the landholders and people whom his military forces conquered. However, many Indians did serve in his army, administration and

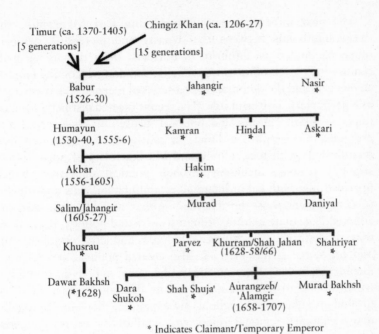

* Indicates Claimant/Temporary Emperor

Chart 1: Mughal Emperors (with Reign) and Imperial Princes (to 1707)

household; most people in north India seem to have accepted his overlordship, at least provisionally, rather than openly oppose him.

The second emperor, Humayun, had a checkered career, as we see in Chapter 3. Still largely dependent on Central Asian commanders, he sought initially to expand the Mughal Empire by conquering down the Ganges into Bengal. But that province remained uncongenial for his closest supporters. Nor did Humayun incorporate very many indigenous people into his court or upper administration. His own brothers repeatedly challenged his authority, trying to divide or take over his empire. Crucially, Indo-Afghans rose up and drove him out. Fifteen years later, briefly before his death, he reconquered much of north India. His final but largely unredeemed vision of the Mughal Empire encompassed the Gangetic plain plus Kabul and the long-lost ancestral lands of Central Asia. Thus, in Part I, the Mughal Empire remained a particularly contingent and fragile process, with little integration between the imperial dynasty and India.

The next three chapters (grouped into Part II) examine the thickening bonds between the dynasty and increasing numbers of people under its authority in northern India during the half-century-long reign of the third emperor, Akbar. Overcoming familial challengers and the domination of a series of regents, Akbar emerged as a particularly powerful ruler. His regime created distinctly Mughal imperial social, cultural and political institutions that spread and grounded the Empire in India. In particular, he innovated new relationships with local Hindu and Muslim rulers of north India's strategic regions, including through political marriages, which provided him with subordinate allies and new officials and officers to complement those he inherited. Akbar and his close advisors adapted Persianate cultural, administrative and political institutions that reconstituted the Empire's military and civil establishments and provincial governance. He also created political and religious ideologies, derived from an array of Islamic and Indic traditions, which bound to him not only his core officials but also many of his Indian subjects throughout his expanding domain. Gradually, many tributary regional rulers and landholders became imperial functionaries, paying systematically assessed revenues and receiving assigned incomes. Growing numbers of people accepted Mughal sovereignty. All these enhanced the Empire's power to govern and to extract resources from the Indian economy, which was predominantly agriculturally based.

Under Akbar, the envisioned extent of the Mughal Empire expanded to encompass the entire subcontinent, which his amanuensis defined as: 'the four corners of India, which is surrounded on three sides by the ocean.'[4] From a series of political capitals—including an entirely new one that Akbar ordered built—he sent out forces to conquer neighboring states in all directions. But Akbar did not substantially push militarily far southward against the still strong sultanates of the Deccan. Thus, by the time of Akbar's death, the Mughal Empire was well established and extensive, but it still faced instabilities inherent in its structure and environment.

The next three chapters (included in Part III) survey three distinct periods of imperial expansion and elaboration, respectively under successive emperors: Jahangir, Shah Jahan and 'Alamgir (popularly known by his princely name, Aurangzeb). Each, while a prince, had impatiently prepared to succeed to his father's throne, and then survived a bloody contest with his brothers and other male relatives to seize it. Each new emperor and his supporters then built upon the institutions and procedures from Akbar's long reign, extending and deepening the Empire. Each also developed his own distinctive court culture and ideology. The first two of these emperors, in particular, patronized the Empire's most elaborate and sophisticated artistic and architectural achievements.

Each of these three successive regimes also undertook initiatives of conquest across imperial land frontiers, which appeared almost limitlessly extendable. Kabul remained a culturally significant component of the Empire. Beyond that, Qandahar, Badakhshan and the ancestral lands of Central Asia remained part of the self-conception of the Mughal dynasty, but only intermittently under its authority. Kashmir, once conquered, became an administratively integral (if geographically isolated) part of the Empire, and various martial expeditions probed beyond that into Ladakh, nearly to the borderlands of China. To the East, Mughal incursions beyond Bengal into Assam met stiff resistance, blocking substantial imperial expansion in that direction. The greatest imperial efforts were to drive the Mughal Empire south, deeper into the Deccan and toward India's peninsula tip.

But as the Empire expanded beyond its heartland in north India, it struggled to stretch imperial ideology and its military and administrative apparatus over a much wider array of Indic cultures, spread across diverse and often challenging environments. The core of the imperial officials and commanders enlarged, but the imperial court only imperfectly amalgamated former enemy commanders and rulers. Governance and control over the entire subcontinent ultimately proved beyond the capacity of the Empire to sustain. Indeed, from the late seventeenth century onward, various groups in the subject population stopped serving Mughal imperial interests, even if they still nominally accepted the sovereignty of the emperor. By the 1707 death of 'Alamgir—who spent the last quarter century of his reign fighting futilely in the Deccan—many of the Empire's earlier strengths had dissipated.

In contrast to these territorial ambitions, an oceanic empire remained only a highly speculative part of the imperial vision. No Mughal emperor made substantial efforts to create a seagoing navy, even as the armed ships of the Ottomans and various Europeans encroached on the Empire's coasts. Nonetheless, economic, technological and cultural exchanges between the Empire and the rest of the globe proliferated, with diverse unforeseen consequences.

Chapter 10 begins the book's final part by tracing the century-and-a-half of imperial fragmentation under a series of weak Mughal emperors, who contrast with the earlier so-called 'Great Mughals.' Yet, such was the Mughal dynasty's cultural power that it remained on the throne, symbolically acknowledged as legal sovereign by many warlords, subjects and invaders, both Asian and European. The book concludes with Chapter 11's analysis of how Indian, Pakistani, Bangladeshi and Western historians, commentators and politicians have regarded the Mughal Empire from its origin to the present. Through this volume, readers will find ways to pursue their own special interests and themselves advance our collective understanding of the fascinating Mughal Empire.

Timeline

1494	Babur inherits Fergana
1504–26	Babur rules in Kabul
1526–30	Babur wins battle of Panipat and successfully invades north India and rules as Mughal Emperor
1530–40	Humayun's first reign ends with him driven from India
1540–45	rule of Sher Shah Suri
1555–6	Humayun's reconquest and second reign in India
1556–1605	Akbar's reign
1562	Akbar emerges from regency and begins policy of Rajput marriages
1566–	creation of new land revenue system
1571–85	Fatehpur-Sikri as new capital
1574–	creation of jagir-mansabdar system
1579	circulation of the document recognizing Akbar's religious authority
1605–27	Jahangir's reign
1611–	rise of Nur Jahan
1628–58	Shah Jahan's reign
1636	treaty of submission by Golkonda and Bijapur
1638	opening of the 'Taj Mahal'
1639–	Shahjahanabad as new capital
1658–66	Shah Jahan imprisoned
1658–1707	'Alamgir's reign
1664, 1670	Shivaji captures Surat
1686–7	'Alamgir defeats Bijapur and Golkonda
1707–12	Bahadur Shah's reign
1713	Jahandar's reign
1713–19	Farrukh-siyar's reign

11

1719	Rafi-ud-Darjat's reign
1719	Shah Jahan II's reign
1719–48	Muhammad Shah's reign
1739	invasion of Nadir Shah
1747–	invasions of Ahmad Shah Durrani, culminating in the battle of Panipat (1760)
1748–54	Ahmad Shah's reign
1754–9	'Alamgir II's reign
1759–1806	Shah 'Alam II's reign
1803	British conquest of Delhi region and establishment of its resident political agent
1806–37	Akbar II's reign
1837–57	Bahadur Shah II's reign
1857	'Sepoy Mutiny' or 'First War for Indian Independence'
1862	Bahadur Shah II dies in exile in Burma

Part I

The Central Asian and Indian Origins of the Mughal Empire, 1526–40, 1555–6

1

BABUR UNTIL HIS CONQUEST OF NORTH INDIA IN 1526

Once you cross the Indus, the land, water, trees, stones, people, tribes, manners, and customs are all of the Hindustani fashion.

Babur[1]

In 1519, Babur, a Central Asian martial adventurer and current ruler of Kabul, raided India and imperiously demanded the submission of young Sultan Ibrahim of Delhi. Sultan Ibrahim's Lodi Afghan clan had for generations been settled in north India and had fought its way to rule. In anticipation, Babur named his new-born son Hindal ('Conquest of India'). Babur based his pretentious claim on the brief conquest of Delhi by his Turkish ancestor, Timur, more than a century earlier. But few Indians had any awareness of Babur and most who distantly remembered Timur's devastating predatory raid, culminating in the general massacre of Delhi's population, dreaded his memory.

Neither Babur's ultimatum nor his gift of a hawk nor his relatively small marauding war band convinced Sultan Ibrahim to surrender north India (then called Hindustan). Indeed, Ibrahim's governor in Lahore contemptuously detained and then rejected Babur's envoy without even conveying him to the Sultan or replying. Babur recorded his frustration: 'These Hindustan people, especially the Afghans, are amazingly devoid of sense and wisdom and far off the path of tactics and strategy. Neither were they able to come out and make a stand like an enemy nor did they know how to adhere

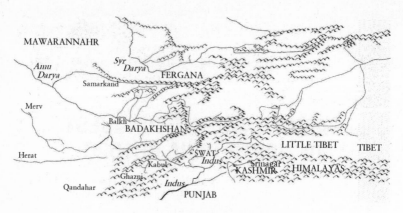

Map 1: Babur's World to 1526

to the path of amity.'[2] Nonetheless, seven years later, in 1526, Babur again invaded Hindustan, slaughtered Sultan Ibrahim's much larger (but disunited) army and seized the vast royal treasuries in Delhi and Agra—suddenly linking his family with people living in those regions, thus creating the Mughal Empire.

CHINGIZID AND TIMURID ORIGINS

Zahir-ud-Din Muhammad Babur (1483–1530) lived most of his life as a would-be emperor striving to reconquer lands he believed had been unjustly seized from his Timurid lineage by rebels (including by rival Timurids). In 1494, 11-year-old Babur inherited tenuous rule over the agriculturally prosperous mountain-fringed Fergana valley (about 130,000 square kilometers) in Mawarannahr ('the land between the rivers' Amu Darya and Syr Darya, known to Europeans as Transoxiana).[3] But he soon lost this patrimony and spent most of his youth capturing and then quickly losing cities in the region. His more lasting inheritance was his imperial ancestry from the revered founders of vast empires: the Mongol 'world conqueror' Chingiz Khan (1162–1227) and the Turkish 'world conqueror' Timur/ Tamerlane (1336–1405).

Chingiz Khan had unified hitherto contending martial Mongol clans. He then enrolled defeated Turkish and other ethnic groups into his armed host that conquered territories stretching from

16

China to Eastern Europe. As his legacy, Chingiz Khan divided his assorted followers among his four male heirs. His second official son, Chaghatai, inherited most of the Turks in Mawarannahr—their language becoming known as Chaghatai Turki. Babur descended in his mother's line from Chaghatai himself and in his father's line from Turks allotted to Chaghatai.

In Babur's day, many Mongols continued to migrate as pastoral nomads around the Central Asian steppe, largely adhering to their traditional Shamanist-Buddhist religious practices. But those Mongols who settled in the urban trading and agricultural economies of Mawarannahr tended to follow Islam. All Mongols valued Chingiz Khan's *Yasa* and *Tura* (collected moral maxims, rules and customs), as did Babur. But he also regarded most of his contemporary Mongols as uncultured and fierce but unreliable warriors, with a strong penchant for predatory looting of foe and friend.

Until the end of his career, Babur recruited Mongol followers as highly mobile and ruthlessly effective light cavalry, best posted in battle as the flanking wings of his main force. In the sweeping *tulughma* maneuver, these wings enveloped the enemy and drove its rear inward, while plundering its encampment. This maneuver would prove decisive in Babur's crucial battle of 1526 that won him north India. Yet, Babur also grimly recounted in his autobiography how his Mongol followers repeatedly rejected his discipline, betrayed his trust, and, when one of his recurrent defeats appeared imminent, looted his supplies and dead and wounded followers. Babur wrote: 'Havoc and destruction have always emanated from the [Mongol] nation. Up to the present date they have rebelled against me five times—not from any particular impropriety on my part, for they have often done the same with their own khans [chiefs].'[4]

Babur even more closely traced his direct male descent from Timur, a Turk. Indeed, Babur devoted his life to emulating Timur's values and practices. Babur's dynasty would for centuries consider themselves Timurids. Timur, a brilliant field commander, had risen from relatively humble beginnings to make himself ruler of much of Central Asia, Kabul and its environs, eastern Iran and (briefly) north India as far as Delhi (youthful Babur heard of Timur's rich Delhi spoils from an aged woman villager). Timur and his largely Turkish warriors terrorized those who opposed him by sacking their cities, enslaving their men, women and children, and building towers of the skulls of those defeated in battle or executed as captives. To stabilize his regime, Timur recruited expert Irani bureaucrats who implemented the sophisticated administrative apparatus developed by Persian empires. Further, Timur married a Chingizid Mongol princess, thereby boasting the honorific *gurgan* ('son-in-law') of Chingiz Khan.

Among both Mongols and Turks, high-born women conveyed the prestige of their male ancestors to their husbands and sons. In elite households, women formed their own sphere, overlapping that of their menfolk. This women's society contained hierarchies among co-wives of different statuses, their young male and unmarried female children, poor relations and servants. While customarily not able to move as openly in the public arena as their husbands, these high-ranking wives linked their natal and their husband's families, often negotiating additional political marriage alliances. Since widows were not stigmatized and divorce and remarriage were generally acceptable in Islam and in Central Asian custom, a woman was potentially able to remain politically active over her lifetime, sometimes acting for a sequence of husbands and her sons by several of them.

Perceptive men followed the advice of the most astute of their senior womenfolk. Babur himself noted: 'For tactics and strategy, there were few women like my [widowed Mongol maternal] grandmother, Esän Dawlat Begim. She was intelligent and a good planner. Most affairs were settled with her counsel.'[5] But Babur in his memoir only occasionally mentioned his many wives or their actions, advice, or personal relationships with him. In contrast, one of Babur's daughters, Gulbadan ('Rose-Bodied') Begum, wrote a history of their family that reveals the substantial influence and agency of those elite women, their cultural values and opportunities, as well as the social constraints on them.[6] These women conveyed their domestic customs and beliefs to the female and male children they raised. Nevertheless, the formal outer worlds of politics and religion tended to be dominated by their husbands and sons.

Timur and most other Turks were relatively recent converts to Islam. They retained many pre-Islamic Central Asian traditions and also adapted many of the values and customs of Muslims coming from Iran and Arabia. As Babur's autobiography repeatedly reveals, they believed all of life was a moral struggle in which good actions, words and thoughts receive rewards and immoral ones punishment, unless expiated. Allah was graciously forgiving to sinning Muslims who resubmitted to Him—even after they broke their previous vows for previous pardons. Effective warlords and rulers, including Babur and his descendants, humbly emulated Allah in this.

Many elite Turks gave patronage to the *'ulama*—Islamic scholars. In this region, most Muslims were Sunni and followed the Hanafi school of interpretation of *Sharia* (Islamic law) which was relatively less strict than some other Sunni legal schools. Timur and Babur admired the personal constraint and piety of the 'ulama, although, as life-long warriors, they themselves did not always adhere to that model of behavior. Additionally, however, both rulers also interacted comfortably with non-Muslims and with people practicing a range of traditions that many strict 'ulama regarded as outside of orthodox Islam.

Like many other Turks and other Central Asian Muslims, Timur and Babur revered Sufi holy men who sought direct experience of the Divine, but also often engaged actively in affairs of this world. In particular, the Naqshbandi Sufi order had gained much spiritual, economic and political power in the region. Charismatic Naqshbandi *pir*s (saintly men, living or dead) guided their followers, among them both Timur and Babur, including by mystically prophesizing through dreams and visions. At several critical times, the late Naqshbandi pir Khwaja 'Ubaidullah Ahrar (d. 1490) appeared to Babur, accurately promising battlefield victory or rescue from threatening death. Babur and other devotees donated land and livestock to these Sufi orders, which pirs then used to reward their followers and intervene politically. In exchange, pirs provided advice to rulers and teachers for their sons. Further, men and women of these spiritual aristocrats intermarried with elite Turkish families, including Babur's.

In addition to more conventional Islamic practices, Babur and many other Central Asians sought to discern divine mysteries and future events through guidance from portents, astrology, auspicious coincidences, people's names, the numeric value of phrases and cryptic dreams. They consulted soothsayers who were expert interpreters of these and other signs of divine will to which the lives of humans remained inescapably subject. Both Timur and Babur lived precarious lives in which every battle involved uncertainty and high risk of death, so they frequently sought super-human interventions to protect or assist them and provide insights into their future.

While conquering and ruling by force, Timur also demonstrated his aesthetic taste and developed his court culture. Timur adorned his illustrious capital, Samarkand, with magnificent mosque architecture and also lush gardens in which the peripatetic conqueror pitched his tents. Timur attracted to his court (and sometimes seized) artists, entertainers, historians and poets of the Persian language as well as his native Turki. These courtiers celebrated martial triumphs, pleasurable arts and personal refinement as they vied for Timur's lavish patronage while trying to avoid his wrath, often fatal. He thus set standards against which later Turkish rulers, including Babur, would measure themselves and each other. Babur, in the course of his tumultuous life, thrice conquered and lost Timur's Samarkand and, at the time of his death, was considering leaving India to recapture Samarkand as the culmination of his achievements.

BABUR'S YOUTH AMONG RIVAL TIMURIDS, MONGOLS, UZBEKS, AND SAFAVIDS

Babur was not alone in claiming Timur's legacy of imperium. Central Asian tradition decreed collective sovereignty for all a ruler's recognized male descendants—rather than primogeniture where only one son, usually the eldest, inherited all. Most Central Asian rulers had multiple wives and concubines, each having a different social status and place in his affections; each of their many sons had a different rank depending on his mother's position, his relative age and accomplishments and his personal relations with his parents. Turkish rulers during their lifetime customarily assigned territories to their main sons as appanages: lands they governed and taxed to support their own courts and armies which served their father. Typically, each son sought to prove himself worthy of rule during his father's lifetime through martial feats and by building a strong following. Subsequent to (or even before) his father's death, each heir sought to expand his own inheritance by defeating his full and half-brothers, uncles and male cousins. Like other ambitious Timurids, Babur's life-long—but unfulfilled—ambition was to reconquer all of Timur's lands.

Babur's father, 'Umar Shaikh Mirza (d. 1494), had inherited precarious power over Fergana. Ruling a small patrimonial state, he spent much of his short and tumultuous life battling bellicose brothers and other male relatives, with the most prestigious and prosperous prize being nearby Samarkand. 'Umar Shaikh died suddenly in the collapse of his pigeon loft, just as he was facing dual invasions by his own elder brother and by Mongol relatives of his main wife, a Chingizid princess, Qutluq Nigar Khanum (d. 1505), who had borne Babur.

Only misfortunes among his invading relatives enabled youthful Babur to rally his father's followers, secure support from his two younger half-brothers, and thus temporarily retain his patrimony of Fergana. As Babur recalled, Fergana was only 'a smallish province,' however 'grain and fruit [were] plentiful.'[7] Although he was born there, he had no special links to the local cultivators, artisans and merchants who paid him revenues (roughly estimated rather than finely calculated). Babur valued Fergana primarily as a source of funds for his expansive ambitions, writing: 'The income of Fergana Province, if justly managed, will maintain three to four thousand [soldiers].'[8] These soldiers were mostly not from Fergana but rather men he hired with its revenues.

Throughout Babur's life, he never had a national or territorially based army. Rather, he amalgamated personal followers of various ethnicities, including former enemies and rivals who temporarily submitted to his leadership (this pattern would endure throughout the Mughal Empire). Babur's promises of military success and predatory plunder attracted to his banner a host of adventurous warriors and other independent warlords; but any setbacks or inability to reward generously meant these forces would melt away or turn against him. Such failures marked his entire youth, reducing him occasionally to only a few followers or even to life as a solitary refugee. But he pragmatically persisted: 'When one has pretensions to rule and desire for conquest, one cannot sit back and just watch if events don't go right once or twice.'[9] He self-identified as a royal warrior, but also as a cultivated prince with recognized cultural attainments.

In Babur's day, many Turks remained rustic nomadic pastoralists but others, like Babur, urbanized and aspired to refinement as connoisseurs of architecture, literature and other arts, including cuisine, music and calligraphy. Although Babur built few mosques, wherever he conquered he constructed pleasure gardens (especially in the sophisticated Persianate *charbagh* design of 'four sections' of flowers and trees divided by water channels). He personally composed 600 poems in his native Turki and in Persian—the prestigious court language. Some of his later verses were bawdy improvisations during his frequent parties drinking wine and eating *ma'jun* (a drug confection). Other poems aspired to high literary art. Late in life, he distributed copies of his best poetry to his sons, honored courtiers and neighboring rulers whom he wished to impress.[10]

Babur's most lasting literary achievement remains his innovative autobiography in Turki, now called the *Baburnama*. Such a humanistic and often self-reflective and frankly revealing written chronological record of the author's hopes, accomplishments and disappointments was almost unprecedented in Turkish culture or in the larger Islamic world. Babur evidently intended this work to inform and educate his descendants about his experiences, successes and mistakes, and how he felt personally about the events of his dramatic life. He also recorded his pleasure from high arts, like elegant calligraphy, fine cuisine, song and dance.

Rivaling the many contending Timurids in Mawarannahr were the leaders of another ethnic group, the Uzbeks, who were immigrating and conquering from the northwest. Uzbeks were Turkish steppe pastoralists whom Chingiz Khan had allotted to his eldest son, Juchi. Some Uzbeks remained rustic, while others urbanized and became Muslims. During Babur's youth, Uzbeks, especially under Shaibani Khan (c. 1451–1510), defeated and incorporated many Mongol forces into the expanding Uzbek empire.

Uzbek chieftains frequently intermarried with Mongols and Timurids. Shaibani Khan himself made a political marriage with one of Babur's Mongol maternal aunts. But when political alignments shifted, Shaibani divorced her and forced a marriage with Babur's elder sister, Khanzada Begum (d. 1545). Besieged and outnumbered in Samarkand in 1501, Babur had given Khanzada, his only full sibling, to Shaibani in exchange for saving himself and their mother. (After fathering a child with Khanzada Begum, Shaibani divorced her and wedded her to a courtier; after both men's deaths at the battle of Merv in 1510, the victorious Safavids returned her to Babur where she married a courtier and remained an honored member of Babur's household.) By Babur's thirties, Shaibani had driven the Timurids from rule throughout Mawarannahr.

In addition to the Mongols, Turks and Uzbeks, the Safavids of Iran were the fourth major power in Mawarannahr. The Safavid dynasty's founder, Shah Ismail (1487–1524), had inherited a small kingdom in Azerbaijan at age 12, and also sacred leadership as pir of the powerful Safavi order of Shi'i Sufis. Some Safavid rulers proclaimed themselves millennial representatives of the twelfth Shi'i Imam. Militant Safavi disciples, known as the *qizilbash* ('redheads' from the distinctive 12 red points of their symbolically folded turbans), formed vital parts of the Safavid state, as both courtiers and cavalry. Babur himself briefly joined the Safavi Sufi order to gain vital military support at a crucial time. He also recognized the prestige of Persianate high culture.

Babur spent his youth alternating among predatory raids, brief conquests, and barely surviving on the run or as a poor relation in his wary, condescending, kinsmen's courts. Only sustained success, which eluded him, would make him attractive to potential followers and provide the wealth necessary to reward and retain them. Repeatedly, Babur nearly died from illness or battle (which would have precluded the future Mughal Empire). At age 19, he candidly wrote

> ...I endured such hardship and misery. I had no realm—and no hope of any realm.... I had had all I could take of homelessness and alienation. 'With such difficulties,' I said to myself, 'it would be better to go off on my own so long as I am alive, and with such deprivation and wretchedness [wander] wherever my feet will carry me, even to the ends of the earth.' I decided to go to Cathay [Khitai, meaning Mongolia] on my own. From my childhood I had had a desire to go to Cathay, but because of having to rule and other obstacles, it had never been possible. Now there was nothing for me to rule.... Impediments to my travel had disappeared, as had my former ambitions.[11]

Two frustrating years later, however, he moved with his household—including his mother and brothers—over the Hindu Kush mountains in the depths of winter toward Kabul, a place he had never visited or much considered, on the very southern edge of the Central Asian world that he knew and valued throughout his lifetime.

BABUR'S KABUL YEARS AND FAMILY

Babur's paternal uncle had ruled Kabul until his death in 1501. Then a rival Timurid prince seized the city and married the late ruler's daughter. In 1504, Babur persuaded two hundred Turks and Mongols to follow him and succeeded in snatching from his cousin-in-law Kabul and its surrounding region plus the smaller town of Ghazni. Initially, Babur dismissively called his new domain 'a petty little province' and Ghazni 'a truly miserable place.'[12] However, late in life, Babur nostalgically wrote: 'There were such conquests and victories while we were in Kabul that I consider Kabul my lucky piece' and he willed his burial there.[13]

For two decades, Babur used Kabul to conduct predatory raids, and to expand his domain, although this base proved precarious and had insufficient resources to support his unbounded ambitions. Babur's occasional victories were interspersed with nearly fatal defeats. Once, he barely escaped a frozen death when unwisely taking a short-cut through mountains in winter. Kabul itself periodically prospered from the intersecting trade routes among the richer lands of India, Iran and the Silk Route to Central Asia and China. But throughout these decades, Babur had to struggle to retain control even over Kabul.

Further, the various Pashtun and other Afghan ethnic groups in the region had always resisted Kabul's authority and revenue demands. Hence, Babur annually led punitive and predatory raids to seize livestock and grain from defiant villagers in the surrounding mountains and valleys. Babur used these spoils to reward his personal followers—mostly Turkish or Mongol relatives, retainers and mercenaries. These warriors had few resources other than their martial skills so they relied for their livelihood on Babur, or any other leader who achieved victories. Babur, to support them with sufficient cash, gifts and honors to keep them loyal, made constant efforts to expand his territories. He tenuously conquered Badakhshan, his frontier region with the still-expanding Uzbeks, and also captured from them the often contested town of Balkh. But Uzbeks repulsed his repeated incursions back into Mawarannahr. In 1522, Babur seized the commercially and strategically significant border city of Qandahar, which the Safavids from the west also claimed.

After four years ruling Kabul and as the senior remaining Timurid ruler, Babur formally claimed clan leadership and the imperial title *Padshah*, which also implied innately superior status (in the Safavid model, semi-divinity). Babur in his autobiography anachronistically used this title for himself from his original accession in Fergana, although he actually spent most of his youth as a kingdomless refugee with only the lesser honorific of *Mirza* indicating his status as a Timurid prince. Further, Babur never relinquished his determination to recover Mawarannahr.

In 1513, in exchange for Irani military support to retake Samarkand, Babur donned the qizilbash turban as a disciple of Safavid Shah Ismail and his Shi'i Sufi order. Once installed in Timur's capital for the third (and last) time, Babur pragmatically acknowledged Safavid sovereignty by having Samarkand's mosques recite the *khutba* (Friday sermon calling down blessings on the sovereign) for Shah Ismail and by minting coins in his name. Babur's opportunistic acceptance of Shi'ism contrasted with his frequent denigration of Shi'as and their theology. (Babur's imperial descendants remained embarrassed by his public acknowledgement of Safavid sovereignty.) Further, the strongly Sunni population of Samarkand rejected Safavid and Shi'i authority and accepted a Sunni Uzbek ruler instead, forcing Babur to flee to Kabul again.

As a patrimonial ruler following Central Asian custom, Babur used his close male relatives as his deputies. Babur appointed his two half-brothers, Jahangir Mirza and Nasir Mirza, to govern appanages under his authority. However, both had their own ambitions and, at various times, fought for autonomy or to displace Babur as Kabul's ruler; on several occasions when Babur was absent, one of his half-brothers seized that city and he had to recapture it. However, Babur needed the support of even those who betrayed him. Thus, acting as a gracious font of imperial forgiveness (and emulating God), he repeatedly pardoned his defeated half-brothers and other opponents who submitted in person before him and vowed fealty, even when they had broken such vows previously. After Jahangir died of alcoholism in 1507, followed eight years later by Nasir, Babur was no longer threatened by male siblings. But he was also unable to use them as subordinate governors. Further, unlike contemporary Ottoman and Delhi Sultans, Timurids did not deploy slave-governors.

Hence, to rule and ensure his dynasty's security, Babur needed legal wives to bear legitimate sons.

While in Kabul, Babur had about 20 children, including four surviving sons, with his legal wives. His official marriages reflected the first three stages of his life and his household's multiple cultures. His earliest wives, whom Babur only briefly mentioned in his autobiography, were close relatives and native speakers of Turki, highlighting his early life as a Central Asian Timurid. His first two weddings were political marriages with his double first cousins (daughters of his father's brothers and their wives who were his mother's sisters).

Like Babur's initial career, these intra-Timurid marriages proved unsuccessful. Babur and Ayisha Sultan Begum were engaged at age five to solidify clan solidarity; they married 12 years later. But even in political marriages, personalities can matter. Babur candidly wrote that they never got on well and, after the death of their newborn daughter, she left him 'at her elder sister's instigation.'[14] Babur also noted that his second political marriage, with Zaynab Sultan Begum, 'was not congenial,' although not to the point of divorce. She died of smallpox after a few years in Kabul.

Babur's next marriage was also with a closely related Timurid, the engagement approved and advanced by their female clan elders. Babur recorded that this wedding resulted initially from the personal attraction between him and Masuma Sultan Begum (the youngest half-sister of his divorced first wife, Ayisha). Babur recorded how they met at a female relative's home while Babur was visiting his cousins in Herat. She responded first (according to him): 'Upon first laying eyes on me she felt a great inclination toward me.' Reciprocating, Babur 'saw her, liked her, and asked for her hand.' Her mother and Babur's aunt discussed the matter and 'decided' to bring her to Kabul where Babur married her.[15] But this marriage also failed to produce a son. Masuma died in her first childbirth, although their daughter, named for her, survived. Babur's next Timurid wife was Saliha Sultan Begum, who also bore him only a daughter, Salima Sultan Begum. Thus, Babur still needed male heirs to sustain his dynasty.

During his next life stage, as ruler of Kabul, Babur had not given up his own aspirations for recovery of Mawarannahr, but Timurids no longer had political power there. So Babur now turned elsewhere for his next three marriages (although the senior women of both households probably had major roles in negotiating them). Significantly, Babur recorded the births of his sons with his next three wives but did not mention any of them in his autobiography. They were evidently not Timurid princesses. Since they bore Persian names, they were probably from respectable families in the Kabul region who spoke Persian (or its Afghan dialect, Dari). Of these three, Babur's main wife, Maham Begum (d. 1533), was probably Shi'a. She claimed descent from a four-centuries-earlier Sufi pir, Shaikh Ahmad, known for his ferocity as Zinda-fil (literarily 'Awesome Elephant'). Maham, who married Babur in Herat, secured her prime position in his household by bearing in 1508 his first surviving son, Mirza Humayun. Around age 12, Humayun went as Babur's deputy in the strategic region of Badakhshan; he spent about a decade there learning how to govern while repulsing Uzbek invasions. Although Maham's four other children died, she fostered several of Babur's children by his junior wives.

Babur's next wedding was to Gulrukh ('Rosy-Faced') Begum, who bore Babur four sons and a daughter. Although only two sons survived—Mirza Kamran (1509–57) and Mirza Askari (1516–58)—both would hold prominent positions in Babur's household and receive appanages. Babur's next wife, Dildar ('Heart-Holding') Begum, bore two sons and three daughters. Of these, Mirza Hindal (1519–51) also served as a commander and administrator under Babur. One daughter, Gulbadan Begum, remained a leading figure in the courts of Humayun and his heir, Akbar.

As Kabul's ruler, Babur spent much energy trying to subdue the surrounding tribes and villages. Babur perennially used brute force and intimidation. But Babur also made personal alliances with local headmen who would then more obediently submit tribute and accept his authority. Thus, Babur's last wedding was a political marriage in 1519 with Bibi Mubaraka, called 'Afghan Begum' by the other women in his household.[16] She embodied the fealty of one of Babur's subordinate allies: her father, Malik Shah Mansur, was a chief of the independent-minded Yusufzai Pashtuns. She spoke Pashto and probably also Dari, plus she learned Turki from her new family. However, she and the much older Babur had no surviving children.

These wives formed a substantial female community, whatever their personal feelings toward Babur and their factional support for their rival sons and half-sons. Gulbadan listed 96 notable women of Babur's household (leaving aside uncounted servants and slaves).[17] Babur entered their world with formality and ritual, as well as occasional intimacy. Only years after he had established himself in north India did he direct the women of his household to join him there from Kabul. As they arrived, he ceremoniously greeted them according to their status and place in his personal regard. During his four years in India, the last stage of his life, Babur made no further marriages. But he did expend much effort in balancing his reliance on each of his four contending sons and in securing his political and cultural legacies for them.

Between the ages of 21 when Babur first entered Kabul and 43 when he left, never to return alive, he cultivated many pleasures and arts. He started frequently savoring convivial parties, often alfresco in gardens or on river-rafts, drinking wine for the first time in his late twenties. With a rare exception, these escalating drink- or drug-fueled revelries, filled with music and poetry, were all-male gatherings. Indeed, Babur, at age 36, recorded his surprise when a woman joined them in drinking for the first (and only recorded) time; repulsed by her inebriated loquacity, he 'got rid of her by pretending to be drunk.'[18] On special occasions, Babur's womenfolk and young children joined him in more decorous picnics in pleasure gardens that he constructed around Kabul.

During his two decades in Kabul, Babur made himself an increasingly experienced and educated ruler. He analysed the nature of authority, both divine and mundane. He presented his state as more than just predatory on the communities around him, expressing a sense of responsibility to impose his own just rule on them. He studied Islamic law which formed the basis of judicial decisions. Three sections of *Rasila-i Mubin*, the Turki-language verse treatise he wrote around 1521, are theological. Nowhere, however, does Babur claim religious authority (as would some of his imperial descendants). The poem's fourth section considers the principles and forms of taxation on land and merchants, indicating his engagement with the pragmatic functions of administration.

Babur also practiced, perfected and praised his own martial skills in leading hunts and raids. Further, Babur enhanced his forces with the latest military science. The Ottomans to the west had developed gunpowder artillery and matchlock muskets fired by foot soldiers for their *janissary* ('new model') infantry.[19] These defeated the Safavids at the battle of Chaldiran in 1514. The Safavids quickly adopted these technologies to supplement their light qizilbash cavalry armed with bows and arrows, lances and swords. Similarly, Babur began recruiting a series of Ottoman *ustad*s (masters) to hand-craft matchlock muskets, to cast and fire expensive artillery pieces, and to deploy techniques for protecting them by binding carts into a barrier in the 'Anatolian manner.'[20] In 1519, Babur noted how his musket-bearing snipers had killing power from a distance and also awed enemy troops in Central Asia and India unfamiliar with them. The cumbersome cannon had limited use in mountainous Afghanistan, but would prove effective for Babur on the Indian plains.

While ruling Kabul, Babur found his most lucrative raids were through mountain passes and across Indus River tributaries into the rich agricultural lands and wealthy cities of the Punjab. When Babur personally first raided India's northwest in 1505, he recorded his amazement: 'I had never seen a hot climate or any of Hindustan before ... a new world came into view—different plants, different trees, different animals and birds, different tribes and people, different manners and customs. It was astonishing, truly astonishing.'[21] Thereafter, Babur occasionally forced several cities in the Punjab and Sind to pay tribute and submit to his authority or be plundered and contribute to the Timurid-style towers of skulls that marked his victories. Over his last 20 years, Babur made increasingly deeper incursions into the subcontinent.

As we have seen, in 1519, Babur vainly called on Sultan Ibrahim to relinquish the territories, including Delhi, briefly conquered by Timur in 1398. In 1523–4, Babur defeated part of Ibrahim's forces, forced the subordination of the Afghan governor of Lahore, but withdrew from his march on Delhi due to an Uzbek threat against Balkh (which he still valued more highly than Delhi). For his fifth Indian incursion in 1526, Babur entrusted nominal governance of Kabul, Qandahar, and his household to his young son, Mirza Kamran. Babur summoned his more experienced son, Mirza Humayun, and his forces from Badakhshan. Babur mobilized his Pashtun allies from Afghanistan and those long settled in the Punjab. He thus assembled 12,000 men (counting 'liege men, merchants, servants, and all those with the army') and successfully invaded this different new world of South Asia.[22]

BABUR'S INITIAL CONQUEST OF 1526

When Babur made his final and finally successful invasion of Hindustan in 1526, he faced a daunting enemy, but remained undaunted: '... we placed our feet in the stirrup of resolve, grabbed the reigns of trust in God, and directed ourselves against Sultan Ibrahim.... He was said to have a standing army of one hundred thousand, and he and his begs [noblemen] had nearly a thousand elephants ...'[23] In addition to Indo-Afghans, this force also contained Hindu allies, most prominently Raja Vikramajit from Gwalior.

Further, Ibrahim had inherited vast treasuries. Babur judged he should have hired an insurmountable number of Indian soldiers, but foolishly did not due to miserliness:

> If Sultan Ibrahim had had a mind to, he could have hired one hundred thousand to two hundred thousand troops. Thank God he was able neither to satisfy his warriors nor to part with his treasury .... He himself was an inexperienced young man who craved beyond all things the acquisition of money ... and neither his march nor his fighting was energetic.[24]

Thus, despite the mass of Ibrahim's army, it and his regime proved fragile.

In contrast, Babur effectively deployed his more limited resources. Babur received wary support from Afghans settled in India who turned against their fellow Afghan, Sultan Ibrahim. However, most of Babur's motley followers were martial adventurers from various lands he had repeatedly ruled and lost in Central Asia, including Turks and Mongols, plus Arab and Baluch mercenaries. They were attracted to Babur by the prospect of plunder. Babur knew the names of his most prominent commanders but individual and groups of soldiers arrived (and departed) at their own volition and received no salaries. Hence, he had no accurate information about their number, which he initially thought was 12,000 but, when he actually deployed them on the battlefield, he realized 'We had fewer men than we had estimated.'[25]

The reliable core of Babur's force was his personal followers. Most prominent was his eldest son Humayun, who had been fighting for five years to control Badakhshan. Babur, having impatiently summoned Humayun, tested him with a detached command, and approved his conduct: 'This was the first time that Humayun saw action, and it was taken as a good portent.'[26]

Babur also innovated in military technology by personally employing specialists in gunpowder weaponry. This was a major financial drain since their salaries and equipment were notably expensive and they could not as easily live by foraging and plundering from the surrounding countryside as did his largely unsalaried cavalry and infantry. When Babur entered north India for this last time, he tested his new military science, which was not yet widespread there. Evidently as an experiment, Babur had a hundred captured enemy soldiers executed by muskets, not as usual with swords or arrows. These were ideal conditions for the musketeers since they had ample time to prop up their awkward weapon, there was no rain to dampen the gunpowder or extinguish the firing match, no pressure of time or distracting threat against them, no need to wait impatiently while the musket cooled before it could be reloaded, and a mass of unmoving bound targets at a fixed and known range.

In the actual Panipat battle in April 1526, Babur used his muskets and cannon to anchor his army's center, protecting them against enemy cavalry with a wall of seven hundred carts linked by ox-hide ropes and interspersed with shielding pylons. Even though the slow firing rate and inaccuracy of muskets and rock-firing cannon were frustrating to Babur, they frightened the enemy as well as killed a few of them. This tactic also assisted Babur at his other major battle in India, at Khanua, but was evidently not the decisive factor in either.

More effective at Panipat against Sultan Ibrahim's unwisely immobile army was Babur's light cavalry, mostly Mongols. They harassed the sultan's entrenched troops and then, when Ibrahim belatedly advanced his army against Babur's well-prepared position, this cavalry executed a tulughma maneuver: sweeping around both enemy flanks, thus forcing them to crowd ineffectively together. In the melee, Ibrahim's war elephants scattered, he died, and his army fled, leaving thousands dead. The remainder of his still armed but demoralized troops dispersed across the region. A vast number of Indian families who lost menfolk at Panipat or who were looted (by victors and vanquished) must have been devastated. The entire north Indian populace must also have dreaded the disorder and lawlessness that accompanied such violent regime change and also earlier Timurid invasions.

Facing no organized opposition, Babur immediately dispatched Humayun to seize more distant Agra while he himself camped at Delhi (a hundred kilometers from the battlefield). As Babur first entered his new realm, he explored what he considered its major features. At Delhi, he prioritized paying reverence to the major Sufi tombs of Shaikh Nizam-ud-Din Aulia (d. 1324) and Shaikh Bakhtiar Kaki of Fergana (d. 1236), both of the India-based Chishti order. Babur explored the fortress, royal tombs, mosques and gardens of earlier Delhi Sultans. He had the royal treasury sealed for later assessment and dispersal. He directed that the khutba in Delhi's mosques proclaim his name as sovereign and graciously 'distributed some money to the poor and unfortunate' of the city.[27] Babur then rushed the two hundred kilometers to Agra where Humayun had entered that city and besieged the inner citadel.

Humayun had allowed the safe departure of the Hindu royal family that had traditionally ruled Gwalior until seven years earlier, when Sultan Ibrahim had forced their submission and confined them in Agra as royal hostages; the head of the clan, Raja Vikramajit, had died at Panipat in Ibrahim's army. In exchange for the family's safe passage out of Agra, Humayun had received 'many jewels and gems, among which was a famous diamond ... that a gem merchant once assessed ... at the whole world's expenditure for half a day' (the Koh-i Nur diamond, after many travails, is now possessed by the English queen).[28] Babur allowed Humayun to keep this treasure. Babur also generously pensioned Ibrahim's mother and then later pardoned her following her nearly successful attempt to poison him.

In the mode of a Central Asian warlord on a predatory expedition, Babur lavishly distributed Ibrahim's hoarded treasuries, without even counting it. He gave the most to Humayun, next to his other major commanders. Babur boasted, 'All the Afghans, Hazaras, Arabs, and Baluch in the army and every other group were given cash from the treasury in accordance with their station. Every merchant and student, indeed every person who was along with the army took away a large share.'[29] Babur continued that he exported to Kabul many gems and dancing women for his womenfolk plus money 'for every living soul, male and female, bondsman and free, adult and child in the province.' Further, Babur publicized his triumph widely, as Timur had done when he looted Hindustan, by sending news and booty to the people of Fergana and elsewhere in

Mawarannahr, as well as to the Islamic holy cities of Mecca and Medina. Babur reportedly even dispatched news of his conquest to the Tsar in Moscow.[30]

Expecting gratitude from Hindustanis for his just conquest, Babur was disappointed:

> ... a strange antagonism and hatred was felt between our soldiers and the natives. The native soldiers and peasants ran away as far as they could from our people. With the sole exception of Delhi and Agra, all the places that had fortresses made them fast and refused obedience ... Neither grain for ourselves nor straw for the horses was to be found .... The people had turned to brigandage and thievery.[31]

Nonetheless, Babur gradually, by force and threats, subdued these fortresses and extracted submission, tributes and revenues from the regional rulers and landholders of Hindustan. Over the next four years, Babur stayed in north India and ruled there. As Babur and diverse people living in north India gradually came together through contestation and cooperation, they produced the dynamic but still uncertain process that was the Mughal Empire.

2

INDIANS AND EMPEROR BABUR CREATE THE MUGHAL EMPIRE, 1526–30

> ... it is agreed that the boundary of a country is the place up to which people speak the language of that country ...
>
> Mughal Emperor Jahangir[1]

After four earlier attempts, Babur had finally entered north India, decisively defeating the Lodi army in 1526. Unlike his distant ancestor, Timur, however, Babur did not pillage and withdraw. Instead, he settled and expanded his conquests there until his death. The Mughal Empire thus emerged from the complex interactions between Babur and the people of these diverse lands, initially largely unfamiliar with each other.

The massive and populous South Asian subcontinent contained various regions, each with its own ecology and complex socio-cultural, economic and political conditions and histories. Never had all the distinct regions of the subcontinent been united under a single language, religion, economy, or ruler. However, with local variations, most of South Asia shared some overarching environmental factors, like extreme rainy and dry seasons, and also cultural features, notably some of the beliefs and social order of Brahminic Hinduism. Further, by Babur's time, most regions had a substantial minority of Muslims. Many earlier rulers had created trans-regional states; a few had built brief empires that nearly spanned the entire subcontinent. Babur's political vision, however, did not extend much beyond north India and its neighboring regions.

Map 2: South Asian macro-regions and main physical features

The types and depths of the relationships between Babur and the increasing number of his assorted subjects varied considerably over time and space. Some people persisted in resistance. Others paid him revenues and tribute. Some, particularly traditional service elite groups, came to join his army and administration, as they had earlier rulers. The Empire, however, still remained thinly fragile when Babur died in 1530.

THE ENVIRONMENTS OF SOUTH ASIA

Neither Babur nor most people living in South Asia conceived of the subcontinent as a single geographical entity, as it appears in today's maps: an entire peninsula bounded by the Himalayas across the north and oceans on the west and east. Instead, distinct physical environments defined each region. Perennial seasonally swollen rivers, mountain ranges and other geological features created South Asia's four macro-regions: the Ganges-Jumna River basin of Hindustan and Bengal; the Indus River basin running from the Punjab south to Sind; the Deccan upland plateau; and the peninsular south with both highlands and coastal plains. Each macro-region was the size of a large nation in today's Europe. Their climates ranged from deserts to fertile plains to dense jungles. Each macro-region also contained ecological micro-regions: each district contained significantly different soil and water conditions. Each macro-region also had particular patterns of rainfall and riverine irrigation, and thus a specific mix of wet and dry agriculture, with profound socio-cultural, economic and political consequences. Nonetheless, some broad characteristics occurred everywhere, albeit with variations.

Previously unfamiliar to Babur, but all too familiar to people living in South Asia, were the extreme temperature and rainfall variations of the monsoons (literally 'season' in Arabic). The subcontinent extends from above the Equator well into the northern hemisphere, with the Tropic of Cancer crossing its midsection. Hence, over the months following the December Solstice, the increasingly direct sun's rays gradually heat the land, creating by June a strong three-month-long updraft that draws in westerly winds from the relatively cooler Indian Ocean. This southwest Monsoon carries extensive moisture onto India's west coast, where intense rain falls along a coastal belt, squeezed out by a steep ridge of mountains—the Western Ghats. This leaves the interior Deccan with less moisture, closer to the dry lands familiar to Babur, although much hotter. These seasonal winds then continue north up the Bay of Bengal, again picking up moisture and energy, hitting the Bengal coast as cyclones and drenching rains. The southwest Monsoon is then channeled by the Himalayan Mountains westward up the Ganges plain, making the new Mughal heartland of Hindustan fertile, but dropping decreasing amount of rain, until the Punjab is relatively dry and Rajasthan and the Indus plain contain deserts.

These seasonal winds then subside and reverse. From September, the land cools, making the relatively warmer ocean the source of the updraft. Thus, colder and dryer Northeast Monsoon winds blow off the Himalayas across north India, with enough rain to enable some areas to produce a second crop. The peninsula's south-eastern plain, which was never well incorporated into the Mughal Empire, receives its heaviest rains in December, when these Northeast Monsoon winds sweep inland from the Bay of Bengal.

While the monsoons follow chronologically predictable patterns, they vary in the annual amount of rainfall in each region. Some years, droughts occur in one or more regions. Transportation of grain from more productive areas to such drought-struck places could be disrupted by wars. Drought-induced disorder and emigration had profound consequences for the local economy, population and administration. Many rulers, including Mughal emperors, provided some charity food-distribution to heavily affected regions, but this was not systematic nor of sufficient scale to alleviate the effects of a famine. Consequently, environmental forces—beyond the power of governments to control, even today—strongly affected the Mughal Empire, year by year. Some reigns suffered more, some less.

Wherever sufficient rain falls on fertile soil, especially on the lower Gangetic plain and the peninsula's coasts, people traditionally cultivate highly productive rice and other wet crops. In dryer regions, including western Hindustan and the Punjab, less water-dependent crops like wheat and millet predominated (prior to the twentieth-century's mechanized irrigation and hybrid plants). In general, wet crops are roughly three times as productive as dry crops, with rural population densities to match. The cuisine of each regional culture also reflected the prevailing crops. The preferred diet of Babur's court initially highlighted wheat-based breads familiar from Central Asia and Afghanistan, but, as the Mughal court settled in India, its cuisine expanded to include more Hindustani-style rice dishes.

THE CULTURES AND COMMUNITIES OF SOUTH ASIA

The substantial majority of the people living in South Asia followed a complex composite tradition that outsiders designated 'Hindu,' since its followers lived beyond the Indus River. Babur evidently never inquired extensively about the cultures or internal social divisions of the people he ruled, although he knew that they included many distinct Muslim and non-Muslim groups. In fact, the elite and popular beliefs, customs and life ways of South Asia's diverse communities varied widely by social class and region.

At the elite level, the overarching tradition centered on a Brahmin-headed religious and social system which extended across most of South Asia, albeit in differing depths. Its heartland was north India, known as Hindustan ('land of the Hindus'). However, Brahmins were always an elite minority: present at the top of the ritual order almost everywhere, but in varying small proportions of the population.

For a thousand years, Brahmin scholars and philosophers using classical Sanskrit-language oral and written texts had been expounding the principle of a universal moral order, *dharma*. Birth and behavior divided all humans into four *varna*s ('social orders'), each with a broadly identified dharma: Brahmins were the highest as priests (although many followed other occupations); next were martial Kshatriyas (including rulers, warriors and landholders); followed by Vaishya merchants and artisans; then Shudra common folk (although historically some Shudras achieved wealth and power). Outside these varnas, and thus considered less human, were various others, including uninitiated children and unmarried women (even those whose parents were in a varna), excommunicated deviants from dharmic practice, forest-dwelling *adivasi*s ('aboriginals,' often called 'tribals'), menial workers, and Asian, European and African foreigners. Each person, divinity and other being had a distinct individual dharma based on ancestry, age, gender and accumulated *karma* ('deeds') from past lives.

In each area, Brahminic and local social systems overlapped in more specific communities—each a distinct *jati* ('birth' group). Each jati had its own particular dharma, for example as weavers, potters, or warriors, and was customarily endogamous and commensal. In each region, a ranked hierarchy of jatis existed by consensus. However, the exact varna identity (if any) of individual jatis was often disputed (many jatis claimed higher varna status than those around them accepted).

In Brahminic Sanskrit texts, this varna system appeared stable. But in practice, as jatis, clans and families settled in India or as they rose or fell in economic or political power, they merged into or shifted among varnas. As a particularly prominent example, many clans of the Rajput ('king's son') jati boasted themselves the eternal epitome of the Kshatriya varna with putative ancestry from the sun, moon, fire, or another deity. Rajput clans often dominated politically and militarily across much of northern, western, and central India. In Babur's time, the two major Rajput ruling clans in Rajasthan were Sisodias based in Mewar and Rathors in Marwar.

Historically, however, many martial immigrants (from elsewhere in South Asia or from Central Asia) claimed Rajput status after they had settled or conquered and became local landholders or rulers. Some Rajputs originated from rising families within communities of indigenous pastoralists, agriculturalists, or adivasis. To demonstrate their Rajput status, these upwardly mobile groups 'Sanskritized': they imitated established Rajput jatis in diet and deportment, employed Brahmin priests, had Kshatriya-specific rituals performed for themselves, and 'rediscovered' long-forgotten descent from legendary Rajputs. When the aspirant clan's daughters were accepted as brides by established Rajputs, this meant recognition as subordinate allies with legitimately Rajput status. Particularly successful rising Rajput clans convinced other Rajputs to give them brides; under hypergamy, bride receivers held higher status than bride givers.

Many established Rajput clans also recognized some non-Hindu martial immigrants as also following the dharma of the warrior and ruler. These newcomers included some Muslim clans, like Babur's dynasty, who were thus partly incorporated into the Indic social order, without being considered Hindu. Indeed, many Rajput and other Hindu oral and written texts identified Turks as a jati, rather than classifying all Muslims collectively as a single community. Additionally, some Rajput families converted to Islam, while still retaining much of their traditional dharma and social status.[2] From Babur's grandson onward, the Mughal dynasty accepted brides from some leading Hindu Rajput families (but never gave brides to Rajput families), thus proclaiming the relatively higher social rank of the Mughal imperial family.

Separate minority communities following other Indic religious traditions also functioned as jatis, even when they did not intermarry or interdine with Hindus. For instance, Jains emerged from Indian origins like Hindus, but formed a small endogamous and commensal religious community. Jains held significant roles in banking and commerce. They were widely respected for their non-violent beliefs, including the avoidance of killing and vegetarianism. Jain practices contrasted deeply with Mughal warrior traditions but Jain leaders and religious teachers attended Mughal emperors and claimed to have influenced their policies toward non-violence.

Similarly, Zoroastrian Parsis traced their origin to pre-Islamic Iran but had long settled in India, particularly as merchants. They regarded the elements of fire, earth and water as sacred, and viewed the cosmos as a Manichean battle between good and evil. They remained a small endogamous and commensal community living among but apart from Hindus.

Each South Asian region also produced thriving popular devotional movements. Some considered themselves broadly within the Hindu tradition but others did not, sometimes explicitly attacking both Brahmin and Muslim religious authorities. For example, the Punjab was the main base of the monotheistic Sikh religious movement. Although Babur did not record this, in his 1520 raiding expedition, he briefly captured (and may have conversed with) Guru Nanak (1469–1538), founder of Sikhism.[3] Followers of the Sikh Gurus were mostly *Khatri*s (a merchant and scribal jati) or *Jat*s (a farmer jati). While in many ways a distinct religion and social community, Sikh families also occasionally intermarried with their equivalent Hindu jatis. The Sikh movement would become a powerful regional political force that increasingly challenged Mughal rule, especially during the seventeenth and eighteenth centuries.

Some immigrants, including Muslims and Christians, tried to fit into their own conceptual categories all these complex Indic systems. Many Muslims differentiated themselves collectively from all others in India, including Hindus, Jains and Sikhs. Further, some orthodox Muslims regarded these Indic communities as not 'People of the Book,' meaning that God had never chosen for them a prophet to convey the Qur'an. In contrast, Christians, Jews, and some other non-Muslim communities had once been selected by Allah to receive the Book. For Muslims, the final Prophet, Muhammad, had conveyed the Qur'an directly in Arabic. However, Babur—like some Delhi Sultans and other Muslim rulers in India—pragmatically reinterpreted the theological status of these Indic communities to permit them to be *zimmi* ('protected subjects') as if they were People of the Book, in exchange for their paying *jizya* (a tax in lieu of service to the Muslim ruler). Further, many Muslim rulers never actually collected *jizya* from their non-Muslim subjects. However, to Babur, the distinctions among the different Indic traditions apparently remained immaterial except that they were clearly not Muslims.

Similarly, when Roman Catholic Portuguese explorers first reached the south-western Indian coast in 1498 (28 years before Babur's final invasion), they initially identified all the non-Muslims there as Christians, whose temples supposedly contained distorted images of the Virgin Mary and various Catholic saints. Moreover, the Portuguese used their term *casta/caste* ('breed') to include all four varnas and the many thousands of jatis. This terminological confusion has remained in wide circulation ever since.

When Babur arrived, a substantial minority of people living in South Asia were Muslims: some were immigrants and their descendants, but most were converts. Many families had accepted Islam through the influence of charismatic Sufis. Often, these Sufis had heterodox Islamic concepts and customs that incorporated many of the converting community's pre-Islamic beliefs and practices, especially domestic customs about birth, marriage and other rituals, and women's roles. Some prominent converts later claimed biological descent from the Prophet Muhammad or another revered Arab, boasting honorifics like Sayyid or Shaikh, despite their Indic biological ancestry. The largest concentrations of Muslims lived in the widely separated regions of India's north-west and eastern Bengal.

Since the early thirteenth century, Muslim Afghan immigrants had established themselves as landholders and rulers across the Gangetic plain. When Babur arrived, a Lodi Afghan sultan ruled in Delhi while other Muslim dynasties ruled in the Deccan. Although Babur would project himself as the model Muslim ruler during some campaigns in north India, many Indo-Afghan Muslims regarded him as alien and fought against him. Babur's descendants would each negotiate the extent and expression of their roles as Islamic sovereigns.

Linguistically, South Asia also contains great diversity, with three major language families, dozens of separate regionally based languages, and thousands of distinct dialects. Most north Indians speak one of the dozen languages derived from Sanskrit. Most south Indians speak one of the four major languages of the separate Dravidian family. Additionally, especially in the Deccan and the north-east, many forest-dwelling groups have their own languages, unconnected to either Sanskrit or a Dravidian language.

From well before Babur's invasion, Persian had begun to dominate at Muslim courts, especially in the Deccan sultanates that had cultural, diplomatic and economic links across the Indian Ocean with Iran. Gradually, the Mughal dynasty would shift from the Turki of Babur to Persian, and adopt many accompanying Iranian administrative and cultural practices. Then, as the Mughal Empire expanded, its imperial Persianate culture and administrative forms became fashionable for other rulers, including Rajputs. Thus, from Babur onward, the Mughal Empire would interact with the distinct traditions in each region, as well as with South Asia's overarching trans-regional patterns.

THE ECONOMIES OF SOUTH ASIA

Throughout India's history, including during the entire Mughal period, the vast majority of its people have lived in an agriculturally based economy. When Babur arrived, he found that settled farmers held customary occupancy rights to plant and harvest (although not full property landownership). Other local people or institutions also held their own separate rights to that same land. Most prominently, one or more levels of *zamindar*s ('landholders') held rights to collect the revenues, retain a portion, and convey the rest to the state's agents. Many zamindars based their claims on having originally settled or conquered the region. The amount of revenue retained by zamindars depended on whether the land was directly managed by them or not, as well as on their power relative to the cultivators and the state. Village headmen, servants, accountants and local religious institutions also often had customary rights to a share of the produce. All these rights could be inherited, exchanged, or sold, with varying degrees of documentation required by various states.

In Babur's time, most regions had much unused but potentially arable land. Hence, the land itself had limited economic value, although farmers often had invested in considerable labor to bring it under active cultivation. Control over people was more valuable than control over land. Thus, the revenue demands by zamindars or the state could not be so high as to drive farmers to emigrate and resettle new lands. Moneylenders and merchants made loans and purchased produce for sale in regional markets (the agricultural economy in many regions would be further monetized under Mughal rule).

Overall, zamindars, peasants, moneylenders and imperial administrators engaged in multi-sided cooperation and subtle or open contestation over agricultural resources. Each had his (or, less frequently, her) own interests in maximizing income while minimizing the economic and cultural costs of defending those interests. Babur, trying to establish his regime quickly, often officially recognized those landholders who would at least pay some tribute, letting them assess and collect revenues from the cultivators. Even in Hindustan, Babur never fully convinced many local rulers and landholders to accept his authority and routinely pay him the revenues or service he demanded. Mughal officials would long struggle even to gain information about the actual local production. Further, while Babur could concentrate his forces to capture cities and conquer territories, he controlled insufficient manpower and authority to prevent the periodic rebellions that necessitated his reconquering them.

Like many other rulers of that age, the Mughal dynasty would favor settled agriculturalists as their main revenue base. But settled agriculture was not strongly separated from other ways of life. For example, at times of drought (or excessive revenue demand), farmers sometimes resorted to the forests, while periods of rain (or promises of revenue relief) could attract former forest-dwellers to settled agriculture.

Further, some individuals, families, or whole communities customarily migrated. During the harvest season, male and female agricultural laborers often followed the shifting wave of ripening crops intra- or inter-regionally. During the fallow season, many village men (with varying military experience and weaponry) joined mobile armies or formed their own bands, seeking plunder. The Mughal state would never fully control this vast seasonal military labor market. Further, itinerant artisans and entertainers provided services to villages. Women and men hand-manufactured cloth and other products for sale which they, or brokers, carried to nearby *qasba*s ('market towns')—centers of regional commerce, concentrated artisan manufacture, inter-regional trade and governance.

Throughout the Mughal period, many migratory communities combined pastoralism with commerce, often over long distances. They also produced meat and dairy products for local and regional markets. Imperial armies relied on huge caravans of bullocks carrying grain on their backs. But such pastoralists and itinerant traders also proved difficult for the Mughal administration to locate and tax.

Many communities lived mainly or provisionally in forests, often forming internal frontiers for the Empire, easily avoiding the heavy cavalry and artillery that became the imperial army's core.[4] Forest-dwelling adivasis hunted and practiced swidden agriculture. In many cases, a leading family had risen to establish its own kingdom and claim Rajput status. Such forest-dwellers had tense relationships with settled agricultural society, both raiding for cattle, grain, women and other booty and also trading forest products like wood and herbs for grain and artisanal products. Further, recalcitrant landholders, political rebels and outlaws took refuge in thick groves, often planted for that purpose, against tax-collectors as well as marauding warlords and recent invaders like Babur. Babur bemoaned the 'forests of thorny trees in which the people ... hole up and obstinately refuse to pay tribute.'[5] Conversely, such forest-dwellers often felt the brunt of Mughal coercive efforts to transform forests into settled, revenue-producing farmland.

In addition to the interrelated agricultural, pastoralist and forest-based economies, extensive long-distance trade routes in high-value, low-volume goods connected South Asia by land with the famous trans-Asian 'Silk Road.' In Kabul, Babur had already taxed this trade. In particular, South Asia imported horses (vital for cavalry but constantly needing replacement due to uncongenial equine conditions) while exporting slaves and valuable man-made and natural products. Babur was initially less familiar with India's sizable and growing overseas trade with Africa, Southeast and East Asia and (especially from the sixteenth century onward) Europe. But, he came to appreciate India's wealth from indigenous production and also its perennial export surplus. To tap into these, Babur had to conquer Hindustan and the prosperous coastal provinces to its south-west and south-east.

THE POLITICAL WORLDS OF SOUTH ASIA

Each South Asian region had its own history of political independence. Over the previous two thousand years, many had been centers of their own trans-regional empires, a few briefly conquering much of the subcontinent. But all empires struggled to govern beyond their original heartland. From the early thirteenth century until Babur's invasion, the Delhi Sultanate, under five successive Muslim dynasties (most ethnically Afghan or Turk), had ruled in north India. They fought, negotiated with, and occasionally ruled many of the diverse Rajput and other regional states across the Ganges and the Indus macro-regions.

Some more expansive Delhi sultans also conquered the Deccan, but such military assertions beyond the Sultanate's heartland proved technologically and culturally unsustainable. Indeed, the Deccani conquests split off as the Bahmani Sultanate in 1347. Coincidentally, just after Babur's invasion, the Bahmani Sultanate itself fragmented into warring successor kingdoms: Ahmadnagar, Berar, Bidar, Bijapur and Golkonda. Cultural, economic and political links across the Indian Ocean to Iran meant more Persian and Shi'i influences in the Deccan than in north India. Nonetheless, several contending Deccani sultans sent ambassadors to Babur soon after his invasion, each vainly seeking his military support against the others. However, Babur had insufficient resources to extend into the Deccan so he dismissed those invitations.

Even further south, at the margins of Babur's knowledge, were many diverse kingdoms. Most were ruled by regionally based Hindu kings from Dravidian-language speaking communities with their own martial traditions and ambitions. The largest was Vijayanagar (until 1565, when it fragmented). Babur's dynasty would never fully incorporate these various southern states.

During Babur's lifetime and thereafter, military and economic battles continued for control over the Indian Ocean. However, neither Babur nor his descendants built blue-water warships or many coastal defenses. In contrast, the Portuguese royal navy proved a rising military and mercantile force in the Indian Ocean, based after 1505 in permanent colonial enclaves along the western coast. The most significant Portuguese bases were Goa (seized from the Bijapur Sultanate in 1510) and Daman and Diu (taken from Gujarat in 1531 and 1535 respectively). The Portuguese also established trading enclaves in Bengal at Satgaon (1550) and Hugli (1579). The Portuguese profited from both their own transoceanic trade with Europe and their participation in Asian commerce in

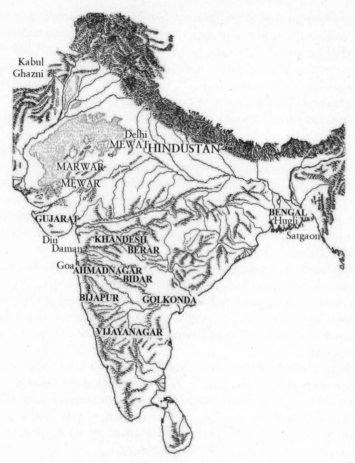

Map 3: Major States and Regions as of 1526

the Indian Ocean. Further, fast and well-cannoned Portuguese warships enforced their demand that all Indian Ocean merchant ships purchase their license (*cartaz*) or else have their cargo, crew and passengers subject to seizure. While the cartaz fee was modest, the document carried Christian images, which offended many Muslims; it could only be purchased in Portuguese colonial ports, which redirected trade routes there. Thus, although the Portuguese did not penetrate inland, they nonetheless affected India's politics, economy and culture.

The still expanding Ottoman Empire sent occasional war fleets into the Indian Ocean from Egypt, seeking political and commercial advantage. But they eventually lost out to the Portuguese, who themselves would be overshadowed by the Dutch, French and English East India companies during following centuries. Later Mughal emperors negotiated with European sea powers for the safety of pilgrims to Mecca and of oceanic trade, with limited success. Thus, the Mughal Empire remained a land power with modest riverine forces.

Babur's shattering of the Delhi Sultanate opened new possibilities for expansion by ambitious rivals. In the lower Gangetic plain, many Indo-Afghan and other local rulers seized the opportunity. Only months after Panipat, Babur sent Humayun to march eastward against these rulers, whom Babur repeatedly called 'rebels'—although they had never been under Babur's rule, he claimed sovereignty across north India, making them 'rebellious.'

The most threatening ruler who marched against Babur in the next campaigning season after Panipat was Maharana Sangaram Singh, 'Rana Sanga' (r. 1509–29). An experienced Sisodia Rajput commander, he bore many battle scars earned in expanding his domain over the key Rajasthan regions of Mewar and Marwar. Rana Sanga pressed north into the heart of Hindustan, leading a coalition of Rajput, Indo-Afghan and Indian Muslim clans. Babur concentrated his forces, now including substantial numbers of Indian Muslims. Babur rightly apprehended a perilous battle against a much larger army, and the reluctance of his core force of Central Asians, many homesick, to remain fully committed to his cause. Dishearteningly, a prominent Central Asian soothsayer arrived and declared the planet Mars to be aligned against Babur.

For the first time, Babur faced a predominantly non-Muslim army. Hence, he sought sectarian and divine support by highlighting his Islamic identity more than ever before. He exempted all Muslims from taxes on cattle and goods. He publicly renounced wine (forbidden in Islam), even destroying a newly arrived shipment of 'three camel trains [of] superior Ghazni wine'; he shattered his gold and silver drinking vessels, distributing the valuable shards to poor Muslims.[6] All the soldiers of what Babur now called his 'Army of Islam' swore on the Qur'an to fight as *ghazis* (Islamic warriors) in a *jihad* until death. Babur also had a supportive audience from Muslim west Asia: Safavid and Uzbek ambassadors attended him.

In 1527, the armies met at Khanua, near Agra. After desperate fighting, Babur's forces prevailed and Rana Sanga fled wounded. In triumph, Babur built a huge tower of enemy skulls in the Timurid mode and seized territories from those who had opposed him, including the strategic region of Mewat, near Delhi.

Featuring his newly emphasized Islamic identity, Babur officially added Ghazi to his own titles and coins. He also composed the verses:

> I have become a desert wanderer for Islam
> Having joined battle with infidels [*kafar*] and Hindus.
> I readied myself to become a martyr [*shahid*],
> God be thanked I am become a *ghazi*.[7]

Additionally, Babur also renamed his most effective cannon 'Ghazi.'

Two of Babur's courtiers separately 'found' the Hijri year of his victory in the alpha-numerical value of *Fath-i Badshah-i Islam* ('Victory of the Emperor of Islam'), thus discovering God's will via chronogram. Indeed, increasingly in India, Babur reduced his earlier emphasis on Timur as his source of authority, which had proved unpersuasive to Indians. Instead, Babur highlighted himself as conquering champion of Islam in the pattern of Mahmud of Ghazni, who had invaded India 17 times around 1000 CE.[8]

Babur still remained oriented toward Muslim Central Asian warrior culture. But, many of his Central Asian followers, having already endured enough of India's uncomfortable and unfamiliar climate, returned home, laden with loot and gifts from Babur. To reinforce his thinning forces in Hindustan, Babur issued a general invitation of employment to all warriors in Central Asia. However, Uzbeks took advantage of Babur's extended absence in Hindustan by seizing Balkh. In response, Babur sent Humayun and his personal followers back to govern Badakhshan and expand the Mughal Empire in Central Asia. Instead, Humayun struggled to hold Badakhshan. As Humayun's grandson, Jahangir, stated: 'it is the temperament of the Badakhshis to be seditious and turbulent.'[9] Further, Humayun failed to recover Balkh or capture Samarkand.

As Humayun left Hindustan, however, he had strengthened his hand against his three rival half-brothers, but imprudently upset Babur, by taking money from the Delhi treasury without authorization. In Humayun's place, Babur summoned his youngest son, Askari (age 12), to prove his worthiness in battle and administration under Babur's direct observation; Askari would remain in India until Babur's death. Through Babur's own writing, we see his growing engagement with South Asia, which he never left alive.

CREATING THE MUGHAL EMPIRE

Babur, his Central Asian followers, and his new Hindustani subjects created the Mughal Empire as an amalgam of their various cultures, traditions and interests. Although Babur's forces had initially triumphed, his rule remained tentative. He and his still mainly Central Asian commanders and troops were alien to his new Hindustani subjects, having different values and speaking different languages. Even many Indo-Afghans did not know the Persian or Turki of Babur's followers. Nor did all Hindustanis regard Babur as their legitimate ruler. Hence, Babur's regime largely relied on the military forces he could command and reward with looted treasuries and forced taxes.

Ruling an expanding empire but lacking a robust land-tax collection administration, Babur needed to keep capturing royal treasuries in order to reward his commanders. During the three remaining campaign seasons until his death, Babur annually led his forces or dispatched his commanders to overawe or crush regional powers—from the Sultan of Bengal in the east to the nomadic Baluch rulers in the west. Many agreed to accept Babur's overlordship and submit tribute—at least temporarily while under immediate threat or assault by his troops.

Babur allotted often still resistant cities to his most prominent remaining Central Asian commanders. They were to extract from these their expenses for maintaining their soldiers, households and pleasures, plus submit a proportion of the revenues to Babur's own treasury. In a patrimonial court like Babur's, the ruler often turned to a courtier or attendant at hand to take military governance over a newly available city. Hence, many Central Asian governors— arbitrarily assigned to control unknown places and having no affinity with the local population—largely remained in beleaguered garrisons. Nor did they typically remain there long, either recalled by Babur for the next campaign or else transferred to another unfamiliar posting.

The most costly component of Babur's forces was his gunpowder division that he paid directly. Babur entered India with innovative musketry and artillery technology, which he continued to develop. This weaponry gave him an advantage over his Hindustani opponents who lacked access to this military science. For a decade before Panipat, Babur had been employing expensive Ottoman-trained gunpowder experts, most prominently Master Ali-Quli and Mustafa Rumi Khan (they and their expertise came from Rum, meaning Constantinople, the second Rome, so the title 'Rumi Khan' indicated his distinctive role and was awarded sequentially to many such artillery commanders). Babur proved especially tolerant and solicitous of these rare professional gunners, noting that Master Ali-Quli 'was difficult to get along with.' For instance, when the experimental casting of a huge cannon seemed to fail, Babur had to cajole: 'Master Ali-Quli went into a strange depression and was about to throw himself into the mold of molten bronze, but I soothed him, gave him a robe of honor, and got him out of his black mood.'[10] Some immigrant artillerymen settled in India—Master Ali-Quli's son serving Babur and then Humayun.

Babur noted the power but also the limitations of his cannon. They provided awe-inspiring long-range covering fire when crossing a river or besieging a citadel. But they were underpowered to batter breaches in major city walls, except under ideal circumstances (like firing down from a height). The cannon barrels needed long cooling between shots lest they crack, so 16 firings per day was a good rate. Further, the cannon were dangerously unreliable. Babur noted while testing one newly-cast weapon: 'Although the shot went far, the mortar shattered and pieces of it wounded some people. Eight of them died.'[11] As these Ottoman experts empirically developed the science of metal casting in India, they made ever larger cannons that could fire ever bigger rocks or expensive metal cannonballs. But, even cast in two pieces (the barrel and a separate powder chamber) and pulled by elephants, these increasingly heavy cannon were difficult to transport: Babur needed to widen roads by cutting 'the jungles so that the carts and artillery might pass without difficulty.'[12]

Further, cannon, muskets and their masters were direct and continuing costs for Babur, unlike cavalrymen under commanders to whom he could assign lands for their income or infantry whom he could hire and dismiss as needed; cavalry and infantry could also be given license to loot conquered lands. But gunpowder-using soldiers moved slower and were too valuable to let loose in the countryside. Hence, after only two years in India, 'To meet the requirements for the army's weapons, artillery, and gunpowder ... [Lodi Sultan] Ibrahim's treasuries in Delhi and Agra ran dry.'[13] So Babur had to demand his governors send him more revenues from their assigned territories.

Others in India also coveted this gunpowder technology. The military science that Babur brought merged with that imported across the Indian Ocean into the Deccan by west Asian experts and the Portuguese.[14] Wealthy Indian rulers began to procure muskets and cannon, escalating levels of violence in warfare. Indian peasant-warriors acquired muskets, forming an armed military labor pool that the Mughals could never contain. However, for the next two centuries, Ottoman and Christian European immigrants largely monopolized the making and firing of large cannon—while Indian commanders directed their deployment and Indian laborers transported and loaded them.

Lacking enough Central Asians to control and manage the lands Babur had so rapidly conquered, he began to recruit Indians for his army and administration. A high proportion of those who joined Babur's forces were Indian Muslims—mostly Shaikhzadas (descendants of earlier Indian converts to Islam) and settled Indo-Afghans. Babur and his successors kept Central Asian-style bow-armed cavalry at the core of their military, but bows were ruined by India's monsoons and horses did not thrive. Far cheaper and more available were Hindustani infantrymen whom Babur's commanders could hire as needed from the abundant military labor market, often as entire military labor gangs under the direct command of their own *sardar* ('headman'). Babur's high-ranked officers (whom he named in his autobiography) were all Muslim, but many of their unnamed subordinate officers and soldiers were not.

Joining Babur's administration were many Hindu scribal families that had served the Delhi Sultanate. They were experienced and informed experts, working in the locality where they had extensive roots, who might provide Babur's governors with the requisite records and advice about past and appropriate revenues paid by each newly conquered city and region. When Babur summoned these military governors for his campaigns, such Indian officials administered the territories he had conquered. In addition, thousands of Indians artisans and servants found employment under Babur, his courtiers and his commanders.

Babur sought spiritual support for himself and his regime from Sufi pirs, including Indian-based orders. He continued until the end of his life to pay reverence to Naqshbandis, as had Timur. Some Naqshbandis joined Babur in India as prominent courtiers. Further, in 1528, when afflicted with a debilitating bowel inflammation that even prevented him from offering *namaz* (prayer), Babur sought again the intercession of long dead Naqshbandi Pir Khwaja 'Ubaidullah Ahrar. When Babur recovered, he vowed to versify the pir's *Risala-i Walidiyya* as a 243-line poem; Babur even attributed liberation from his lingering desire for wine to this poetic act of devotion.[15]

Additionally, Babur began occasionally to honor India-based Chishti, Shattari and Suhrawardi pirs. He renewed many of the revenue grants given by Delhi Sultans to these pirs, other religious worthies and institutions. Each Sufi order had its own distinctive practice of mystical devotion and widespread network of shrines and disciples across much of north and central India. Gaining the support of these revered men and institutions provided Babur (and, even more so, his successors) with wider legitimacy among Muslim and also non-Muslim Indians of many social and economic classes. Conversely, these pirs were often rivals of each other and the Naqshbandis. Various pirs vied for Babur's financial and political support.

During Babur's four years before his death, he remained personally ambivalent about settling in Hindustan, but he displayed a remarkable openness to new experiences there. He inquisitively explored selected aspects of his new domain, fascinating for their unexpectedness. He devoted many pages of his autobiography to describing in meticulous detail the nature and utility of distinctive Hindustani animals, plants, monumental buildings and systems of weights and measures. Significantly, he wrote relatively little about India's diverse people or their cultures, except for critiquing the shocking near nakedness of peasant men and women and the full nakedness of some sacred sculptures (he ordered some nude statues in Gwalior destroyed for prudish rather than religious reasons). Strikingly, given their high proportion of the population, Babur in his *Baburnama* names relatively few non-Muslims, with the exception of his opponents and a few Hindu royal families.

Indeed, while living in India, Babur sought to create pleasurable refuges in the Central Asian style that would isolate him and his household from India's physical discomforts, especially its hot, dry winds and dust. As he explored his new realm, Babur constantly sought promising sites where he could construct water-cooled gardens, step-wells and bathhouses. He was surprised and pleased by how abundant, inexpensive and skillful were the thousands of Indian stone-masons and other artisans and workmen whom he employed (but did not name except collectively by their professions). Babur assembled his court and commanders around him in these gardens. They also reflected his efforts to control the Indian environment. But Babur also recognized the distance between the people of Hindustan from himself and his courtiers, noting that the complex of walled gardens they built for themselves outside of Agra was called 'Kabul' by locals.[16]

Babur retained close interest in the actual Kabul region. He established a direct communications relay, with a string of watchtowers, *caravanserai* (walled compounds for travelers to secure protection, water, storage and sleep), and post-stations equipped with horses and messengers along the entire way. Only after two years in Hindustan did Babur order his sister, wives and their household staff to immigrate from Kabul to join him.

Babur expressed his mixed feelings about living in and ruling Hindustan. He wrote: 'The one nice aspect of Hindustan is that it is a large country with lots of gold and money.'[17] A poem in his 1528 collection candidly reveals his sense of moral failure for remaining in seductive Hindustan:

> I deeply desired the riches of this Indian land.
> What is the profit since this land enslaves me.
> ... Excuse me my friend for this my insufficiency.[18]

While Babur repeatedly complained about India's discomforts, this same poetry collection includes a contrasting celebration of its seasonal pleasures:

> Winter, although a time of the brazier and the fire,
> Yet this winter in India is very amiable.
> A season of pleasure and pure wine.
> If wine is not permissible, yet ma'jun [drug-confection] is also fine.[19]

Other seasons also had their attractions:

The weather turns very nice during the monsoon. Sometimes it rains ten, fifteen, or twenty times a day; torrents are formed in an instant, and water flows in places that normally have no water. During the rainy season, the weather is unusually good when the rain ceases, so good in fact that it could not be more temperate or pleasant.[20]

But Babur continually longed for the more congenial climate of Central Asia.

An inevitable problem for any patrimonial state, including the Mughal Empire, is succession. Babur needed sons as his deputies during his lifetime, but knew first-hand that they could become deadly rivals, especially after his death. Babur thus tried to settle his legacy by his posthumous allocation of his territories among his sons: Humayun, the eldest, was to receive Hindustan and the status of Padshah, and Kamran was to continue to hold Kabul, with territorial provisions for his two youngest sons, Hindal and Askari, as well. Babur also directed them to support each other according to Central Asian principles of corporate sovereignty.

As Babur repeatedly sickened in Hindustan, some courtiers briefly conspired for the succession by another Timurid nobleman, Mir Muhammad Mahdi Khwaja, current husband of Babur's only full sister, Khanzada Begum. In the end, however, Babur's main commanders respected his will and the authority of the direct patrilineal Timurid line. But no succession was secure for any of Babur's sons (or later descendants).

As Babur seriously ailed in 1529, he called Hindal to his side. Instead, Humayun rushed from Badakhshan without authorization. Further, while passing through Kabul, Humayun ordered Hindal to take his place in distant Badakhshan. Overruling Humanyun's order, Babur again summoned Hindal. Gulbadan recorded both Babur's annoyance at Humayun's willful actions (until his mother interceded) but also Babur's personal affection for him. Gulbadan further recalled how, when Humayun himself sickened to near death, Babur ritually transferred that illness to himself. While Humayun recovered, Babur died in Agra in 1530, after directing that his body be returned to Kabul for burial, where it lies today. Despite Babur's testament, but following Timurid practice, his four sons would fight desperately for supremacy. His successor, Humayun, proved unable to sustain the Mughal Empire his father had initiated.

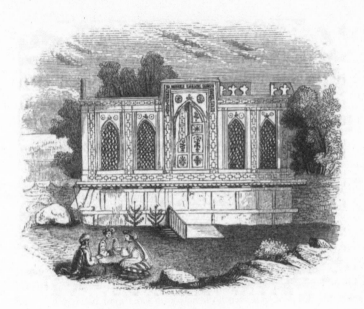

Tomb of the Emperor Babur, Kabul, ca.1844[21]

3

EMPEROR HUMAYUN AND INDIANS, 1530–40, 1555–6

> I have rarely, even in dreams, seen [Emperor Humayun's] like for innate
> talent. However, since he allowed in his retinue … self-seeking individuals,
> evil, vile and profligate men … he had contracted some bad habits … that
> ha[ve] occasioned talk on the part of the people …
> Mirza Muhammad Haidar Dughlat about his cousin, Humayun[1]

Following Humayun's enthronement as Mughal Padshah and
ruler of Hindustan in 1530, he failed to stabilize his regime.
When Humayun acceded at 22, he was largely unfamiliar
with India; he spent 80 per cent of his life outside it. He had
accompanied Babur's initial conquest of Hindustan in 1526 but,
after a year fighting there, returned to Central Asia. Only just
before Babur's death had Humayun rushed back to Hindustan.
As emperor, Humayun had some early military successes but he
did not secure the consistent loyalties of his father's powerful
Central Asian commanders or his three half-brothers. Nor did he
mobilize sufficient financial and manpower resources from India
to rule there. After a tumultuous decade of growing opposition,
particularly from resurgent Indo-Afghan forces, Humayun
fled India. He did not return for 15 years, when he reinvaded
Hindustan to restart the Mughal Empire, just months before his
own death.

HUMAYUN'S SUCCESSION AND COURT CULTURE

As dying Babur had decreed, Humayun succeeded as Mughal Emperor in north India. But also following Babur's authoritative testament and Central Asian custom, the males of the imperial family shared sovereignty. Newly enthroned Emperor Humayun reconfirmed the authority given to his three half-brothers by Babur. Then, Humayun repeatedly and graciously forgave their bloody betrayals.

Each half-brother had dynastic ambitions of his own, at times claiming independent sovereignty. Humayun's eldest half-brother, Mirza Kamran, largely ruled (or sought to regain) Kabul, where Babur had posted him. During periods of ascendancy, Kamran extended his rule over Qandahar, other parts of Central Asia and the Punjab; but he also spent years as a refugee. Their younger and lower-ranked half-brothers, Mirza Hindal and Mirza Askari, each shifted over the decades among serving Humayun, serving Kamran, and asserting his own independence. Eventually, Kamran's forces killed Hindal then Humayun exiled Askari and Kamran.

Further, Babur had entrusted their cousin and adoptive brother, Mirza Sulaiman, with Badakhshan. Mirza Sulaiman sometimes accepted overlordship by Humayun or Kamran, but sometimes asserted his autonomy against Babur's sons. He outlived them all.

Gulbadan—half-sister of Humayun, Kamran and Askari and full-sister of Hindal—described in rich detail in her book, *Humayunnama*, the lives of the often contending male and female members of their clan.[2] Her account reveals how the family's leading women provided political and emotional bonds and arranged marriages. These women guided the education of children, teaching them their appropriate roles and deportment. They also supported the ambitions of their favorite male and female relatives. At times, they interceded with the patriarch for advancement or forgiveness on behalf of their close male kin. Gulbadan's book also highlights how relationships were often cross-cutting: cousins married each other; widows and divorcees remarried; wives occasionally favored their natal kin against their husbands; higher-ranked wives became foster-mothers of their co-wives' children; slaves and concubines and their sons by the patriarch rose in power; lower-ranked women became milk-nurses and their own biological children formed foster kinship and emotional bonds with the patriarch's sons they attended, often with lasting influence.

Effectively administering an empire the size of Hindustan required practical policies and techniques unfamiliar to Humayun. Instead, he sought to locate himself symbolically within the cosmic order, reflecting his own mystical claims to be the millennial sovereign.[3] He constructed his court as a microcosm of the universe, centered on his own sacred self. He draped a veil over his turban and face, sheltering his courtiers from his divine splendor, occasionally ritually raising his veil to reveal his effulgence. He identified each weekday with an astral body, himself wearing self-designed robes of the conforming color while conducting the corresponding imperial functions. For instance, on Tuesday, identified with the astrological planet Mars, Humayun wore red garments, sat 'on the throne of wrath and vengeance,' and directed the sentencing of each criminal and war-captive to imaginative punishments, guided by Humayun's own inspired insight into the otherwise hidden essence of the prisoner and his alleged deeds.[4] Humayun ordered his tents to be symbolically made in twelve sections, each representing a zodiac sign. Humayun's model, which stressed mystical powers, evidently resonated with the transcendent doctrines of his favored Shattari Sufi order, which specialized in interpreting and channeling cosmic forces through yogic practices. Thus, he used various novel rituals to create an imperial cult as his regime's core.

Additionally, Humayun innovated with administrative structures. He issued various mundane rules and ordinances, which he ordered compiled by his courtier and historian Khwandamir into the *Qanun-i Humayuni* ('Laws of Humayun').[5] But additionally, he devised elaborate organizational schemes. In one, Humayun arranged his court and administration into three divisions of the Order of the Arrow, each with 12 sections, each signified by an arrow of diminishing purity: from his own arrow of unadulterated gold down to those of his lowly gatekeepers having the most amalgam.[6] In another scheme, he divided the branches of his administration according to the prime natural elements: fire (the military), air (his household), water (irrigation) and earth (buildings and lands). Each branch's officials were to wear robes of the corresponding color. But his imaginative rituals failed to prove his authority to his brothers, Central Asian commanders, new Indian Muslim and non-Muslim subordinates, or many Hindustani subjects. In particular, leading Central Asians still asserted their own right to a share in governance and resisted Humayun's efforts to centralize authority in himself. Indeed, Humayun faced repeated rebellions throughout his reign.

Like Babur, Humayun presented himself as the imperial font of repeated gracious forgiveness for those rebels he deemed worthy and who submissively begged for pardon. Some defeated opponents were beneath his notice and were summarily executed. But others attracted his mercy because they were relatives, noblemen, women, children, or performed especially persuasive forms of submission (like approaching him bearing a shroud or hanging their sword from their neck). Thus, he recovered their (nominal and often temporary) support but lowered the moral hazard of opposing him since, if defeated, they could again expect forgiveness.

HUMAYUN'S EARLY MILITARY SUCCESSES

Immediately on his accession, Humayun determined to conquer much of South Asia, despite the many powerful rulers and warlords pressing against him and despite his limited knowledge of his new domain. Threatening Humayun from the central and lower Ganges plain were shifting coalitions of Indo-Afghans and the Sultan of Bengal, supported by local landholders and cultivators. Continuing Babur's military momentum, Humayun's imperial forces under his direct command gained some initial victories. But another threat impinged from the south-west: Sultan Bahadur Shah of Gujarat (r. 1526–35, 1536–7).

Earlier, as a refugee prince fleeing his father and then his succeeding elder brother, Bahadur Shah had fruitlessly sought Babur's aid. Nonetheless, Bahadur Shah eventually seized the throne, prompting Babur's assessment: 'a bloodthirsty and audacious young man.'[7] Bahadur Shah's coastal domain was wealthy, controlling major ports for India's trade across the Indian Ocean. He thus had access to benefits, and was exposed to dangers, from the contending Ottomans and Portuguese. He used his wealth to purchase the loyalties of various other regional rulers, to hire extensively from the Indian military labor market, and to collect expensive artillery— commanded by Rumi Khan (one of many artillery commanders bearing that title). Twice (1533, 1534) Bahadur Shah besieged Chittor, a fortress controlling strategic access to Hindustan.

Map 4: Humayun's World during His Indian Reigns

Belatedly responding to Bahadur Shah's challenge, Humayun abandoned his inconclusive eastern expedition and marched to defend Chittor. Arriving too late to save that fortress, Humayun decided in 1535 to conquer Gujarat instead. When the two armies met in Malwa, Sultan Bahadur followed Rumi Khan's advice to entrench his army behind cannon-reinforced walls. However, Humayun's more mobile forces surrounded and starved them until they fled. Thereafter, Rumi Khan shifted to Humayun's service as his artillery commander. The escaping Bahadur Shah sought refuge in a series of his cities, each time driven out by Humayun's pursuing forces. Finally, Bahadur Shah turned for aid to Portuguese Viceroy Nuno da Cuna (r. 1528–38), at the fortified island of Diu, which Bahadur Shah had earlier ceded to the Portuguese in exchange for military support. However, as fleeing Bahadur Shah negotiated with the Viceroy in Diu harbor in 1537, a clash erupted; Bahadur Shah drowned (either assassinated by the Portuguese or accidentally killed while fleeing them).[8]

Humayun's plan to continue subduing prosperous but turbulent Gujarat met opposition from his major Central Asian commanders, who insisted Mughal forces return to Hindustan where rebels had arisen in his absence. When Humayun hesitated, these generals supported his half-brother, Askari, who rode to Agra and proclaimed himself sovereign. Humayun then perforce followed to subdue and forgive his brother and recover his throne. Their cousin explained 'because of discord among the amirs [Humayun] abandoned Gujarat without achieving anything and returned empty-handed at the height of his power. This resulted in a falling off in his fortune, and the awe he had inspired in the hearts of the people suffered a diminution.'[9] Seeking to restore his regime's confidence and his ability to reward his supporters with looted treasuries, Humayun led his main forces down the Ganges again toward Bengal.

Eastern India still largely remained in the hands of hostile Indo-Afghans who had rallied under the dynamic leadership of Sher Khan, an Indian-settled Afghan of the Sur clan. Humayun's first major battle was to capture the massive and strategically located fortress of Chunar, held by Sher Khan's son. Chunar's walls were defended by cannon (showing the dissemination of gunpowder technology over the previous decade). Nonetheless, Humayun's artillery was more extensive and powerful. Further, Rumi Khan (now in his service) innovatively mounted cannon on riverboats to batter the fortress into a negotiated surrender. This also forced Sher Khan's nominal submission.

Showing Humayun's appreciation of the rising significance of artillery and Rumi Khan's special technical expertise, Humayun rewarded him with command over the captured fortress and its captive garrison, empowered to do 'whatever he thought best.'[10] Rumi Khan reportedly ordered the three hundred imprisoned artillerymen to have their hands amputated (or executed, according to some accounts), evidently thus retaining his own exclusive control over this military science. But Humayun had earlier granted them pardon through an act of imperial grace (and incentive to surrender). Hence, 'The Padishah was pained by this act of Rumi Khan's and said, "Since these men were under amnesty, it was not appropriate to cut their hands off".'[11] Further, technician Rumi Khan clearly stood outside of the cultural circle of Humayun's major Central Asian commanders, who reportedly assassinated him with poison while in imperial disfavor.

Soon, however, other artillery commanders, also conventionally bearing the title Rumi Khan, replaced him and Humayun continued to pour money into his artillery park. At its peak, Humayun commanded seven hundred caissons, each drawn by four pair of oxen. On every caisson was a small Anatolian cannon that shot a ball weighing [2.25 kg] ... [plus] eight mortars, each drawn by seven pairs of oxen. Stone balls could not be used in these because they would be pulverized. They shot [seven-metal-alloy] balls weighing [22.5 kg] .... With these they could hit anything visible within a league.[12]

While impressive, Humayun's developing arsenal inevitably entailed increasing logistical support and expense.

Humayun, 'hoping that he could repair the damage to his reputation' and seize enemy treasuries to pay for his mounting costs for men and equipment, continued eastward to conquer the wealthy Sultanate of Bengal.[13] Although his army achieved some victories, many of his Central Asian supporters felt uncomfortable in humid, riverine Bengal. On his part, Humayun reportedly withdrew from active leadership, shutting himself off with his wives in a pleasure palace, indulging in opium.

As the political and military situation back in Hindustan deteriorated, Hindal claimed his own sovereignty in Agra. As explained by Humayun's grandson:

> When [Humayun] conquered ... Bengal, he took up his abode there for some time. Mīrzā Hindāl, by his order, had remained at Agra. A body of avaricious servants ... working upon his base nature (shaking the chain of his vile heart), led the Mīrzā on the road of rebellion and ingratitude .... The thoughtless Mīrzā had the _khutba_ recited in his own name ... and openly raised the standard of rebellion and strife.[14]

Abruptly, Humayun decided to move his army up the Ganges, unwisely too late to avoid the monsoon that made roads virtually impassable. An increasingly powerful Sher Khan, supported by growing numbers of other Indo-Afghan commanders who had abandoned Humayun, blocked his way.

HUMAYUN LOSES HIS EMPIRE

Throughout his reign, Humayun did not effectively incorporate non-Central Asians into his court and administration, most notably Sher Khan. During Babur's reign, Sher Khan had come to join his service. But more polished Central Asian courtiers ridiculed him for his rustic manners. A relative of Sher Khan recalled hearing him recount his experiences: '... it happened that they placed before [Sher Khan] a solid dish, which he did not know the customary mode of eating. So he cut it into small pieces with his dagger, and putting them into his spoon easily disposed of them.'[15] Babur also recalled this incident as revealing Sher Khan's innovative boldness, so Babur ordered surveillance over him.

Alienated, Sher Khan fled Babur's court. Thereafter, Sher Khan pursued his own independent rule, opportunistically opposing and negotiating with Humayun. Following Sher Khan's loss of Chunar, he had agreed to rule Chunar and Bihar province under Mughal sovereignty, but soon repudiated his submission. Based on his direct knowledge of Babur, Humayun, and their regimes, Sher Khan later claimed that he had rightly predicted:

> I will shortly expel the Mughals from Hind, for the Mughals are not superior to the Afghans in battle or single combat; but the Afghans have let the empire of Hind slip from their hands, on account of their internal dissentions. Since I have been among the Mughals, ... I see that they have no order or discipline, and that their kings, from pride of birth and station, do not personally superintend the government, but leave all the affairs and business of the State to their nobles and ministers .... These grandees act on corrupt motives in every case .... Whoever has money, whether loyal or disloyal, can get his business settled as he likes by paying for it ...[16]

In June 1539, as Humayun's weakened forces marched westward from Bengal, they met Sher Khan's more effective army at Chausa. Humayun's sodden, dispirited and out-maneuvered Mughal army lost badly, with many of his commanders and one wife killed and another captured (Sher Khan gallantly returned this surviving wife, Hajji Begum). Fleeing with his scattered army, Humayun nearly drowned struggling across the Ganges, only rescued by a poor water carrier named Nizam.

Fleeing to Agra, Humayun ineffectively regrouped his disheartened and much diminished forces. Alienating many commanders and courtiers even further, Humayun dramatically rewarded Nizam by making him emperor for a day. For many leading courtiers, this raised fundamental questions about Humayun's conception of sovereignty: if he could transfer sovereignty at will (especially to a man of low birth), was it really inherent in his own person either as the unique embodiment of divine authority or as a Timurid? Further, Humayun's military disaster, loss of territories with which to his reward followers, challenges by his half-brothers, and periodic opium-induced withdrawals from active rule all spread doubts about his reign's future among his supporters and Hindustanis generally.

Seeking to recover his lost territories and prestige, Humayun marched against Sher Khan again, losing even more decisively at Kanauj in May 1540. His demoralized imperial army scattered even before serious combat began. Again, Humayun barely escaped, being rescued by an Afghan soldier, Shams-ud-Din. To the further dismay of his few remaining commanders, Humayun later insisted on lavishly rewarding Shams-ud-Din and inducting him into the imperial household (eventually as foster-father to Humanyun's first surviving son). Driven out of Hindustan by Sher Khan (who acceded in Delhi as Sultan Sher Shah), Humayun fled west to the Punjab, losing supporters at each stage.

Still nominally Padshah, Humayun deliberated where to find refuge and then reconquer a realm. Mirza Kamran held Kabul and blocked Humayun from the family's Central Asian homeland. Humayun considered invading the trans-mountainous region of Kashmir, but his remaining commanders rejected that. He even contemplated renouncing the world to become a *qalandar* (wandering holy man) or making the pilgrimage to Mecca. Finally, he moved with his ever-shrinking entourage across the Rajasthan desert into Sind. The Central Asian commanders who had supported Babur and then Humayun, but lacked bonds to Hindustan, had virtually all left. So thin was the layer of imperial administration over Hindustan that, after Humayun's departure, few traces of his regime remained. The Mughal Empire virtually ended, just 14 years after it commenced with Babur's invasion.

Even as a refugee, Humayun still had some jewels. But his main remaining asset was continued recognition by some key people of his imperial status, despite his much diminished prospect for providing any rewards. Most notable among the handful still attending on him was Bairam Khan, a Shi'i Turcoman (Persianized Turkish) warrior, whose family had long served Babur and Humayun. As Humayun wandered the wastelands of Sind, Bairam Khan and his personal followers joined Humayun's camp.[17] Some local rulers and landholders drove his small band away, but others supplied him with food, willingly or perforce.

In Mirza Hindal's entourage was a Persian-speaking family with a daughter, Hamida Banu. Like Humayun, she was distantly descended from Sufi Shaikh Ahmad 'Zinda-fil.' According to Humayun's half-sister, he was attracted to Hamida, then in her early teens, and proposed to her family and patron, Hindal. But Hindal objected that Humayun was too poor to marry. Hamida also asserted her personal objections and refused Humayun for weeks, despite the urgings of Humayun's womenfolk. Hamida reportedly thought his social status too high: 'I shall marry someone ... whose collar my hand can touch, and not one whose skirt it does not reach.'[18] Humayun, however, persisted until she finally wed him in desert exile.

Within a year, in October 1542, Hamida Begum bore Humayun his first surviving son (and fourth child), Akbar. But only months later, Askari, who held Qandahar under Kamran's overlordship, nearly captured Humayun's entire band. Humayun, Hamida and about 30 followers hurriedly escaped, abandoning unweaned Akbar. Askari kept his nephew as a royal hostage for a year before passing him on to Kamran, then ruling in Kabul. Askari also ordered the local Baluch chieftains to seize Humayun.

Reduced to eating horsemeat parboiled in a battle helmet, Humayun and his small band crossed the Safavid frontier unannounced in 1544, hoping for honorable treatment. Humayun's personally hand-written and submissive note to Emperor Shah Tahmasp (r. 1524–76) impressed the Safavid court:

> Although I have never enrolled myself formally among your Majesty's servants, nevertheless strong ties of love and devotion have always drawn me to you. Now, through the caprice of fate, my realm has been reduced from the broad lands of India to the narrow confines of Sind .... I trust that, when we meet, I may be able to explain my situation to you.[19]

Continuing his humble tone and alluding to Shah Tahmasp's ancestor, Shi'i Imam Ali, Humayun later again requested an imperial audience. A Safavid historian noted Humayun's request was 'accompanied by a number of verses alluding to the story of the miraculous rescue of Salman by Ali from the grip of the lion, and the aptness of this allusion will not be lost upon intelligent persons.'[20]

After negotiations, Shah Tahmasp provided an imperial welcome to his 'younger brother' (although Humayun was eight years older); a deferential visiting emperor (even a deposed one) added luster to the Safavid court. To repay this gracious hospitality, Humayun presented to Tahmasp 250 rubies, his last remaining treasure.[21] Further, Humayun accepted the Shi'i Safavid monarch as his pir, just as Babur had done for Tahmasp's father (these dual submissions to Safavid sovereignty and Shi'i pirship would rankle subsequent Mughal emperors). While in exile, Humayun visited Iran's major Sufi shrines. He also learned to appreciate Safavid aesthetics (he would later extensively recruit Iranian courtiers, artists and historians).

HUMAYUN CAMPAIGNS TO RECREATE THE MUGHAL EMPIRE

In 1545, after Humayun had spent about a year in Iran, Shah Tahmasp sent a qizilbash army of 12,000 to assist Humayun by successfully recapturing Qandahar from Askari. However, Humayun then took Qandahar from the Safavids (the two emperors eventually compromised that Bairam Khan would govern under their joint sovereignty). Later that year, Humayun recaptured Kabul from Kamran, recovering his imprisoned son, Akbar, as well.

For the next decade, Humayun lived largely as his father had done for 20 years—as Kabul's insecure ruler, launching predatory raids in order to attract and reward warriors with loot. Humayun considered reconquering Hindustan on several occasions but prioritized recovering Balkh and other parts of the family's homeland in Mawarannahr from the Uzbeks. Instead, Humayun twice temporarily lost Kabul (and custody of Akbar) to Kamran. In 1551, a raid by Kamran killed Hindal, currently supporting Humayun. But Humayun repeatedly forgave the recurrently rebellious Kamran and Askari until, finally, even Humayun's grace exhausted, he reluctantly had Askari exiled and Kamran blinded and exiled by 1554. Only after Humayun's three half-brothers had all been eliminated, and he had recruited Iranians and a younger generation of Central Asian warriors, did he actually invade Hindustan in 1555—when Sher Shah Suri's successors were particularly divided and weak.

Having driven Humayun from India 15 years earlier and killed or exiled most of his supporters, including Indian Muslims, Sher Shah had constructed a more effective state. During his five-year reign, he developed a more efficient administrative apparatus, including more accurately assessed land revenues, stabilized currency, and enhanced transportation and communications infrastructures. All these fostered the economy and enabled him to extract and control more income, which he used to recruit extensively from the north Indian military labor market. This freed him from dependence on other Indo-Afghan chieftains, whom he subordinated to his royal authority. Improving the efficacy of his core cavalry, he instituted a system of inspection and branding of warhorses to ensure their serviceability. His strengthened military won him victories and captured royal treasuries in the surrounding territories. Before his death in 1545 (by accident, while besieging a Rajput fortress), Sher Shah developed many institutions and procedures later central to the Mughal Empire.[22]

But, over the next decade, Sher Shah's successors fell into disarray. At the time of Humayun's invasion, Muhammad 'Adil Suri, the nominal Sultan, held little loyalty from contending Indo-Afghan governors or commanders. Hence, despite 15 years of exile, Humayun easily captured Lahore in February 1555. In July, Humayun's diverse forces defeated the main Indo-Afghan army at Sirhind and seized Delhi.

Hindustan's society and economy were deeply disordered. Remnants of the Suri forces quickly regrouped and many other Indo-Afghan and Rajput rulers and warlords remained unvanquished. Rising Mahdist and other Islamic millennial movements in Hindustan and Afghanistan challenged the established religious, political and social orders. Further, extreme drought, famine and plague had been recurring for years.

During the remaining months until his accidental death in 1556, Humayun sought to re-establish his rule over Hindustan. He innovatively reached out to Indian Muslims. He welcomed Suhrawardi Sufi leader Shaikh Gadai Kamboh (a Punjabi whose ancestors had converted to Islam), whom Sher Shah had driven into exile for Mughal sympathies. Similarly, Humayun created a political alliance with the powerful Indian Muslim clan based in Mewat (a region strategically near Delhi) by marrying a daughter of their chief (as his last of many wives).

Humayun's last scheme for governance was decentralization. Six relatively autonomous governors would each manage one of

Sher Mandal, built by Sher Shah, site of Humayun's library and fatal fall

his newly reconquered provinces—Delhi, Agra, Kanauj, Jaunpur, Mandu, Lahore—while Humayun himself, as paramount ruler, would circulate among them with an imperial army to supervise and reinforce as necessary. In the critical words of Abu-al-Fazl (who later advocated a centralized Mughal state): 'From the beginning of his [Humayun's] career till now his mind was exercised in strange inventions and in showing forth recondite truths.'[23] Humayun allocated Kabul to his infant second son, Hakim, who nominally governed under a trusted guardian. In addition, Humayun sent Bairam Khan to Lahore to secure strategic and economically crucial but still turbulent Punjab, accompanied by Humayun's young but eldest son, Akbar. Humayun also betrothed Bairam Khan (whom Humayun entitled Khan-i Khanan, 'Nobleman among Noblemen') both to Salima Sultan Begum (a granddaughter of Babur), as well as to Humayun's new sister-in-law, a Mewati noblewoman.

Only seven months after Humayun's decisive victory at Sirhind, he tripped while descending a steep stone staircase from his library in Delhi, reportedly when responding to the call to prayer. He died from his injuries days later in January 1556. Bairam Khan then emerged as regent while Akbar began his half-century-long reign that would truly establish the foundations for the Mughal Empire.

Part II

Establishment of the Mughal Empire under Emperor Akbar, 1556–1605

4

EMPEROR AKBAR MAKES HIMSELF
THE CENTER OF THE MUGHAL EMPIRE

[Emperor Akbar] was of middle height, but inclining to be tall; he was of the hue of wheat; his eyes and eyebrows were black, and his complexion rather dark than fair; he was lion-bodied, with a broad chest, and his hands and arms long. On the left side of his nose he has a fleshy mole, very agreeable in appearance, of the size of half a pea. Those skilled in the science of physiognomy considered this mole a sign of great prosperity and exceeding good fortune. His august voice was very loud, and in speaking and explaining had a particular richness. In his actions and movements he was not like the people of the world, and the glory of God manifested itself in him.

Akbar's eldest son, Emperor Jahangir.[1]

In May 1562, 19-year-old Emperor Akbar was napping inside his harem when he heard an unprecedented disruption just outside. His maddened foster-brother and prominent commander, Adham Khan Kokaltash, with bloody unsheathed sword, was threatening the eunuch guards. Moments earlier, Adham Khan had led his henchmen into the adjacent imperial offices where they assassinated Shams-ud-Din Ataka Khan, the Empire's leading minister and head of a rising rival faction of the young emperor's foster-relations. Immediately, many leading courtiers fled the city, terrified of a bloody succession war. Akbar's authorized biographer wrote, 'His Majesty was awakened by the dreadful clamour,' rushed out, saw the gory corpse, grappled with Adham Khan, and then 'struck him such a blow on the face with his fist that that wicked monster turned a summersault and fell down insensible.'[2] Akbar had his remaining personal attendants toss Adham Khan over the parapet. When he barely survived, Akbar ordered him dragged upstairs by his hair and thrown over again, 'headlong so that his neck was broken, and his brains destroyed.' While Akbar forgave Adham Khan's mother, Maham Anaga (Akbar's ailing former wet-nurse and thus foster-mother), she died grieving weeks later. Respecting their long, close personal service to him, Akbar built substantial tombs for her and her son, in the architectural style of the preceding Afghan dynasty. Further, Akbar used this traumatic event to empower himself after six years under the domination of his regent-guardians.

Tomb of Maham Anaga and Adham Khan, Delhi, *c.* 1562

During Akbar's five-decade reign (1556–1605), he and his key supporters firmly grounded the Mughal dynasty in Hindustan. Akbar's grandfather, father and their leading supporters had mostly lived outside India, largely oriented toward Central Asia. In contrast, Akbar was born in Sind (western India) and remained within

Map 5: Akbar's World on Accession, 1556

Hindustan throughout most of his life (his longest period away was as a royal captive in Kabul during early childhood).

After Akbar's succession was eventually secured and he had emerged from regency, he and his close advisors innovated key policies. Akbar expanded his household, court, administration and army through wide-ranging recruitment, particularly through many political marriage alliances and cultural policies that attracted various Muslim and non-Muslim Indians. He and his courtiers reconstituted the Empire by developing more centralized fiscal and administrative systems. Over each phase in his imperial career, based in a different capital, he commanded expanding Mughal armies that remained almost constantly engaged in defensive and offensive warfare against his ambitious relatives, rebellious imperial officials, elite and popular uprisings and neighboring rulers. Most of his life, Akbar personally entered the battlefield and directly commanded military campaigns until just before his death. Thus, Akbar and his supporters established and expanded the Mughal Empire as a complex synthesis of Central Asian, Islamic and diverse Indian processes, cultures and people.

AKBAR'S SUDDEN ACCESSION IN 1556 AND IMPERIAL RIVALS

Using hindsight, many commentators regard the Mughal Empire as Akbar's birthright. However, his succession was by no means certain following Emperor Humayun's unexpected death in January 1556. Many leading commanders feared destructive disorder and the collapse of the nascent Empire—frequent outcomes of Central Asian successions and, more generally, of patrimonial conquest states with little local loyalty. More than half of Humayun's high officers and officials were Central Asians, another third were Iranians, and few were Indian Muslims or Rajput Hindus.[3] Some Central Asians and Iranians had migrated to Hindustan due to personal fealty to Humayun, so they prepared to return home. Humayun's remaining rival courtiers sought to delay the succession crisis by concealing his death for two weeks. They spread false reports of his good health and costumed someone who resembled the deceased emperor in his imperial robes for public display (a deception reportedly recommended by visiting Ottoman admiral, Sidi Ali Rais, as occasionally done in his imperial court).[4] Some commanders saw Humayun's death as an opportunity to follow Timurid tradition by dividing his territories among his sons, other close male relatives, or themselves.

Bairam Khan, Humayun's most powerful companion, was fortuitously in nearby Punjab. Further, Bairam Khan was personal guardian of 12-year-old Akbar, the most promising claimant: Humayun's eldest son and clearly intended heir as Padshah in Hindustan. Humayun had groomed Akbar to rule, awarding him at age nine his recently deceased uncle Hindal's entourage and appanage. Humayun had also appointed Akbar as governor of Kabul and Ghazni, albeit nominally and under the actual charge of trusted and experienced guardians. Thus, Bairam Khan, on receiving secret news of Humayun's fatal injury, immediately installed Akbar on a makeshift throne, then rushed him to the Agra court, fended off rival courtiers and claimants, and formally installed Akbar as emperor—with himself as controlling regent. Nonetheless, other biological and adopted relatives and favorites of Humayun, evoking the Central Asian tradition of collective sovereignty, would powerfully assert their own claims to parts or all of Akbar's legacy for three decades, until he had outlived virtually all of them.

At Humayun's death, the most plausible alternative to Akbar was Humayun's younger son, Mirza Hakim. But Hakim was in distant Kabul and, at age two, as yet unsupported by a sufficiently powerful faction to claim more than that region, which Humayun had intended for him. For much of Hakim's early youth, he nominally ruled in Kabul, first under the regency of one of Humayun's favorite courtiers, Munim Khan, and then under Hakim's mother, Mah Chuchak Begum. Next, Hakim lived under the control of Shah Abdul Ma'ali, yet another contender for the Mughal throne. Finally, during Hakim's teens and twenties, he emerged occasionally as Kabul's de facto independent ruler, generally recognized by the Safavids and Uzbeks. Emperor Akbar's court had mixed attitudes and policies toward Hakim: treating him as Akbar's subordinate but outside the official administrative hierarchy; occasionally supporting Hakim when he was vulnerable but also repeatedly repulsing his martial incursions into India.

Throughout Hakim's life, he provided a focus for ambitious dissidents within the Empire who resented Akbar's policies.[5] Hakim invaded the Punjab whenever Akbar appeared weak. Among those in north India who periodically proclaimed Hakim's sovereignty (and denied Akbar's) were prominent Uzbek, Turkman and Indo-Afghan commanders, members of the 'ulama, powerful Naqshbandi Sufi pirs and other orthodox Sunni Muslims. Especially dangerously, Uzbek officials entrusted by Akbar with governing Malwa and eastern India periodically rose up during the 1560s, rejected his authority, and declared Hakim's reign. In 1579–82, a rebellion in Bengal led by the Indo-Afghan Qaqshal clan again evoked Hakim's sovereignty. Only major military expeditions led by Akbar personally or by his loyalists eventually drove back these recurrent threats from the west and east.

Akbar graciously pardoned Hakim after each betrayal, explaining: 'Hakim Mirza is a memorial to the Emperor Humayun. Though he has acted ungratefully, I can be no other than forbearing.'[6] Only after Hakim's death (at 31 in 1585 from chronic alcoholism) did Akbar integrate Kabul with the rest of his Empire. This death also weakened conservative Sunni factions and independent-minded commanders, enabling Akbar to innovate administratively and religiously with less overt opposition. Beyond Mirza Hakim's challenges, other major rebellions by high courtiers marked the first half-dozen years of Akbar's reign following the regency.

Prominent among Humayun's leading commanders who challenged Bairam Khan's regency and Akbar's authority was Shah Abdul Ma'ali, Humayun's adoptive son and a high-born Sayyid (claiming descent from the Prophet Muhammad). Although at Humayun's death he proved unable to rally sufficient force to mount the throne himself, he pointedly rejected participation in Akbar's enthronement. Subsequently, Bairam Khan had Shah Abdul Ma'ali imprisoned. But, recognizing his relationship with Humayun and his potential as a focus of dissidence, Bairam Khan then had Akbar allow Shah Abdul Ma'ali to withdraw honorably on pilgrimage to distant Mecca.

Following Shah Abdul Ma'ali's return, however, he mobilized several serious challenges to Akbar. Most dangerously, he seized Kabul and Mirza Hakim, married Hakim's elder sister, Fakhr-un-Nissa Begum, and had Hakim's regent-mother assassinated. But then he himself was executed by yet another contender for Humayun's legacy, Mirza Sulaiman. Even then, Shah Abdul Ma'ali retained sufficient prestige for burial next to Babur.

Mirza Sulaiman, another of Humayun's relatives and adoptive sons, held power in politically turbulent but strategic Badakhshan during much of his career, as prince Humayun had done. When Humayun died, Sulaiman besieged Hakim's Kabul, only retreating after his sovereignty was recognized through the khutba, albeit just once.[7] Later, whenever opportunities arose, Sulaiman seized Kabul or the Punjab. During one of his repeated captures of Kabul, Sulaiman assassinated Shah Abdul Ma'ali, married his daughter to Mirza Hakim, and used Hakim as a puppet. Later, Sulaiman was displaced from Badakhshan by his own grandson, Mirza Shahrukh, who eventually succumbed to the Uzbeks. Ultimately, both Shahrukh and Sulaiman fled to refuge with Akbar. Akbar honored these Mirzas in especially distinguished welcoming ceremonies, reviving for the occasion the court customs of their shared Chingizid and Timurid ancestors. Akbar then incorporated both men into the Mughal imperial hierarchy with high ranks and gave a daughter to Shahrukh in marriage.

Thus, Akbar, especially during his reign's the first three decades, faced challenges from other claimants to Humayun's legacy and from dissident imperial commanders. Then, during Akbar's last decade, his own maturing sons would form foci for fissiparous factions.

Most prominently, Akbar's eldest surviving son, Salim, would reign virtually independently in Allahabad for five years (1599–1604), even claiming the title Padshah, before resubmitting to Akbar and eventually receiving his forgiveness. Throughout the Mughal dynasty, every imperial succession would remain an extended, uncertain and dangerous event. Fortunately for Akbar, Bairam Khan loyally managed Akbar's accession and administration during his early teenage years.

AKBAR UNDER REGENCY, 1556–62

For four years following Akbar's enthronement, Bairam Khan acted in Akbar's name to extend the Empire as well as Bairam Khan's own power. Although Akbar's grandfather, Babur, had immediately asserted his independent rule while even younger, Akbar remained largely unengaged in imperial administration until the dramatic 1562 events recounted above. Instead, Bairam Khan governed as Wakil-us-Sultanat ('Agent of the State,' effectively regent).

Various Indo-Afghan and Rajput rulers and commanders had recovered following their defeat by Humayun at Sirhind in July 1555. Their forces rallied around Hemu, who had risen up dramatically through the Suri administration to become chief minister. Contemporary sources concur that Hemu came from a Hindu non-Rajput trading community, but identify his early career variously as greengrocer, itinerant trader, or market master.[8] In October 1556, just months after Akbar's accession, forces under Hemu defeated the Mughal army holding Delhi and recaptured that city. Hemu then took the illustrious title Raja Vikramajit, evoking legendary Hindu sovereigns. Responding, Bairam Khan executed the defeated Mughal commander, Tardi Beg Khan (a rival at the Mughal court), and used Akbar as a symbol to rally the remaining imperial troops in desperate fighting at Panipat the next month. The battle only favored the Mughals after an arrow struck Hemu's head, incapacitating him. His followers panicked. Wounded Hemu was dragged before Bairam Khan and Akbar and decapitated (sources differ about whether Hemu was beheaded by Bairam Khan or by Akbar, who would thus earn his title Ghazi).[9] Substantial opposition, especially by Indo-Afghans, continued for decades, repulsing repeated Mughal assaults.

Bairam Khan, strengthening his own control even further, posted his own Central Asian and Iranian supporters as governors of key provinces. He also extended Humayun's policy of incorporating Indian Muslims, for instance appointing Suhrawardi Sufi Shaikh Gadai Kamboh as chief *Sadr* (managing revenue-grants for Muslim clerics and other worthies).[10] Bairam Khan so generously distributed revenue lands to his supporters that the treasury emptied significantly. The Safavids took advantage of Mughal weakness to retake Qandahar in 1557. But in north India, Bairam Khan expanded the Empire, seizing Ajmer, Jaunpur and Gwalior in 1558. While Bairam Khan governed, Akbar frequently hunted far from court.

Throughout Akbar's life, he combined hunting with military expeditions. Hunts, besides the pleasure of the chase, effectively honed his virile and martial skills and reputation while simultaneously familiarizing him with Hindustan's hinterland and rural people.[11] One distinctive form of hunting that Akbar savored was the massive Mongol-style *qamargha*. This required considerable organizational skill since hundreds (or even thousands) of beaters were systematically linked in a great circle, enclosing all the wild animals within. Subordinate officers then maneuvered these beaters simultaneously and evenly inward, concentrating the animals for Akbar and his chosen companions to slaughter *en masse* with arrows, spears, swords and guns. Another distinctive, dangerous and also productive form of hunting was capturing wild elephants. In Indic royal ritual and iconography, elephants represented sovereignty; they were the distinguishing vehicle for rulers entering battle, prominently displaying inspiring leadership to the surrounding troops. Akbar, throughout his youth, risked his life capturing wild elephants, riding elephants into battle and also taming domesticated bull elephants in *mausth*—seasonally aggressive behavior associated with testosterone surges in the elephant (and perhaps in the rider as well).

During his hunting tours and also while residing in his main capital, Agra, Akbar met diverse Indians. These ranged far wider than the constricted circle of primarily Central Asians and Iranians surrounding Babur, Humayun and now Bairam Khan. Even while Akbar was under regency, he appeared to some Hindu Rajputs as a potential ally against Rajput rivals (within their own clan and from other Rajput clans) and also against Bairam Khan's administrators.

Historically, many Hindu ruling and landholding Rajputs fiercely defended local autonomy, pragmatically combined with degrees of subordination to more powerful rulers. Priding themselves on their Rajput warrior dharma, they often based themselves in commanding fortresses, many dangerously near Delhi or Agra. Rajputs had fought both against and also allied with Delhi Sultans. When Babur arrived, some Rajputs fought him at Panipat. Many more rallied against him under Rana Sanga at Khanua. Many supported Hemu. But various Rajputs eventually joined Mughal armies, seeking better opportunities than those available in their resource-poor homelands. The relatively weak Kachhwaha Rajput clan had been among the earliest to support Humayun during his first Indian reign.

In 1557, Raja Bihari Mal (r. 1547–74), the beleaguered Rajwat dynasty ruler of Amber and disputed head of the Kachhwaha Rajput clan, approached Akbar at Agra, promising personal loyalty to the young emperor. Akbar then supported Bihari Mal in his intra-clan conflicts, in his struggles against more powerful Rajput neighbors in Mewar and Marwar, and against the domineering Mughal governor of nearby Mewat. Their bond later strengthened when Akbar wed Bihari Mal's daughter. As Akbar developed his own regime, he would continue to incorporate many Hindu Rajputs into his court and army, creating a much wider manpower base than his father or grandfather had attempted.

From Akbar's youth onward, he prided himself on his personal courage, periodically plunging into combat. For instance, in 1562, while hunting a hundred kilometers from Agra, he was approached by a Brahmin complaining about oppression from local brigands who had murdered his son and plundered his property. As Akbar personally recounted, he drove his elephant and small personal bodyguard against thousands of entrenched bandits: 'Seven arrows hit [Akbar's] shield ... five went through ... and two stopped in the shield .... At last [Akbar's elephant] broke down the wall and entered ... and a large number of the audacious rebels were killed .... Nearly a thousand of them were sent to the abode of annihilation by the fire of the Divine anger.'[12] Akbar would repeatedly prove his personal courage in battle, and in politics.

Akbar always treated Bairam Khan as a foster-father, affectionately and respectfully calling him Khan Baba ('Nobleman Father'). However, as Akbar matured through his teenage years, competing courtiers conspired to arouse his resentment against Bairam Khan's continued paternalism. Among those challenging Bairam Khan's regency were two rival clans within Akbar's household, each opportunistically supported by factions among the imperial commanders.

One ambitious clan was led by Shams-ud-Din, who had saved Humayun's life during the disaster at Kanauj in 1540. Two years later, Shams-ud-Din had requested as his reward that his wife would become a wet-nurse and foster-mother of baby Akbar, making Shams-ud-Din his foster-father and their children Akbar's milk-siblings. When Humayun and Hamida Banu had to abandon newborn Akbar, Shams-ud-Din's family remained with him, even during his years of confinement in Kabul, earning his grateful affection. Especially after Shams-ud-Din's faction eventually helped displace Bairam Khan, more of the clan received high ranks in Akbar's administration than almost any other.[13]

Even more decisive in ousting Bairam Khan from regency was the rival faction, centered on another of Akbar's wet-nurses and foster-mothers, Maham Anaga. These foster-relatives highlighted for Akbar the alleged arrogance of Bairam Khan and also instigated a series of affronts to Bairam Khan's prestige. Bairam Khan's assertively proud and resentful responses to these perceived insults led to heightened tensions between him and Akbar. As a courtier later recounted: 'the Emperor himself (because he had not absolute power in his own kingdom, and sometimes had no voice in some of the transactions relating to expenses of the Exchequer, and because there was no privy purse at all, and the servants of the Emperor had but poor fiefs, and were kept in the depths of poverty, while [Bairam Khan's] were in ease and luxury) wished that the circle about him should be put on a different footing. But he had no power to accomplish this...'[14]

As the factional forces concerted against Bairam Khan began to push him aside, he stubbornly resisted demeaning himself by begging submissive forgiveness in person before his protégé Akbar. Instead, Bairam Khan futilely marshalled his remaining forces against the imperialist army that Akbar sent to subdue him. But when Akbar issued an imperial *farman* ('decree') against Bairam Khan, many of his supporters deserted and joined Akbar, while the remnant was easily defeated. In 1560, Bairam Khan surrendered his symbols of rank, relinquished his official offices and assigned revenue lands, and requested permission to make the pilgrimage to Mecca.

Akbar retained his gratitude for Bairam Khan's surrogate parenthood, but also recognized the need to remove him honorably from Hindustan. Akbar reassigned him some land revenues as a pension during his pilgrimage and in retirement after his return. Bairam Khan, however, was assassinated *en route* in Sind by hostile Afghans. Reflecting Bairam Khan's cultural identity, his family sent his body for burial to Mashhad, an Iranian city sacred to most Shi'as.

Even as Akbar struggled to assert his own control, Bairam Khan's displacement occasioned even more conflict among those vying to replace him as regent. Initially successful in asserting her personal influence over Akbar, Maham Anaga supported Munim Khan, an old favorite of Humayun, as official Wazir, while she largely dictated policy and promoted her younger son and Akbar's milk-brother, Adham Khan. During this period, Mughal armies conquered Malwa (1562) from Rajputs and also the Chunar fortress in the east from resurgent Indo-Afghans. But Adham Khan clashed with Akbar over the division of captured royal and slave women and other spoils; Adham Khan reportedly killed some of these women rather than relinquish them to Akbar. Then, seeking even more power, Adham Khan and his companions assassinated Shams-ud-Din in 1562 (recounted above).

The consequent dramatic assertion of Akbar's personal power, and the embarrassing flight of many leading courtiers and powerbrokers, enabled him to emerge as dominant in his own court. He expanded his supremacy during the next four decades in the face of many challenges and through almost constant battlefield and ideological wars. Akbar never again allowed any single official to concentrate power. Rather, he carefully divided the consolidated authority held by Bairam Khan among ministers who worked under Akbar's direct supervision and usually held nearly equal power and rank: *Wakil* ('agent'), *Diwan-i Kul* ('overall revenue and finance minister') and *Mir Bakhshi* ('minister in charge of supply, logistics, personnel, news-gathering and the emperor's personal security').[15] Further, Akbar relied for advice on an inner circle of courtiers who did not necessarily hold the highest offices or ranks. Little evidence has survived about how much influence and practical power Akbar's mother, step-mothers, leading wives and other female relatives exercised.

Akbar himself was illiterate (possibly due to dyslexia). Yet he had a remarkably retentive memory, mastering the vast volumes of records, documents and official letters that his attendants read out to him. Imperial chroniclers attributed omniscience to Akbar, so their accounts may be exaggerated, but they recorded that Akbar personally dictated all important orders, appointments, promotions, demotions and awards of titles to the hundreds of high-ranking imperial officers and officials. He directed overall diplomatic and military strategy and commanded campaigns (either in person or through designated deputies). He also intervened in all other matters brought to his attention by his courtiers and by an elaborate network of newswriters, with regular and confidential reports coming to him independently from separate offices in every province. Fawning accounts credit Akbar with inventing many weapons in the imperial arsenal and with master superintendence of the imperial horse and elephant stables. Akbar also expanded his pool of loyal supporters, binding diverse men and women to him through strong personal affinities, including through political marriages.

AKBAR EXTENDS HIS HOUSEHOLD AND SUPPORTERS THROUGH POLITICAL MARRIAGE ALLIANCES

Especially in a patrimonial state, the ruler's various political marriages can provide him with significant ways to define and extend his household, allies and body of officials and officers. Conversely, the ruler's new relatives by marriage link themselves to his regime and can gain access to its power and prestige. Often affecting the consequences of a political marriage are the relations between the ruler and his bride, including personal affection. Apart from that, a wife who bears sons, especially if one of them is favored as heir or inherits the throne, customarily enhances her position. Surviving source material does not describe fully the lives, roles, or political influences of most of Akbar's many brides, or how their lives in the imperial harem (and bed chamber) changed when political relations between him and their natal family flourished or turned hostile.

Neither Akbar nor his first bride had much choice in their wedding, although the Islamic *nikah* is legally a personal contract between groom and bride, willingly accepted by both. Following the convention of intra-Timurid marriages, Humayun (while still ruling only in Kabul) wed Akbar at age nine to Shahzadi Ruqaiya Sultan

Begum, the equally young daughter of Hindal. While this marriage solidified family bonds, lasted until Akbar's death, and provided her with an honored and influential place as senior begum in the imperial harem, it did not produce any surviving children. Instead, Ruqaiya Sultan Begum later fostered prince Khurram, a grandson of Akbar and a junior co-wife.

As Akbar reached his late teens and was emerging from regency, he chose his own second marriage, probably still influenced by his first wife, his foster-mothers and other senior Timurid women. After Bairam Khan's displacement and subsequent assassination in 1561, Akbar married one of his widows, Salima Sultan Begum (a granddaughter of Babur and thus both Akbar's and his first wife's cousin).

While this wedding followed intra-Timurid marriage conventions, it also showed Akbar taking over Bairam Khan's establishment. Thus, Akbar informally adopted Bairam Khan's four-year-old son (by another wife) 'Abd-ur-Rahim. Later, Akbar enhanced these personal ties by giving a foster-relative as bride to 'Abd-ur-Rahim. He proved loyal throughout his long career, attaining his father's premier title, Khan-i Khanan, and high administrative posts. Further, Akbar selected for imperial service members of Bairam Khan's staff, including his Iranian fiscal supervisor, Khwaja Muzaffar Khan Turbati; Akbar perceived him to have 'aptitude for business, and [so] granted him his life.'[16]

Salima Sultan Begum held a prominent place in the imperial harem, made herself a respected poet under the penname Makhfi ('Hidden/Concealed One'), and long outlived Akbar. However, she had no surviving children. Thus, Akbar's first two marriages defined his household within Timurid traditions, but neither perpetuated his dynasty nor extended his political alliances among Indians.

In contrast, one of Akbar's key pioneering policies was to negotiate many political marriages for himself and his sons with Hindu Rajput rulers. Some earlier Muslim sultans had taken Hindu Rajput noblewomen as wives or concubines, often as war booty, and customarily converted them to Islam. But Akbar innovatively honored his Rajput wives by respecting their religious traditions and choices; some converted to Islam, but others freely performed Hindu rituals in his harem, often with Akbar's participation. He also recognized their sons as his legitimate heirs, and enrolled their menfolk into the highest levels of imperial service.

Additionally, Akbar supported his Rajput in-laws against other branches of their clan, against other Rajput clans, and against those of his Muslim courtiers who held anti-Hindu sentiments. Further, Akbar recognized the hereditary right of loyal Rajputs to rule their traditional kingdoms with some autonomy, albeit under Mughal sovereignty. Historically, aspiring Rajputs had long practiced hypergamy, giving brides to more powerful Rajput clans; now many Rajputs related similarly to the Mughal dynasty.[17]

As we saw, 14-year-old Akbar had been approached by Raja Bihari Mal of Amber, successfully seeking his support. Five years later, as Akbar emerged from regency and was making a pilgrimage to the Sufi shrine of Khwaja Mu'in-ud-Din Chishti at Ajmer (near Amber), Raja Bihari Mal again approached. He proposed a more personal and enduring alliance by offering as a bride his eldest daughter, Harkha Bai (d. 1613, also known as Hira Kunwari, 'Diamond Princess,' and Mariam-uz-Zamani, 'Mary of the Age'). According to Akbar's approving amanuensis:

> The Rajah from right-thinking and elevated fortune considered that he should bring himself out of the ruck of landholders and make himself one of the distinguished ones of the Court. In order to effect this purpose he ... [placed] his eldest daughter, in whose forehead shone the lights of chastity and intellect, among the attendants on the glorious pavilion [i.e., Akbar's harem].[18]

No surviving evidence shows how much senior women on either side influenced the wedding negotiations or if the bride had any voice in them.

Bihari Mal also sent his son and heir, Bhagwantdas (r. 1573–89), to serve Akbar, followed by his 11-year-old grandson and future ruler of Amber, Man Singh (r. 1589–1614). Man Singh grew up within the imperial household, rising to the highest ranks and offices over his lifetime of service, to the advancement of his imperial Mughal relatives and his Kachhwaha clan.

Despite Akbar's growing number of wives, as he reached his late twenties he still had no surviving children—a daughter and twin sons having died soon after birth. Seeking divine intervention, Akbar humbly made a pilgrimage from Agra 36 kilometers to the Chishti Sufi Shaikh Salim, who dwelled near Sikri village. Harkha

Bai soon became pregnant. For the birth, Akbar sent her to a palace he built near Shaikh Salim's home. Akbar named his first son and eventual heir Mirza Salim (1569–1627, r. 1605–27), pet named Shaikhu Baba. Akbar then appointed Shaikh Salim's daughters and daughters-in-law as the baby's wet-nurses, the Shaikh's second son as the child's tutor, the Shaikh's grandsons as the child's foster-brothers, and other male descendants of the Shaikh as high-ranking imperial officials. Further, Akbar erected an entirely new capital city, Fatehpur Sikri, adjacent to Shaikh Salim's grave. Similarly, Akbar's two other sons, Mirza Murad (1570–99) and Mirza Daniyal (1572–1604), were soon born respectively at the Chishti shrines of Shaikh Salim and Shaikh Daniyal (a disciple of Khwaja Mu'in-ud-Din) at Ajmer. These long-awaited births bound Akbar to Shaikh Salim and the Chishti order.

As Akbar's sons matured, he married each to many Hindu Rajput wives (and also many high-born Muslim spouses). Fifteen-year-old Mirza Salim's first Rajput marriage was with his mother's brother's daughter, Manbhawati Bai. The wedding combined Islamic and Indic-Hindu wedding rituals:

> ... the Emperor celebrated the [nikah] ceremony of [Salim and Manbhawati Bai's] marriage in the presence of the Qazís [Muslim clerics] and nobles. And the sum of [500,000 Rupees] was fixed as the marriage settlement [*mehr*]. And they performed all the ceremonies, which are customary among the Hindús, such as lighting the fire &c .... Rájah [Bhagwantdas] gave as his daughter's dowry, several strings of horses, and a hundred elephants, and boys and girls of Abyssinia, India, and Circassia, and all sorts of golden vessels set with jewels ... the quantity of which is beyond all computation.[19]

Political marriage alliances with Rajput brides meant all subsequent Mughal emperors had Hindu ancestors and many had Hindu mothers and wives.

Following the same political marriage strategy as the Kachhwaha, other aspiring Rajput clans also offered daughters as wives to Akbar and his sons. Of Akbar's many official wives, at least 11 (and probably far more) were from Hindu Rajput families, and he married his sons to at least six Hindu Rajput brides. Many Rajput clans also supplied sons to serve Akbar, but no clan proved as successful as the Kachhwahas. At Akbar's death in 1605, 27 Kachhwahas held high rank in Akbar's service out of 61 from all royal Rajput clans.[20] On their part, Rajput imperial wives, their male relatives in Mughal service and outside of it, and various other Hindus amalgamated into their own Indic-Hindu cultural traditions many of the Persianate customs developing in Akbar's court.

These Rajput clans located the Mughal imperial clan in the same social and divine order as themselves, with similar martial dharma. Bards wrote praise poems to their Rajput patrons, in Rajasthani, Braj Basha and Sanskrit, sometimes celebrating heroic opposition to the Mughal emperor, sometimes lauding valiant service to him, both as justified by Rajput dharma. For instance, Amrit Rai's 1585 biography of Raja Man Singh—Kachhwaha ruler of Amber, repeatedly a bride giver to the Mughal house and a leading imperial general—identifies Akbar as a worthy divine master within the Indic-Hindu cosmic order:

> a portion of the supreme being descended to earth
> to destroy the suffering of others.
> He is the rightful universal emperor [*chakravartin*] of the Chaghatay clan,
>   a protector of the entire earth.
> Long live Shah Jalal-al-Din [Akbar], the world-conqueror, the jewel of
>   the world![21]

This poet continues:

> His measureless power adorns the three worlds ....
> The emperor upholds dharma. His rule stabilizes the earth ....
> The goddess Lakshmi shares her time between Vishnu's embrace and
>   nestling at Akbar's breast.[22]

Such praise singers thus glorified their Rajput patrons by elevating their employer and sovereign Akbar to semi-divine status and intimacy with Hindu goddesses. Significantly, such praise poems avoided mentioning the giving of Rajput brides to the emperor, since that had negative gendered implications, whatever the practical political benefits to both parties.

The growing presence in Akbar's harem of Hindu Rajput wives and in the Mughal administration of their male relatives and other Rajput and non-Rajput Hindus correlates with Akbar's religious and political policies from early in his reign. In particular, Akbar terminated several levies and regulations that discriminated against non-Muslims including his ending the prohibition on the construction of new Hindu, Jain, Parsi and other non-Muslim temples. Akbar made *inam*s ('endowments of land revenue') to Hindu temples (including at Vrindavan) and to non-Muslim holy men. In 1564, Akbar halted the collection of *jizya*, regarded as a discriminatory tax by many non-Muslims, including Akbar's growing number of Rajput officials. In contrast, some orthodox Muslims regarded *jizya* as an appropriate and legally required penalty on subjects who refused to convert to Islam; they convinced Akbar to re-impose it in 1575. However, these imperial orders largely went unenforced and Akbar officially reconfirmed its abolition in 1579. We can never know the full extent that Akbar was influenced by the increasing number of Hindus in his household and service, but these policies evidently gained support from many non-Muslims, who comprised the vast majority of his subjects.

The wealth and territorial acquisitions gained by some Rajput ruling clans through imperial service afforded them status, resources and political power unavailable to their merely locally based ancestors, especially since their Rajasthan homeland was not agriculturally rich. Further, the concept 'Rajput' changed through their interactions with the Mughal Empire, evident in: clan genealogies and histories highlighting sacred ancestry; Persianate literary, artistic and administrative vocabulary and expertise; sartorial and other fashions emulating imperial court style; and the primacy of the royal clan head above his tributary kinsmen.[23] Moreover, Rajput imperial officials increasingly served far from their homelands, often forming marriage and other alliances with Rajputs they met there. They used incomes and rewards from imperial service to fund the expansion of their natal estates and to patronize Hindu temples and other devotional sites. They thus gained financially and politically, particularly compared to rival Rajputs who disdained participation in the Mughal Empire and expended their limited resources resisting it.

Among the leading Rajput clans longest to fight against the Empire were the Sisodias of Mewar. They suffered a major military defeat by Babur in 1527, lost their stronghold of Chittor to Akbar in 1568, and received devastating battlefield losses in 1576 from an imperial army commanded by Raja Man Singh. (Man Singh won the battle, but did not capture the Sisodia ruler nor allow Mughal forces to pillage Mewar, leading to temporary disfavor by Akbar.) Thereafter, the Sisodias resisted from their Mewar base until 1614. Even after they finally perforce submitted to Akbar's successor, they negotiated that their clan would never provide a bride to the Mughal family and that the reigning Sisodia Rana would not personally serve in the Mughal army or administration (although other Sisodias did). Especially after the power and prestige of the Mughal Empire declined during the eighteenth century, the Sisodias celebrated their resistance to the Mughals as indicating cultural superiority over other Rajput clans who had hypergamously given their womenfolk as imperial brides.

Significantly, Akbar and his strong successors never gave their womenfolk as brides to Rajputs or any other non-Muslims. Instead, Akbar informally adopted some daughters of close Rajput courtiers and arranged their marriages with Rajput royal houses.[24] Later, Emperor Jahangir, although himself the son of Akbar's first Rajput wife and having many Rajput brides of his own, wrote condemning Muslim clans which reciprocated by giving brides to Hindus: 'They ally themselves with Hindus, and both give and take girls. Taking them is good, but giving them, God forbid! I gave an order that hereafter they should not do such things, and whoever was guilty of them, should be capitally punished.'[25] Moreover, regardless of the mother, Mughal emperors raised their sons and daughters as Muslim Timurids.

Akbar also made many political marriage alliances with high-born and strategically placed Muslim rulers, preferring but not limited to Timurids. For instance, during imperial campaigns to conquer Upper Sind and Thatta (Lower Sind), the two competing Muslim royal families each offered Akbar a bride.[26] Rejecting one offer and accepting the other, Akbar was also choosing which family to accept as subordinate ally.

But even such intra-Muslim marriages did not necessarily produce lasting amity between the dynasties. For example, Khandesh Sultanate stood strategically between Akbar's Hindustan and the Deccani sultanates he distantly coveted. In 1564, Khandesh Sultan Miran Mubarak Shah II of the Faruqi dynasty (claiming prestigious descent from the second Sunni Caliph, 'Umar) gave his daughter as a bride to Akbar. Despite this marriage, Mughal relations with the

Khandesh dynasty remained fraught and they fought periodically for four decades.

In sharp contrast to Akbar's marriages with Rajputs (where only Rajputs provided brides), Akbar gave his sisters and daughters as wives to Timurids and other high-born Central and west Asian Muslims. In Islam, Muslim men can take nikah wives from non-Muslims (if they are People of the Book) but Muslim women cannot legitimately marry outside the faith. Further, giving brides hypergamously had more cultural force in Indic than in Timurid Islamic traditions (although in most cultures, families customarily feel degraded when their womenfolk are taken by an enemy). Thus, Babur and Humayun had married their womenfolk to Timurids without acknowledging those men's superiority.

Akbar intended giving his sisters and daughters as brides to advance the Mughal agenda, but in practice, these political marriage alliances did not ensure that these in-laws proved useful or loyal to Akbar. Around 1561, Akbar had married his full sister, Bakhshi Banu Begum, to a close Timurid relative, Mirza Sharaf-ud-Din Husain. But this brother-in-law had his own imperial ambitions and alternately led Mughal armies against their mutual enemies and conspired with Akbar's foes, before fleeing for his life to Mecca. Further, in 1564, one of Sharaf-ud-Din's freed slaves shot Akbar in the back—the arrow wounding but not killing. Akbar's courtiers suspected but could not prove Sharaf-ud-Din's instigation. But, such was the prestige of Timurids that Sharaf-ud-Din, after a decade away and a period of imprisonment, eventually received imperial forgiveness and returned to Akbar's service. Likewise, around 1593 Akbar married a daughter to Mirza Muzaffar Husain Khan, a Timurid former ruler of Gujarat who subsequently spent his life alternately in Akbar's service and in Mughal prisons for rebellion. Then, Akbar married another daughter, Shakr-un-Nissa Begum, to Mirza Shahrukh, the Timurid deposed ruler of Badakhshan; but Shahrukh never recovered Badakhshan nor proved especially useful to Akbar.

Similarly, Akbar gave a daughter in marriage to his own brother-in-law Raja Ali Khan of Khandesh. Raja Ali Khan reciprocally gave a daughter to Salim, Akbar's eldest son. Despite these three political marriages, Raja Ali Khan only accepted incorporation into the Mughal hierarchy after being forced militarily to submit.

Akbar's many marriages produced a vast women-centered world: the imperial harem containing thousands of women. Each of the hundreds of imperial wives had a separate sub-household, filled with female attendants and supported by a salary appropriate to her status. The harem also contained eunuchs as attendants, guards and intermediaries with the outside world. Akbar's closest male companions, particularly senior relatives by birth or marriage, might receive the honor of visiting parts of his harem. Through the personal influence of some imperial womenfolk over the emperor and through other indirect interventions into imperial affairs, the harem penetrated the Empire's public space.

Beyond relatives by marriage, Akbar also worked to recruit diverse loyal and effective officials who enabled him to manage and expand his Empire. He and his core officials built on the work of Sher Shah to create a more efficient and stable system of land revenue extraction. They created a unified military-administrative hierarchy focused on Akbar himself. These elevated the Mughal Empire to levels of power and authority unprecedented in India. But the Mughal armed forces and administration had to struggle to penetrate north India's multi-layered and deeply entrenched economic, political and social systems, and to expand beyond Hindustan.

5

EMPEROR AKBAR AND HIS CORE COURTIERS BUILD THE MUGHAL ADMINISTRATION AND ARMY

In the profession of fighting, a defeat is not considered to be a dishonor.
Emperor Akbar consoling a defeated imperial commander[1]

Emperor Akbar and his close advisors were dedicated to expanding the Mughal Empire through territorial conquest and through the imposition of what they proclaimed to be his righteous regime. The Empire was primarily a military-fiscalist state that required a vast and growing army and administration in order to extract tribute and revenues from the diverse areas they kept conquering. That income then supported the imperial army and administration, as well as Akbar's household and court. Under Akbar's close direction, Mughal armies attacked neighboring states and suppressed popular rebellions and resistance by landholders and other local magnates in newly acquired territories as well as the imperial heartland. Simultaneously, Akbar and his central courtiers innovatively strove to create stable, efficient and uniform administrative processes throughout the Empire. Despite their overarching imperial models, however, in practice there was much regional and local variation since officials had to adjust pragmatically in order to both satisfy their superiors and yet economically maintain order and collect revenues. Crucially, out of the diverse body of mainly immigrant followers whom Akbar inherited, he and his key courtiers synthesized a single, largely integrated Mughal hierarchy of soldier-administrators with a balance of ethnic origins and overriding devotion to the Emperor himself. Thereby, Akbar's regime created processes and procedures that empowered the Mughal Empire for over a century.

THE RURAL POLITICAL ECONOMY

Historically, most states in India lacked the administrative manpower, expertise, and coercive or cultural force to extract the maximum revenues. Rather, many rulers of conquest states, like Babur, Humayun and many of their predecessors and contemporaries, seized the treasuries of defeated enemies and coerced regional rulers and landholders into paying whatever tribute could be economically extracted for the expenses of their royal household and to reward their commanders. If initially predatory conquerors remained to rule, which not all did, many awarded each commander with an appanage (often called an *iqta*) whose estimated revenues generally seemed to accord with his status. Each military governor had charge over that territory and often appropriated its resources largely in his own short-term interest. Sometimes (as in Japan and feudal Europe) these appanages became hereditary fiefdoms. Some became autonomous kingdoms. But such conquest states and appanage-holders often had trouble penetrating below the upper levels of regional rulers and landholders to deal directly with cultivators and other primary producers.

Throughout Akbar's reign (and those of his successors), Mughal commanders struggled to defeat or incorporate regional rulers. With few exceptions, every north Indian ruler who persisted in overt resistance was eventually displaced since concentrated Mughal forces could eventually overpower any one of them. Many defeated rulers either had their domains taken under direct imperial administration or were replaced by more compliant relatives. Some submitted to Mughal sovereignty but retained a degree of local autonomy, like the many royal Rajputs who served Akbar. Thereafter, Mughal emperors arbitrated their dynastic successions but also provided cooperative ruling families with protection and opportunities for advancement. Even in those regions where Mughal forces did displace regional rulers, imperial officials encountered various levels of zamindars, who dominated the rural economy.

Often, zamindars belonged to locally powerful martial clans holding one, a few, hundreds, or perhaps thousands of villages, acquired as original settlers or subsequent conquerors.[2] Akbar, and his successors, also granted uncultivated lands, especially on external and internal frontiers, to zamindars (and to holy men and other notables) at concessional revenue rates until the lands became fully productive. Most zamindars lived as warrior-aristocrats, albeit locally based ones, with long traditions of armed and other resistance to outside revenue collectors. Since the Mughal Empire never established a monopoly over coercion or the military labor market within its conquered territories, it often faced overt resistance. By one count, there were 144 armed revolts by landholders during Akbar's reign that were large enough to be recorded by his central administration; additionally, lesser conflicts were frequent, particularly after each harvest (but often unreported by local officials concerned about their own reputations and careers).[3]

THE MUGHAL LAND REVENUE AND PROVINCIAL ADMINISTRATION

Throughout Akbar's reign, as during those of his predecessors and contemporary Indian rulers, his commanders seized enemy treasuries to help fund the Mughal army, administration and court. But Akbar also supervised the innovative development of a more centralized and bureaucratized model of revenue extraction that was not predatory, but rather had explicit rules and records for revenue payers and collectors both. In addition to Akbar's inherited supporters, his administration also recruited new Hindu and Muslim officials with local administrative experience and knowledge, often having already established links with landholders. Whenever possible, the Mughal administration constrained the authority of zamindars, striving to turn them into functionaries of the Mughal state.

During Bairam Khan's regency, the Mughal administration had largely used land revenue information from Sher Shah's earlier reign, which was often outdated and inflated. These inefficiencies weakened the state's finances while Bairam Khan disbursed resources lavishly to gain support. Hence, when Akbar emerged from regency, his treasury was severely depleted. To improve the land revenue system, he assembled a growing body of officials, most prominently Khwaja Muzaffar Khan Turbati (a Shi'i Iranian who had served Bairam Khan) and Raja Todar Mal (a Hindu Khatri who had served Sher Shah).

From around 1566, Akbar's revenue officials began reaching below zamindars to measure and assess individual fields in those areas where land revenue collection was under direct imperial management, *khalisa*. Information there was more accessible than from territories already assigned as *iqtas* or other revenue grants. However, this was still a lengthy and contested process; only after a decade had the imperial administration actually measured and accurately assessed substantial amounts of land even in the most secure khalisa territories.

Even this limited local information, however, enabled the administration to tap into the agricultural economy more systematically. The administration strove to produce an official record for each village, listing its arable, inhabited, forested, pasturage and uncultivated lands, and exactly who was responsible for paying revenues for each. Akbar's officials classified each field into one of three categories of revenue rates, depending on the degree of fertility and value of crop. This produced that field's assessed demand. Groups of villages formed a *pargana* ('district'). But powerful zamindars sometimes proved able to obscure these details for unsurveyed villages under their control and themselves pay the revenues as tribute or at rates they negotiated with imperial officials.

As richly but over-optimistically described by Akbar's publicist, Abu-al-Fazl, this revenue system was objective, standardized and smoothly effective across the Empire. In contrast, a contemporary critic described both the theoretical model and also the haphazard and exploitive practice:

> ... [in 1574] an order was promulgated for improving the cultivation of the country, and for bettering the condition of the *raiyats* [cultivators]. All the *parganas* of the country ... were all to be measured, and every such piece of land as, upon cultivation, would produce one *kror* of *tankas* [10,000,000 copper coins] was to be divided off, and placed under the charge of an officer to be called *Krorí* .... Officers were appointed, but eventually they did not carry out the regulations as they ought to have done. A great portion of the country was laid waste through the rapacity of the *Krorís*, the wives and children of the *raiyats* were sold and scattered

abroad and everything was thrown into confusion ... many good men died from the severe beatings which were administered, and from the tortures of the rack and pincers [and] from protracted confinement in the prisons of the revenue authorities ...[4]

A Jain merchant confirmed how kroris simply confiscated his cash.[5]

The imperial administration evidently had even more difficulty getting accurate information about lands already distributed as *iqta* or other revenue assignments. In order to gain more direct data about actual yields, around 1575, the central administration resumed most such grants, with the former grantee receiving in lieu a cash salary from the imperial treasury. Many former grant holders objected, particularly those whose incomes actually exceeded their official grant. About five years later, after the central administration had secured more accurate agricultural productivity figures and, if the former grantee could provide documentary proof of his rights, it reissued most of the reassessed revenue assignments as *jagirs*— the term henceforth widely used for the temporary assignment of land revenue and other taxes from a designated territory. *Jagirdar*s ('jagirholders') then collected these revenues or parceled them out among their followers.

Not all lands were reassigned to jagirdars. A varying proportion remained khalisa—supporting the imperial administration itself, the emperor and his household, the special branches of the military including the imperial artillery and *ahadi*s (4,000–5,000 elite cavalry reporting directly to the emperor), to replenish the imperial treasury reserves and to pay salaries to officials not currently holding a jagir or needing supplements to bring their income to its official level. The central administration evidently selected khalisa lands from those most productive and trouble-free in the imperial heartland. The proportion of land revenues in khalisa (versus those assigned as jagirs) reflected a measure of the emperor's own consolidated control over land revenues and provided him with a fiscal buffer. Under Akbar, between a quarter and a third of the Empire's total assessed revenue remained in khalisa.[6]

For the Mughal revenue system to function effectively, the central administration had to judge accurately the maximum proportion of the actual crop to demand. Eventually, under the *zabt* ('regulation') system, Akbar's administrators systematically calculated the average production of each measured field over the past ten years and settled its revenue demand on that basis. These Mughal revenue extractions absorbed a significant share of the GDP (historians differ about the proportion of the harvest demanded under zabt; reasonable estimates range from a third to half, with the proportion varying in practice among territories).[7]

Eventually up to ninety per cent of territories in Hindustan were reportedly under zabt. In more recently conquered or less fully controlled territories, none or little land was under zabt. Instead, the revenues actually extracted seem to have been annually negotiated between collection agents and local revenue payers—either zamindars or cultivators. Armed confrontation, while expensive to both sides, frequently remained a seasonal event. Revenue collectors needed to extract as much as they could with the minimum of costly enforcement. Conversely, revenue payers had to balance resistance costs against what they kept. Nonetheless, zabt—in contrast to tribute-paying by semi-autonomous chiefs and zamindars to semi-autonomous *iqta* holders which had earlier prevailed—reflected the novel degree of centralized control exerted (or claimed) by Akbar's administration.

Imperial officials increasingly demanded that land revenues be paid in cash at fixed times with written accounts kept by village and provincial accountants, rather than in kind as had often prevailed earlier. This monetized the rural economy; wholesalers based in qasbas purchased local crops so revenue payers would have money for taxes. These wholesalers transported the crop to towns and cities, imperial armies, or markets in food-deficit regions. Large banking houses also transferred considerable amounts of capital throughout the Empire through *hundi*s (an early form of cashier's check).

During Akbar's last decade, about a hundred metric tons of silver flowed annually into the Empire—mostly originating in the Americas or Japan and imported via European merchants purchasing Indian hand-manufactures and natural resources. Imperial mints accepted any amount of bullion and, for a fee, coined silver (or gold or copper) currency of uniform purity and weight, standardized throughout the Empire (with some special exceptions). This silver inflation lowered interest rates and raised prices for producers, stimulating the Empire's economy, enhancing the dynamic innovations by Akbar's administration.

During the early 1580s, Akbar's officials also worked to develop and implement a standard model for provincial governance. They divided the territories currently under imperial authority into 12 geographically well-defined *suba*s ('provinces')—in many cases simply adopting traditional provincial divisions. Later in Akbar's reign, three more subas were created from conquered Deccani sultanates. Each suba in principle had a *subadar* ('governor'), diwan ('chief revenue official'), *faujdar* ('military commandant'), chief *qazi* ('head of the judicial establishment'), sadr ('manager of revenue-grants') and staff of newswriters. During Akbar's early years, some posts were shared between two officials, but thereafter only one man generally held one post. Each official reported independently to his counterpart at the imperial center, forming a system of checks and balances. Within each suba were sub-divisions—*sarkar*s and, within them, parganas—with parallel administrative offices. Regular networks of runners and other communications systems, including carrier pigeons, linked the imperial bureaucracy into an effective information order.[8] In actual practice, however, there remained wide variation by province (particularly those outside Hindustan) in the duties and powers of all these officials. Further, in order to function, officials negotiated pragmatically with local magnates and revenue payers.[9] An official's inflexible demand, overruling local custom, or other perceived oppression, often led to rebellion that could be costly to suppress, both for the Empire and also the official's career.

In principle (although not always in practice), the Mughal judicial system applied the *Sharia* of the Hanafi school of Sunni Islam, as interpreted by 'ulama (and later by Akbar). This was the basis both of criminal law for all and also of civil law for Muslims. But Hindu and other religious communities often provided legal advisors to assist Muslim judges when their members were involved. Further, many matters internal to jatis or villages or other communities were settled by their own *panchayat*s (councils conventionally composed of five male elders). Yet, the Mughal administration occasionally also chose to supervise some intra-community matters. They chose, for example, to determine the volition of a Hindu widow before she was permitted to demonstrate her fatal fidelity to her late husband as a *sati* ('true wife'). In theory, at least, she had to appear personally before the emperor or his representative to seek permission, proving that her act of immolation was her own choice, rather than coerced.[10]

Akbar's officials instituted the use of Persian language, script and technical terms to standardize records throughout the expanding empire. This spreading utilitarian use of Persian helped amalgamate society, as local accountants and officials learned this language in order to function within the Empire. Noted experts wrote numerous technical manuals, *Dastur al-'Amal*, that provided guidance for scribes, with model templates for official documents and correspondence.[11]

Many middle- and lower-level administrators who joined the Empire were from Hindu Khatri and *Kayastha* jatis, with long traditions of state service. They worked in salaried positions, earned by merit or influence, subject to periodic performance reviews. While their profession was hereditary, the office they currently filled was not necessarily so. Even beyond the Empire, Persian terms and categories began to enter local revenue and other records of other kingdoms, although local languages might be retained as well in what often became bilingual or multilingual documents. Further, Persian learning by men in qasbas and even villages also focused widespread attention on the imperial court as the cultural exemplar for deportment, literature and other arts.[12]

As Akbar's officials asserted imperial control down toward the local level, they used 'political socialization': converting zamindars into quasi-officials who routinely collected taxes for the Empire and maintained order in Akbar's name.[13] Indeed, as imperial service careers appeared more promising, zamindars and their sons sometimes aspired to enroll and to attend the imperial court. Given the relatively small number of Mughal officials compared to the vast subject population (roughly one high official per hundred thousand subjects), the imperial administration relied heavily on the willing or coerced cooperation of zamindars and other local elites in order to function.

THE MUGHAL MANSAB SYSTEM

Most earlier Indian rulers gave each commander titles, rewards and *iqta*s ad hoc according to the ruler's personal assessment of his worth. Even while Akbar's close courtiers were developing the combined land revenue, jagir and provincial administrative systems, they also innovatively created one integrated decimal hierarchy for top officer-administrators: the *mansab* ('rank') system. Four centuries earlier, Akbar's distant ancestor Chingiz Khan and more recently Sher Shah had used a basic decimal organization for their armies, but this Mughal system became far more sophisticated and bureaucratic.[14]

From about 1574, Akbar assigned each of the top thousand or so Mughal appointees a numerical grade from 10 up to 5,000. Only about 33 numerical values were actually used, each with a specific income and required number of cavalrymen (or other soldiers) recruited and paid by the *mansabdar* ('mansabholder'). Mansabdars of 500 or more ranked as *amir* ('nobleman'). This mansab system thus created ranks through which a man could move during his career, which customarily combined administrative and military responsibilities (the judiciary was largely distinct in training and duties). A specific office did not have a fixed rank: a governor might hold one mansab but his successor a lower or higher mansab. However, officials often received temporary promotions when their current mansab was inappropriately low for their new office. Further, mansabdars had no fixed terms in office and often very varied careers—Akbar might transfer them suddenly in response to a campaign or crisis or else their reported misgovernance. Once the system was in place, this hierarchy provided the emperor with a finely regulated process for rewarding through promotion or punishing through stagnation or demotion in mansab.

While Akbar's innovative mansab system had many new bureaucratic features, it also contained many personalistic and patrimonial characteristics. There was no entrance examination (unlike the contemporary Chinese imperial civil service). Rather, appointments and promotions were all (theoretically) based on Akbar's personal inspection and superhuman insight about the man's true worth, usually supported by recommendations from high officials whom Akbar trusted. When this system was first being implemented, many established commanders objected to their assigned rank as unworthy of them. Further, this hierarchy now put each mansabdar specifically and overtly above, equal to, or below every other one. Thereafter, rival mansabdars jostled for precedence and complained about their rank and promotion rate.

The mansab system was not routinely hereditary, although heredity clearly affected one's initial ranking and subsequent career. By birthright, Mughal imperial princes usually held the highest mansabs (above the 5,000 cap for others) and thus the most income to support their households, military forces and political factions. But princes often held unequal ranks, reflecting their relative ages, mother's status and their current esteem in the emperor's mind. Defeated but now submissive rulers also usually received very high initial ranks.

The sons and grandsons of mansabdars often followed them into service, thereby becoming *khanazad* ('house born,' implying lifelong loyalty to the emperor). Customarily, sons initially held lower ranks than their fathers and had to earn promotions through battle and effective administration. However, sons of high mansabdars often started with higher rank than other recruits and customarily had accelerated careers. Junior kinsmen often served their seniors as lower-ranked mansabdars with their own smaller military contingents—relatives often moved together from one region to another. Additionally, at a mansabdar's death, the emperor might honor him by deeming a son worthy of appointment or promotion, sometimes to his late father's mansab and titles.

Crucially, Akbar ritually bound each mansabdar to him personally. Each offered Akbar deep prostration and *nazr* ('ritual presentation to a superior,' usually of gold coins but sometimes jewels or other high-value items). Mansabdars (and also tributary rulers and landholders) also offered *peshkash* ('presentation gift' of money, valuable goods, or rare animals) when approaching the emperor, especially on special occasions like imperial birthdays or coronation anniversaries. Conversely, Akbar bestowed gifts, especially sets of *khilat* ('robes of honor') by which he clothed the recipient in a garment symbolically worn by Akbar and thus imbued with his bodily essence. This Mughal practice built upon Central Asian traditions, but achieved sophisticated gradations of qualities and quantities.[15] Mansabdars aspired to attend personally on Akbar. Catching Akbar's eye through distinguished deportment in court could garner a desirable appointment. However, incurring his displeasure from misbehavior could ruin a career.

The single mansab hierarchy incorporated officer-administrators of various ethnicities as Akbar's direct servants—partially cross-cutting their other loyalties. Nonetheless, mansabdars also developed factions through long- or short-term alliances, often based on kinship, ethnic identity, compatible religious beliefs, and/or mutual interests.

Akbar's many wives and female kin participated in these factions, lobbying Akbar personally and his courtiers indirectly. But tensions arose among personal loyalty to the emperor, individual aspirations and factional solidarities.

The central administration assigned each mansabdar one or more jagirs (occasionally replaced or supplemented by cash from the treasury) that totaled his mansab's official income. Mansabdars (except for the lowest-ranked) had their own agents collect the assessed revenue from their jagirs. These agents received payments from zamindars and provided written receipts, under the supervision of the Mughal provincial administration. To prevent abuses in revenue collection, mansabdars governing a territory were conventionally not the ones assigned jagirs there, although for practical reasons, jagir assignments were often located nearby or even within an official's jurisdiction.[16]

Despite official policy for central administrators, in practice disparities between a jagir's assessed value and its actual income occurred. Particularly prestigious mansabdars received more lucrative jagirs; mansabdars less respected by the central assigning officials received jagirs that sometimes generated less than the official revenue, or were expensive to extract revenue from. Additionally, actual expenditures incurred in different postings varied considerably; some mansabdars had surplus income, while others overspent. Over time, repeated modifications in the jagir system proved necessary to redress imbalances or address changing circumstances.

Either from inadequate income or self-interest, many mansabdars neither employed the number of cavalrymen specified by their rank nor provided adequate cavalry horses. Although the central administration calculated a fixed rate per man, mansabdars hired soldiers at negotiated salaries. To ensure that each mansabdar fulfilled his military obligations, the central administration from around 1574 instituted periodic inspections of each mansabdar's inventory, with an official muster roll (describing each man's appearance, domicile and ethnicity) and the branding (*dagh*) of each horse with an indelible mark of approval (and to prevent double counting). Further, there were general ethnic quotas, for instance Central Asian and Rajput mansabdars should only (or predominately) employ men of their own ethnicity. Such bureaucratic checks often evoked resentment, especially from mansabdars who either regarded themselves as entitled noblemen and resented administrative questioning of their honor or else were gaming the system.

Historian Badauni (who once held office as muster roll and horse inspector) described prevailing abuses:

> ... Amírs did as they pleased ... [putting] most of their own servants and mounted attendants into soldiers' clothes, brought them to the musters .... But when they got their *jágírs* they [dismissed them] and when a new emergency arose, they mustered as many 'borrowed' soldiers as were required, and sent them away again, when they had served their purpose. Hence, ... a lot of low tradespeople, weavers and cotton-cleaners, carpenters, and green-grocers, both Hindú and Musalmán, ... brought borrowed horses, got them branded, and were appointed to a command ... and when a few days afterwards no trace was to be found of the imaginary horse and the visionary saddle, they had to perform their duties on foot. Many times it happened at the musters, before the Emperor [Akbar] himself ... it was found that they were all hired, and that their very clothes and saddles were borrowed articles. His Majesty then used to say, 'With my eyes thus open I must give these men pay, that they may have something to live on.'[17]

Indeed, Akbar's administration recognized such disparities and inequities and in 1585 appointed an imperial commission to investigate abuses in the interconnected zabt, jagir and mansab systems. However, few substantial improvements ensued.

As mansabdars rotated among postings in the expanding Empire, their jagirs also moved. Early in his reign, Akbar celebrated as a major accomplishment his dislodging and dispersing to distant provinces some clans of mansabdars who had settled themselves in particular regions, forming deep connections there. But later, Akbar's administration recognized that such locally knowledgeable mansabdars could be more effective in revenue collection, governance and territorial defense; so the pace of rotation diminished.

Furthering the Emperor's control, he inherited by escheat each deceased mansabdar's personal property. This discouraged mansabdars from building palaces, which, after their death, the Emperor would likely award to current favorites. Consequently, some mansabdars built religious buildings—tombs or mosques by

Muslims and temples by Hindus—to perpetuate their legacy since the Emperor would not confiscate these.[18] For a particularly favored mansabdar, however, the Emperor might restore much of his property to his family at his demise. All this reinforced the dependence of mansabdars on lifelong service to the Emperor. His regard, their martial and administrative skills, personal treasury, and support base of followers and allies were their major resources, rather than any territorial possession (as in a classically feudal context).

As a major variation from this system of temporary and rotating jagirs and escheat, starting around 1596, many royal Rajputs, a few Indianized Afghans and other former regional rulers, received recognition of their family estates or kingdoms as their permanent *watan jagir* ('homeland jagir'). While nominally this land came under imperial authority and regulation and was only assigned back to the jagirdar, in practice, a watan jagir largely continued his pre-existing relationships, both cultural and fiscal, with local zamindars and cultivators. Further, as watan jagirdars rose in mansab (so their official income exceeded the revenue assessment of their watan jagir), they received additional temporary jagirs elsewhere.

The ruler of an expansion-dependent state, Akbar constantly sought to annex his neighbors by force or threat. He stated 'A monarch should be ever intent on conquest, otherwise his neighbors rise in arms against him .... The army should be exercised in warfare, lest from want of training they become self-indulgent.'[19] Conversely, various rulers on the Empire's external and internal frontiers resisted its invasions or counterattacked.

Akbar expected virtually all mansabdars to perform military duties, often in addition to administrative ones. Some mansabdars clearly excelled in warfare, continuing their martial traditions as Central Asians, Rajputs, or Indian Muslims (most notably Mewatis and the Sayyids of Barha). Although some mansabdars specialized in administration, even these were most honored when they were 'promoted from the pen to the sword ..., masters both of peace and war ...'[20] For instance, Mahesh Das, a Brahmin poet (probably from the *Bhat* jati of genealogists and praise singers) was recruited by Akbar based on his literary reputation in other courts.[21] Akbar, impressed by his artistry, entitled him Kavi Raj (Sanskritic 'King of Poets') in 1572. But he not only brilliantly composed Braj-language prose and poetry and enlivened the court with witticisms, he was also assigned as an administrator of cattle markets and a judge of civil disputes. Further, Akbar appointed him an officer in various military expeditions, bestowing on him the additional Sanskritic title Raja Birbal ('King Renowned Warrior'). Birbal proved a competent military commander, reaching the high mansab 2,000. But in 1589, about age 60, he misguidedly led his troops into an ambush during a Yusufzai Afghan popular uprising on the northwest frontier. He and his 8,000 soldiers all died—arguably Akbar's biggest military disaster.

Similarly, Raja Todar Mal earned repute as an expert civil administrator. But he also alternated as a military engineer and battlefield commander. He reached mansab 4,000, dying in office at age 66 (Akbar refused him retirement).[22]

However, as Akbar's Empire expanded and his administration grew more complex, the divergence between non-military and military duties grew. Hence, around 1595 the central administration significantly modified the mansab system to allow personal rank to rise without necessarily increasing the mansabdar's military obligations: assigning each mansabdar both a *zat* ('personal') rank and also a separate *sawar* ('cavalry') rank [hereinafter indicated, e.g., 3,000/2,500]. The latter specified the number of soldiers to be recruited, paid and commanded in the Emperor's service. The two ranks were not always equal, with more martial appointments bringing a (sometimes temporary) increase in the sawar. But the zat determined the order of precedence among mansabdars and was never less than the sawar.

The warrior-ethic remained central for mansabdars; their assigned jagirs provided their major source of income. But many mansabdars also engaged directly or indirectly in money-lending, commercial speculation and the production of luxury goods.[23] To manage culturally distasteful 'trade,' many mansabdars used a Hindu or Jain 'man of business,' to their mutual profit. Indeed, when traditional-minded amirs complained to Akbar in 1564 that he was demeaning himself by employing Todar Mal to run his finances, he replied: 'Every one of you has a Hindú to manage his private affairs. Suppose we too have a Hindú, why should harm come of it?'[24] But such business agents remained dependent on the mansabdar's favor: he could seize their property at will, with little recourse (as an abused agent's son bemoaned).[25]

Many mansabdars also used their official posts for personal profit. Some compelled merchants to sell their goods at concessional prices, or to purchase goods from them at above market rates. Some notoriously never paid their bills. Nonetheless, mansabdars largely recognized their official duty to protect and foster commerce, particularly by policing roads and punishing theft in lands they administered.

Additionally, higher mansabdars (like Akbar himself) had their own *karkhana*s (artisanal and artistic workshops) that produced luxury goods for their households, gifts, or sale. Some courtiers, including imperial womenfolk, invested in ocean-going ships and commerce. However, the Mughal Empire (unlike some contemporaries) did not allow rich merchants to purchase rank, thus largely excluding commercial classes from direct political power.[26]

Imperial service in the field or at court, while potentially richly rewarding, remained uncertain and dangerous. Many mansabdars died in battle and they occasionally assassinated each other. In court, they constantly jockeyed for Akbar's attention and patronage. Indeed, Akbar demoted, dismissed, imprisoned, exiled, or executed many mansabdars, including most of those holding the highest ranks. Some survivors eventually obtained his pardon, reinstatement and subsequent promotions. Akbar himself barely survived at least one assassination attempt, multiple serious wounds in battle and various reckless encounters with wild or maddened beasts, some of which left him severely injured. His death from any one of these would have substantially altered the course of the Mughal Empire, or even shattered it. Akbar's three surviving sons maneuvered and conspired against each other, knowing that only one would succeed as Padshah; two died before he did.

Thus, Emperor Akbar and his core mansabdars devised and imposed an unprecedented, extensive and advanced administrative-military structure. The imperial center envisioned its models for land revenue, jagirs, provincial administration and mansabs as just and uniform throughout the expanding Empire. But in practice, there were many deviations and regional variations. In addition, even as Akbar personally changed as he reigned from ages 14 to 64, he and his close advisors built capitals, developed ideologies, and waged wars.

6

EMPEROR AKBAR'S COURTS, IDEOLOGIES AND WARS, BY MAIN CAPITAL

I am only seeking for the truth...
            Akbar speaking to Father Antonio Monserrate, S.J. (1581)[1]

Over Akbar's long reign, in a series of capitals, he and his selected advisors constructed around him distinctive and evolving imperial cultures, policies and bodies of mansabdars, even while his reorganized armies expanded his empire. The Central Asian tradition that Akbar inherited valued the ruler's movement through his domain, with the state always centered on his court, wherever located, and the emperor often in direct command. Indeed, Mughal emperors organized their palace complexes like their military encampments, and vice versa.[2] Akbar also made his court elaborately ritualized and hierarchic, rather than collegial like Babur's.

Akbar's developing ideologies and his relationships with various ethnic communities reflected his imperial career and his personal spiritual journey. After Akbar and his supporters made his throne more secure, he had expanded scope to implement his current vision of his empire and his role within it and the cosmos. Yet he always faced constraints from powerful groups inside and outside his domain, each with its own agenda. Overall, Akbar's relationships with various religions proved highly controversial; from his day until the present, people holding strong but irreconcilably opposing convictions have struggled to shape Akbar's image.

Many long-term developments spanned Akbar's half-century-long regime—including repeated challenges from Timurid relatives, his political marriages, and his evolving land revenue, jagir, provincial administrative and mansab systems. Nonetheless, broadly distinct phases marked Akbar's composition of his mansabdars, military deployments and religious beliefs and practices. Those phases correlate with his four major capitals. Agra was the main imperial center during both Humayun's reigns in Hindustan; Akbar remained based there for his first 14 years on the throne, although he often visited elsewhere. Akbar then decisively shifted to his new purpose-built court-capital of Fatehpur Sikri, where he largely remained for another 14 years. Both nearby cities stood strategically central to the imperial heartland of Hindustan, but Akbar's court culture in each clearly differed. In 1585, Akbar suddenly left Fatehpur and eventually based his court in Lahore, nearer the unstable western frontier. Over his nearly 14 years based in Lahore, he developed his court and empire in striking ways, including by acquiring Lower Sind, Kashmir and Qandahar. Finally, he spent his last seven years personally commanding the Mughal drive into the Deccan and then, back in Agra, holding off his rebellious eldest son, Salim, who was based down the Jumna River in Allahabad.

THE AGRA PERIOD, 1556–71

Akbar, as youthful emperor under regency and then during the first decade of his own rule, largely lived in Agra, although he made periodic hunting, military, inspection, pleasure and devotional journeys beyond its walls. Asserting control over Humayun's legacy, Akbar authorized construction (*c.* 1562–71) of a magnificent tomb for his father, near Humayun's Din Panah complex in Delhi. Architecturally, this monument evoked the dynasty's current culture: primarily Islamic Timurid traditions with additional Iranian elements.

Simultaneously (1565–73), Akbar invested vast resources in extensively rebuilding and strengthening Agra's defenses. This reflected young Akbar's well-founded concerns over military security.

Within Agra's citadel, Akbar created his court complex, demonstrating his early architectural aesthetic: uniform red sandstone surfaces, highlighted with white marble. Rather than a single palace with interior rooms for each function, the varied buildings stood

Agra, from South West, Engraved by J. Walker from Painting by W. Hodges, 1793[3]

Humayun's Tomb, Delhi, *c.* 1570.

apart, each housing a distinct component of his court, administration and household. He daily presided in his *diwan-i am*, 'general audience hall' (although access required permission). Deeper in the complex, Akbar sat enthroned in his *diwan-i khas* ('special audience hall') before his assembled mansabdars and honored visitors. Each deferentially stood with crossed arms in hierarchically arranged semicircles centered on his throne, moving outward from the highest to the lowest. Akbar's major domo or he himself summoned individuals to approach the throne, make the kind of obeisance appropriate to his status and current fashion, present nazr and other offerings, respond deferentially to any words Akbar might bestow upon him, and receive a *khilat* or other award. The courtier then withdrew to his previously or newly designated place. Even more protected were inner buildings where only very select men and women could enter. His private audience chamber (*ghusal-khana*, 'bath chamber,' from its original purpose) provided a still highly ceremonial place where the emperor conducted business or conversed with specially invited dignitaries or companions. Beyond were the imperial harem buildings, containing the many women's suites. Visits among women of the harem and by wives of high dignitaries created a lively society. But Mughal imperial women were gradually becoming more secluded from the public world than in earlier generations.

Akbar customarily dined alone, meaning only he dined, but he was usually surrounded by attendants and high courtiers. Since Akbar ate substantial amounts of opium over most of his life, imperial dinners might end with his sinking into a stupor, his guests withdrawing deferentially, and his personal servants discretely conveying him into his sleeping chambers. On ceremonial occasions, and in the few instances when Akbar evoked earlier Timurid traditions, select high courtiers dined with him.

Akbar also built within the palace complex a free-standing mosque for his own devotions and those of his household and courtiers, a *hamam* ('bathhouse') for their cleanliness and kitchens to produce meals of quality appropriate to the diner's status. A functional fortress, Agra's citadel contained living quarters and an arsenal for the sizable imperial bodyguard and garrison, with stables for a multitude of elephants, horses and other animals. Akbar famously supervised all these stables personally. The numerous imperial servants, artisans and other workers had lodgings in the palace complex or surrounding city, depending on their status. Within the citadel or nearby were many imperial karkhanas where artificers and artists worked on imperial commissions, making valuable items for the imperial household or as gifts for other monarchs or mansabdars. Occasionally, Akbar might honor a high mansabdar by permitting him to commission art in these imperial workshops. Mansabdars had their smaller versions of the imperial complex, often a mansion surrounded by karkhanas and the houses of subordinates, thus forming neighborhoods in the imperial or provincial capital. Further, Mughal ceremonial, sartorial, artistic and architectural fashions spread across north India.

Akbar awarded mansabs to men from various ethnic backgrounds in gradually shifting proportions. Emerging from regency, Akbar inherited from Bairam Khan a body of high commanders and officials: the majority were Sunni Turanis (Central Asians) while a third were Shi'a Iranis, who were often administrative specialists. Some Iranians had immigrated with Humayun, others came to Bairam Khan. Only a scattering of Indians had joined Bairam Khan's administration.

Over Akbar's Agra years, the total number of mansabdars of each ethnicity rose, but their percentages shifted, reflecting availability and Akbar's own preferences. For the 1565–75 period, Turani mansabdars declined to 38 per cent—reduced from the majority but still the plurality.[4] Iranis also declined, to 27 per cent. However, among high-ranking amirs, Turanis and Iranis were each about 40 per cent. Akbar's Rajput political marriages grew their proportion, until they (and a few other Hindus) comprised 10 per cent of his mansabdars. In addition, even more Indians whose families had converted to Islam became mansabdars, reaching 14 per cent of the total (but only 9 per cent of amirs). All this reflects the gradual but substantial incorporation of north Indians into the Empire.

To make his Agra court culturally preeminent, Akbar recruited the finest and most expensive artists from across India and the Islamic lands to the west. Among his most famous courtiers was the singer entitled Mian Tansen (born Ramtanu Pandey, later, after conversion, renamed Mohammad Ata Khan).[5] He is still revered for creating many *raga*s (the tonic and aesthetic foundation for classical Indian music). He had trained at the Gwalior court and then been enticed by Rewa's ruler. In 1562, Akbar sent that ruler and him a mandatory invitation. For the rest of Mian Tansen's career, he adorned Akbar's court, being lavishly rewarded and honored (although evidently never with a mansab).

In 1567, Akbar invited a budding poet of Persian, Shaikh Abu-al-Faiz, pen-name Faizi (d. 1595). This invitation was controversial since his father, Shaikh Mubarak, had been repeatedly punished for heterodoxy, including by Akbar. Indeed, when the imperial summons arrived, Abu-al-Faiz was reportedly unsure whether to evade or obey it.[6] When a younger brother, Shaikh Abu-al-Fazl, came of age, he too joined the court, rising to become Akbar's main publicist, amanuensis, ideologue, historian and trusted confidant.

Similarly, Akbar also patronized many of the finest painters, both on paper and on interior walls. He attracted to his atelier artists from the prestigious Safavid court. He also sponsored many Indian artists, recruiting some from other Indian courts. After about 1582, his atelier innovated by attributing works to individual artists, rarely done previously in Indic traditions.[7] Gradually, Akbar promoted a distinctive style combining Persian and Indian aesthetics. Additionally, Akbar patronized astrologers, calendar-makers, calligraphers, chronogram-creators, and jewelers.

Simultaneously, like Akbar's predecessors, he led or launched armies in every direction that threatened danger or promised plunder or rich revenues. Many of Akbar's early martial expeditions westward fought Rajputs, the counterpoint to his concurrent policy of political marriages with more cooperative Rajputs. In 1562, Mughal forces captured Jodhpur from the Rathor Rajputs of Marwar, returning this city when they submitted to Mughal sovereignty. In 1567–8, Akbar personally commanded a bloody three-month-siege of the strategically located and supposedly impregnable fortress of Chittor, main bastion of the Sisodia Rajputs of Mewar. Although the Sisodia ruler escaped before the siege, Akbar and his commanders were impressed by the bravery of the fort's remaining defenders and the mass male and female suicide, *jauhar*, of many rather than surrender. The victorious Mughals slaughtered the survivors, but Sisodia rulers resisted in their hinterland for five decades longer.

Other Rajput rulers apprehended the proven Mughal siege technology and ruthless perseverance at Chittor, and were attracted by the rewards of alliance and imperial service. In 1569, the Hada Rajput commander of the famed Ranthambhor fortress negotiated an honorable surrender after a month-long siege, as did the Baghela

Rajput ruler of Bhatta who gave up Kalinjar citadel. In 1570, the Rathor Rajputs of Bikaner and the Bhati Rajputs of Jaisalmir also negotiated recognition of Akbar's sovereignty. Further, Akbar later strengthened his own fortress at Ajmer, in central Rajasthan, to secure intimidating dominance over Rajput lands, and to pursue the remaining holdouts.

From 1564, Akbar's commanders also drove southward into Gondwana, the heavily forested homeland of the Gonds (an amalgam of adivasi communities). Like previous empires (and the Indian Republic today), the Mughal state always found controlling such foresters frustrating since they were hard to locate, difficult to move armies against, and resistant to outside authority. But their lands contained many wild elephants—highly valued for their utility and long associated with royalty—and some rulers had amassed large treasuries. To resist this Mughal invasion, numerous Gond rajas rallied behind the widowed Rani Durgavati of Garha-Katanga, whose dynasty boasted being Rajput. She personally led the combined Gond forces, dying in battle; her followers fought until death, committed mass suicide, submitted, or evaded the invaders. Her younger sister, Kamla Devi, reportedly entered Akbar's harem. In 1567, Akbar recognized the brother of the late Garha-Katanga king in exchange for promised acceptance of Mughal sovereignty. But this region remained an interior frontier for the Empire.

Akbar also pressed south against the Khandesh Sultanate, strategically located between Hindustan and the Deccan. This dynasty had exchanged brides with the Mughals, but relations remained occasionally hostile nonetheless. However, Akbar postponed extensive commitment of Mughal forces into Khandesh and the Deccan beyond.

To the east, Jaunpur, Bihar, Bengal and Orissa had long attracted but also resisted Mughal invasions. While environmentally varied, these territories included agriculturally rich lands, with qasbas and urban centers of well-established artisanal manufacturing (especially cloth) and a strong overseas export trade (increasingly via European merchants). In the Bay of Bengal, Portuguese, Arakanese and other maritime powers had also long plundered commercial shipping.

Even after Bairam Khan had conquered parts of eastern India, Mughal administration there remained thin. Many Central Asian, Irani and even Hindustani mansabdars found Bengal's humid climate and riverine terrain alienating. Repeatedly in the mid-1560s, imperial officials governing eastern India themselves rebelled against young Akbar, evoking instead Mirza Hakim's sovereignty. Even after Akbar's loyalist forces restored his authority (albeit temporarily), imperial officials posted in eastern India had difficulty penetrating the power structure of settled Indo-Afghan and other local rulers and zamindars.

Simultaneous with these military campaigns, Akbar strove to build loyalty among influential men who had long supported his family and shaped his own early beliefs. During Akbar's twenties based in Agra, he largely respected the orthodox Sunni traditions of his ancestors, shared by the majority of his mansabdars and Muslim subjects. These orthodox Sunni policies proved politically advantageous as Akbar mobilized backing against Bairam Khan, known for his Shi'i sympathies, and then as Akbar established his own corps of mansabdars.

Through the 1570s, Akbar gave both financial and ideological support to Sunni 'ulama. His state needed 'ulama to staff judicial courts, lead congregational prayers, invoke divine blessing on the sovereign, teach Islamic sciences, instruct children in basic literacy and numeracy and make Hindustan a moral society. To secure their support and services, Akbar appointed orthodox Sunni men as Sadr, empowered to give revenue grants to 'ulama, Sufi pirs (Naqshbandi and also India-based) and indigent but worthy Muslims. Akbar personally observed conventional Sunni forms of worship, including the prescribed five daily prayers. Under the guidance of strongly Sunni 'ulama (including Shaikh 'Abd-un-Nabi), Akbar punished sects they claimed were deviant, including millennial Mahdists and outspoken Shi'as. During this period, Akbar also characterized as jihads some military campaigns against non-Muslims, including some fought on his behalf that included Hindu Rajputs fighting against other Hindu Rajputs.

Concurrently, however, from his early youth Akbar also incorporated into his household, court and administration non-Sunni people, ideologies and practices, to an extent unprecedented for either his Mughal predecessors or Delhi sultans. During his lifetime and down to today, those who regard Akbar as an ecumenical man and ruler have seen early Shi'i influences on him from his mother, his guardian Bairam Khan, and several other close companions.

Commentators who highlight Akbar's later heterodox beliefs find them inspired by charismatic and eclectic mystics, both Muslim and non-Muslim, whom Akbar chose to meet.

Further, many of his policies from this period explicitly favored some Hindus and offended some orthodox Sunni 'ulama. From 1562 onward, Akbar contracted political marriages with numerous Hindu Rajput brides and promoted to high rank many of his new male in-laws and other Hindus; although relatively few obtained major offices in Akbar's central administration, many led or served in military campaigns and provincial administrations. Additionally, Akbar gave substantial financial support to some Hindu temples (although he evidently never worshiped in any), ended *jizya* and the pilgrim tax on Hindus, and prohibited the slaughter of cows and peacocks.

But Akbar's prohibitions on cow slaughter and temple destruction did not protect Hindus who openly opposed him. In 1572, Akbar sent forces north against Kangra, a kingdom in the Himalayan foothills. After occasional submissions and then revolts, Kangra's Raja Jaichand pushed too far, so Akbar imprisoned him. Akbar then awarded Kangra in jagir to favored courtier, poet and commander Raja Birbal. When Jaichand's young son, Badhchand, rebelled, Akbar sent an army under the current governor of the Punjab, a Turk named Husain Quli Khan. Seeking to dishearten and punish the defenders, Akbar's commander assaulted Kangra's prestigious Mahamai temple. Imperial soldiers reportedly slaughtered the temple's Rajput guardians, Brahmin priests and hundreds of black cows. A contemporary recorded: 'Some savage Turks ... took off their boots and filled them with the [cow's] blood, and splashed it on the roof and walls of the temple.'[8] The defenders finally negotiated surrender and the Mughal commander erected a mosque near Jaichand's palace. Akbar continued to honor and promote Husain Quli Khan, soon awarding him mansab 5,000 and successively two governorships. In contrast, local Hindus reportedly cursed the jagirdar, Raja Birbal, himself a Brahmin, for these desecrations. We do not have evidence about how Raja Birbal reconciled his devotion to Akbar with these events but they suggest how contingent were Akbar's policies and relationships with diverse religiously identified communities.

From Akbar's early teens until his early forties, along with his patronage of orthodox Sunni traditions and increasingly (but not uniformly) of Hindu ones as well, he also sought out intense spiritual relationships with leading Sufi mystics, living and dead. Significantly, he gradually shifted his devotion from the more orthodox Sunni Naqshbandi order favored by his ancestors to India-based orders, particularly the Chishti, who embraced a more incorporative vision of Islam, and refrained from overt political engagement.

From 1566, for 14 years annually, Akbar visited Khwaja Mu'in-ud-Din Chishti's shrine in Ajmer—including a 1570 pilgrimage on foot, some 360 kilometers from Agra. Additionally, Akbar's devotion to Shaikh Salim Chishti took material form in Akbar's new capital at Sikri.

THE FATEHPUR SIKRI PERIOD, 1571–85

During Akbar's thirties and early forties, he was exceptionally innovative, designing and building at Sikri his entirely new court and administrative city as the embodiment of his own changing policies and widening personal religious beliefs.[9] Babur had built a garden at Sikri celebrating his 1527 victory at Khanua. But Akbar located his new city directly in homage to Shaikh Salim, who died there in 1571. Over time, Akbar erected for Shaikh Salim an exquisitely carved white marble grave monument in the courtyard of the vast new congregational mosque. As Akbar expected, his courtiers and amirs constructed their own mansions and gardens around the many imperial buildings. Significantly, Akbar, now more securely on the throne, did not strongly fortify Sikri (although the entire city had a surrounding wall to regulate entry). Nonetheless, Akbar kept his armies active, with pitched battles every year.

On Akbar's south-west frontier lay Gujarat, long frustratingly hostile to Mughal forces. Like Bengal, Gujarat produced great wealth from agriculture, hand-manufacturing and overseas trade via European, Indian and Arab ships. The Gujarat Sultans had briefly succumbed to Humayun but then reasserted independence after his expulsion from India. In Gujarat during Akbar's early reign, the Sultan, locally settled Abyssinians (often liberated slave-warriors) and rival Timurids all contested for power on land, while Ottoman and Portuguese fleets fought to control the sea coast and overseas trade.

Tomb of Salim Chishti in Fatehpur, Main Mosque, *c.* 1581

In 1572, one faction in the fragmenting Gujarat Sultanate appealed to Akbar, who personally led a military expedition from Sikri that seized the Sultan's capital, Ahmedabad. After receiving submission from the Sultan and most local rulers, Akbar returned to his new expanding capital, now called Fatehpur ('City of Victory') Sikri. Almost immediately, however, revolts erupted across Gujarat.

Early in 1573, Akbar led another lightning campaign (dashing 800 kilometers in 11 days) that ended in his bloody victory and retribution: 'Nearly 1,000 [enemy] heads fell on that battle-field and the Emperor ordered them to make a minaret out of those heads, that it might serve as a warning to rebels.'[10] This was the last time Akbar personally entered combat (although he commanded military expeditions until age 60). Akbar then directed Raja Todar Mal to assess the land revenues of those parts of Gujarat and adjacent regions under imperial control. Nonetheless, Mughal administration in Gujarat remained threatened by local uprisings and periodic incursions from Deccan Sultanates and the Portuguese.

Eastern India also remained dangerous for Akbar's officials. In 1574, the Bengal Sultan repudiated Akbar's sovereignty. Akbar personally commanded the siege and capture of Patna fortress in Bihar, then sent Raja Todar Mal to defeat the Sultan. Punctuating repeated Mughal battlefield victories were resurgences by the Sultan and other local leaders. Eventually, in 1576, after a hard-fought victory, Mughal forces executed the Sultan and reconquered the region.

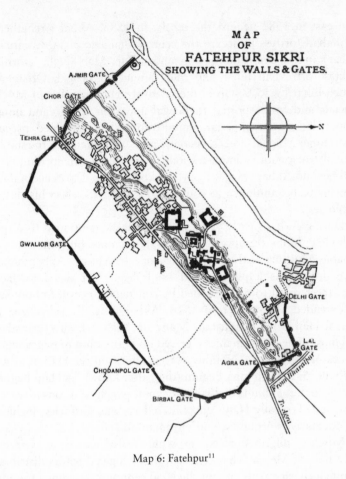

Map 6: Fatehpur[11]

Nonetheless, eastern India remained resistant to Mughal authority. Imperial officials pushing too hard for revenues or obedience led to armed resistance. The largest revolt occurred when aggressive governor Khwaja Muzaffar Khan Turbati provoked an extended popular insurrection (1579–82). The insurgents again evoked Hakim's sovereignty, supporting his concurrent incursion into the Punjab. Further, the prominent Sunni Qazi of Jaunpur issued a *fatwa* ('religious ruling') legitimating for Muslims the rejection of allegedly apostate Akbar's authority. In response, Akbar personally led successful expeditions west to Kabul in 1581 against Hakim and then east in 1582 against the rebels. In 1583, Akbar strengthened Allahabad fortress to secure the central Gangetic plain. Eventually, Akbar's in-law and leading commander, Raja Man Singh, refortified Rohtas fortress in Bihar and then conquered Bengal, Orissa and Cooch Bihar by 1592. Given the relatively small number of Mughal officials and forces posted to Bengal and their fragile and limited support locally, the imperial administration there remained insecure. Each time Mughal forces reconquered, they had to re-establish virtually their entire administration; eastern India remained unsettled well beyond Akbar's reign. Even as Akbar led or dispatched military campaigns, he continued to construct Fatehpur to reflect his shifting ideologies.

During Akbar's early years in Fatehpur, he continued to respect orthodox Sunni traditions. A central religious obligation for all capable Muslims is the Hajj pilgrimage to Mecca. Akbar himself once dressed as a pilgrim and symbolically set out for Mecca, allowing himself to be dissuaded by courtiers concerned about such an extended absence. From 1576, Akbar officially subsidized the annual Hajj from Hindustan. Many of Akbar's family, attendants and most dangerous enemies received his permission to pilgrimage to Mecca or settle there. Notably, Akbar approved the Hajj of at least one wife, Salima Sultana Begum (thereafter known as Hajji Begum), and his paternal aunt, Gulbadan Begum, which took seven years to complete. Typically Hajjis encountered various obstacles, including uncooperative Portuguese and Ottoman officials.

Mughal pilgrims faced growing resistance from Ottoman governors of Mecca. They reported that Mughal visitors distributed so much charity as to disrupt the local economy, remained too long, did not respect Ottoman sovereignty, and were spying for a joint Mughal-Portuguese invasion of Yemen.[12] Indeed, some Mughal officials did discuss an alliance with the Portuguese against the Ottoman Empire, although other Mughal officials in Gujarat also repeatedly clashed with the Portuguese.

In 1581, Akbar ceased underwriting the Hajj. He resented the demeaning necessity to seek unreliable Portuguese protection while crossing the Indian Ocean (or uncertain Safavid permission for the more onerous overland route) and then submit to Ottoman authority once there. In 1582, Akbar wrote to the hereditary Sharifs of Mecca (who governed under the Ottomans) diplomatically apologizing

Rare Partly Surviving Fatehpur Interior Wall Fresco (detail)[13]

for the absence of a Mughal Hajj party the previous year and also requesting written receipts for his lavish financial donations, which remained unacknowledged and unaccounted for.[14] Despite this deferential letter, Akbar never sponsored another Hajj (although many courtiers went anyway). His personal and political policies by this time had largely shifted away from orthodox Islamic practices, as his Fatehpur palace complex reveals.

Akbar constructed about 60 free-standing structures, each reflecting his current ideologies and architectural taste. Some evidently served the same purposes as their counterparts in Agra, including a diwan-i am, diwan-i khas, ghusal-khana, harem, hamam and karkhanas. But in Fatehpur, some had distinctive architectural forms. About 40 structures remain standing (in remarkably good condition four centuries later and mostly unchanged by later reconstruction) and contemporary paintings and narratives described some of them. Nonetheless, Akbar was so innovative that today's scholars cannot concur about which structure housed which function, with widely varied names now applied to many buildings. Further, while the red sandstone exteriors are mainly intact, most decorative and religious paintings on interior walls have faded, while the cloth and wood canopies, partitions and furnishings that shaped their use are gone.

From Babur onward, many Mughal palaces and gardens featured sophisticated use of water, often perfumed and conducted over illuminated cascades. Some water could be heated for bathing. At Fatehpur, Akbar dammed a stream and constructed a dozen step-wells with complex hydraulic lifting-systems and piping to supply water for drinking, cooking, sanitation, bathing and pleasure.

His distinctive Anup Talao ('Peerless Pool') was a square 3,000 cubic meter reservoir with four walkways leading to a nine-square-meter central pavilion. There Akbar sat coolly, while courtiers, musicians, dancers, or other entertainers performed across the water before him. Famously, Akbar once filled this reservoir with coins for distribution in charity.

Nearby, Akbar constructed a remarkable square, central-columned, single-chambered, two-story building, measuring 175 square meters. This building also contained four walkways leading to a platform—a circular dais atop a single, intricately carved central column. Apparently, Akbar looked magisterially down over assembled courtiers below.

Akbar had two elaborate portals, *jharoka*, from which he revealed himself. From one, atop an outer wall, he appeared daily to his subjects on the ground below, who thus reassured themselves of his good health, savored his latest sartorial fashion, or worshipped him. Akbar's publicist described this as Akbar bestowing 'the light of his countenance' by giving *darshan* (Sanskrit for the 'auspicious sight' that a deity bestows on devotees).[15] From this balcony, Akbar also observed spectacular elephant and other animal combats. Akbar had another jharoka looking into the diwan-i am.

Around 1575, Akbar built in Fatehpur another highly controversial building, called the *'ibadat-khana* (Arabic 'divine worship hall'). This

Anup Talao with Columned Building in Background

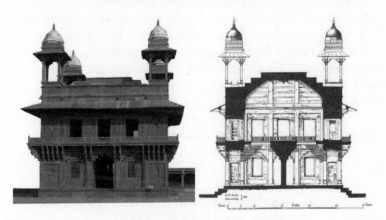

Columned Building Today and Transected[16]

building's location remains uncertain but it housed fiery evening debates among leading religious scholars and leaders, over which Akbar arbitrated.[17] At first, Akbar only invited prominent Sunni 'ulama and Sayyids. Representing various Sunni legal and philosophical schools, they disputed bitterly, as Akbar moved among them listening and also setting contentious questions. One difficult issue he posed was how many wives a Muslim man may legally marry by nikah. Since he was unwilling to divorce any of his hundreds of nikah wives, he thus challenged these orthodox Sunni authorities either to dare rule against him or else find a legalistic way to justify his condition. Akbar reportedly punished Shaikh 'Abd-un-Nabi and other prominent advocates of Sunni orthodoxy who refused to approve more than four wives. The Mughal clan and most Sunnis in India followed the Hanafi school of Islamic jurisprudence but, after much debate, more compliant 'ulama found Maliki rulings that could be interpreted as allowing multiple temporary marriages, nikah al-mut'ah (Arabic 'joyous marriage'), which were legally contracted for a fixed period in exchange for specified compensation to the wife. Shi'i theologians (evidently not included in these early debates) also accept mut'ah marriages. The inflexibility of some Sunni 'ulama and the unseemly casuistry of others apparently reinforced Akbar's shift from his earlier conformity with Sunni orthodoxy and spurred his religious search.

In 1578, amid a massive qamargha hunt, Akbar collapsed unconscious, to the consternation of his attendants: 'suddenly all at once a strange state and strong frenzy came upon the Emperor .... And when news of this became spread abroad ... strange rumours and wonderful lies became current in the mouths of the common people and some insurrections took place among the [peasants], but these were quickly quelled.'[18] Earlier, Akbar had similar experiences, although contemporary sources are vague about their severity and duration since any weakness in the heir apparent or emperor would be perilous for the state. This time, after regaining consciousness, he suddenly ordered the enclosed animals freed rather than killed *en masse* as usual, he designated the site as sacred, and he had the top of his head shorn (reportedly to enable his soul to escape at death). Akbar's publicist proclaimed this a transfiguring infusion of the divine spirit into Akbar. Most recent scholars doubt a supernatural cause. Rather some explain this physiologically, for example Akbar was epileptic. Others use psychology, that Akbar was undergoing inner struggle to reconcile his earlier orthodox Sunni beliefs with his growing crisis of faith and mystical searching.[19] However, no further similar episodes were recorded and insufficient evidence exists for definitive diagnosis four centuries later.

Akbar apparently felt empowered by this experience. He was already extending his own control over the orthodox Sunni 'ulama, whose services Akbar's administration still needed but whose authority he was questioning. Some subsequent innovations arose from Akbar and his close advisors. But others came from courtiers hoping to anticipate Akbar's approval or wishing his patronage for their own ideologies or factions. Since the stakes were so great, many competing factions maneuvered, allied, conspired or strongly advocated policies that they favored or would favor them.

Many Sunni 'ulama, like other religious figures, had received or inherited revenue grants from earlier rulers or from Akbar. Periodically, but particularly after 1578, Akbar ordered the Sadr to investigate all these grants, reducing or confiscating many lacking documentation or where the current recipient appeared unworthy. Akbar then lavishly redistributed grants to Muslim and non-Muslim worthies who earned his respect and demonstrated loyalty (some grants were for uncultivated lands that he wished to make productive, thus extending and developing his Empire's agricultural base). Many 'ulama who lost grants, and even some who received renewals, resented being judged by the state instead of just recognized and supported. Additionally Akbar added to his many titles *Amir al-Muminin*, 'Commander of Faithful,' asserting leadership over the Muslim community in Hindustan and globally.

On Friday, 26 June 1579, in Fatehpur's main mosque, Akbar publicly demonstrated both his sovereignty and also his right as *imam* ('prayer leader'). A few earlier rulers had personally done this, but no previous Mughal emperors. Court poet Faizi composed a khutba which Akbar recited, calling down Allah's blessing on the sovereign (Akbar himself):

> The Almighty God, that on me the empire conferred;
> A mind of wisdom, and an arm of strength conferred!
> To justice and to equity, He did me guide;
> Expelled all but justice, from my thought;
> His attributes beyond all comprehension soar!
> Exalted His greatness, Allah-o-Akbar![20]

The last phrase (which Akbar also minted on his coins) conventionally means 'God is Great' but also, controversially, 'Akbar is Allah.'

According to a contemporary advocate of Sunni orthodoxy, however, Akbar's performance went awry: 'His Majesty began to read the *khutbah*. But all at once he stammered and trembled, and though assisted by others, he could scarcely read three verses ... but

A Square Silver Rupee of Emperor Akbar with 'Allah-o-Akbar' and 'Jalal-ud-Din,' 33rd Regnal Year, 996–7 H (1587–9 CE)[21]

came quickly down from the pulpit, and handed over the duties of Ímám ...'[22]

Nonetheless, continuing this trend of subordinating Sunni 'ulama, in September 1579, a *mahzar* circulated at court; this was an 'attestation,' a religious decree whose authority was endorsed by all who signed and/or affixed their personal seals. The original disappeared and the actual authorship was unstated, but Badauni claimed the handwriting was Shaikh Mubarak's—allegedly the only one of the dozen signatories who added that he fully and willingly approved the document. It asserted in part:

> ... Hindústán is now become the centre of security and peace .... We, the principal 'Ulamá ... have duly considered the deep meaning, *first*, of the verse of the Qurán: 'Obey God, and obey the prophet, and those who have authority among you,' and, *secondly*, of the genuine tradition [Hadith]: 'Surely the man who is dearest to God on the day of judgment is the *Imám-i 'ádil* ["just leader"]; whosoever obeys the Amír, obeys Thee; and whosoever rebels against him, rebels against Thee' ... [therefore] we declare that the ... Amír of the Faithful, Shadow of God in the world, *Abu-l-Fath Jalál-ud-din Muhammad Akbar Padsháh Gházi* whose kingdom God perpetuate!) is a most just, a most wise, and a most God-fearing king. Should therefore in future a religious question come up ... and His Majesty in his penetrating understanding and clear wisdom be inclined to adopt ... any of the conflicting opinions, which exist on that point, and issue a decree to that effect, we do hereby agree that such a decree shall be binding on us and on the whole nation ... and further, that any opposition ... shall involve damnation in the world to come, and loss of property and religious privileges in this.[23]

Badauni asserted that he and most 'ulama signed unwillingly, under severe threat to their offices, income, or lives.

Scholars (then and now) have debated the nature, meaning and legitimacy of this mahzar and the extent of Akbar's ambitions. The text explicitly recognizes Akbar's authority to arbitrate any religious issue whenever the 'ulama were not unanimous—as long as his interpretation accords with the Qur'an and Hadith. Some commentators designated this Akbar's 'Infallibility Decree,' implying he modelled his claims on the concept of Papal infallibility (which, though not yet Roman Catholic doctrine, was explained by Jesuits at Akbar's court).[24] Some later scholars argue that Akbar intended to be Caliph over all Muslims in his own domain; others that Akbar claimed authority over all Muslims globally and thus rejected subordination to the Ottomans, Safavids, or Uzbeks; yet others assert Akbar proclaimed himself the millennial sovereign, equal to his ancestor Timur.[25] Whatever the precise intention of this mahzar, it accorded with Akbar's efforts to subordinate the Sunni 'ulama; but some still resisted, even those who signed the mahzar. This further motivated Akbar to seek additional political support and religious knowledge outside Sunni orthodoxy.

Akbar's shifting ideology and policies affected the proportions of various ethnic groups among his mansabdars. By 1580, Sunni Turanis had shrunk to 24 per cent of mansabdars, less than half the proportion at his accession. Similarly, Shi'i Iranis had also halved to 17 per cent. In contrast, Hindus and Indian Muslims had risen to 16 per cent each.[26] With some small variations, these proportions remained relatively stable through the rest of Akbar's reign.

By the late 1570s, Akbar had also broadened his 'ibadat-khana debates to include scholars and holy men from various other religious communities. He listened closely, challenging each speaker's assertions, testing them against his own developing theology, and adopting parts of their ideology when they confirmed or advanced his own.

From 1578 onward, Akbar welcomed leading Jains to court. Subsequently, Akbar reconciled divisions within the Jain community and endowed some of their sacred sites.[27] Jains (then and now) credit their leaders' personal and spiritual influence on Akbar for his empire-wide ban on animal slaughter during the annual Jain holy season.

Indeed, Akbar experimented with vegetarianism, explaining:

> It is not right that a man should make his stomach the grave of animals .... Were it not for the thought of the difficulty of sustenance, I would prohibit men from eating meat. The reasons why I do not altogether abandon it myself is that many others might willingly forego it likewise and thus be cast into despondency .... From my earliest years, whenever I ordered animal food to be cooked for me, I found it rather tasteless and cared little for it. I took this feeling to indicate a necessity for protecting animals, and I refrained from animal food.[28]

He thus explained vegetarianism in ethical and aesthetic terms, rather than by invoking the authority of any particular religious community.

Around 1583, Akbar reportedly ceased performing the five daily Islamic prayers and began publicly worshiping the sun four times daily and divine light more generally.[29] Akbar's new rituals may have multiple sources. Mongol tradition proclaims divine luminescence as impregnating the Mongols' mythic mother. Leading Indian Parsis, who worship fire, also attended on Akbar. Some of Akbar's Rajput Hindu wives claimed descent from the sun, and performed Brahminic fire- and solar-worship in his harem. Indeed, Akbar reportedly included in his noon-time ritual the recitation of the sun's 1,001 Sanskrit names. Further, Akbar invited Portuguese Jesuits to court, and questioned them about Mary's sinless impregnation by the Spirit, among other topics.

Akbar evidently first encountered the Portuguese in Gujarat in 1573. He even briefly ventured into Surat harbor in a Portuguese vessel. In 1578, some Portuguese came from Bengal to Fatehpur and the Portuguese viceroy sent an ambassador from Goa. Seeking more educated informants, Akbar requested the viceroy in 1579 to 'send me two learned priests who should bring with them the chief books of the Law and the Gospel, for I wish to study and learn the Law and what is best and most perfect in it.'[30] In response, the Viceroy sent three Jesuits (their young order had worked to convert India since 1542). This delegation included a Persian-speaking Iranian convert to Catholicism. The Jesuits reported (in the third person):

> Akbar, from his throne, ordered them to come nearer to him, and asked them a few questions .... Having retired ... into an inner apartment, he ordered them to be conducted to him ... in order that he might exhibit

them to his wives. Then he ... put on Portuguese dress—a scarlet cloak with golden fastenings. He ordered his sons also to don the same dress, together with Portuguese hats .... He also ordered 800 pieces of gold to be presented to them; but the Fathers replied that they had not come there to get money ... whereupon he expressed admiration at their self-control ...[31]

During their three years at court, these Jesuits diligently but ineffectively pursued their usual strategy for the conversion of the entire kingdom by starting with its ruler.

Akbar appeared very open to learning about certain topics from these Jesuits, treating them as he did many other diverse courtiers he allowed to attend upon him. He quizzed them about an atlas they presented (probably Abraham Ortelius of Antwerp's 1570 *Theatrum Orbis Terrarum*), showing inquisitiveness about European geography and how the cartographer could know the names and locations of Indian cities.[32] Akbar also learned about the Americas; Mughal courtiers heard:

Of late years the Europeans have discovered an extensive and populous insular continent which they have called the New World. Some shattered vessels have been here driven ashore. A man mounted on horseback was seen by the inhabitants. Mistaking the man and his horse for a single animal they were overcome by fear and the country fell an easy capture.[33]

But Akbar evidently made no practical use of the atlas or European-style globes he later received, treating them as curiosities, like the European-made musical organ that one of his courtiers brought back from the Hajj.

Akbar admired European-style art for its unfamiliar perspective and figuration. He had some of his best artists copy European paintings and incorporate their conventions. He reportedly displayed special veneration towards pictures of Christ and Mary (traditionally revered in Islam, although not considered divine). He also commissioned a Jesuit to compose a biography of Christ in Persian.[34]

Showing the Jesuits favor, Akbar ordered them moved from their distant lodgings to nearer his own living quarters, converting a perfume workshop for them. There, they installed a small chapel, before whose altar Akbar reportedly prostrated himself, with head uncovered (as Europeans showed respect and Hindustanis showed abject submission). Akbar appointed Jesuit Father Monserrate (who wrote a detailed report for his superiors) as tutor for his second son, Mirza Murad. But Akbar found unconvincing the Jesuits' insistence on monogamy (even for Akbar), the Trinity, the divinity of Christ and the low status of the Prophet Muhammad. Ultimately, Akbar frustrated Jesuit expectations for his conversion.

Akbar, however, recognized the value of some Portuguese worldly knowledge and their potential as allies, or troublesome adversaries. In 1582, he dispatched two envoys to King Philip II (ruled Spain, 1556–98, also Portugal, 1581–8), proposing regular diplomatic exchanges and requesting Arabic and Persian translations of the Pentateuch, Gospels and Psalms.[35] Akbar's emissaries, however, never got further than Goa. Additionally, skirmishes erupted in Gujarat over Portuguese seizures of Mughal ships, confiscation of a village and blockade of Surat.[36] Akbar received another short-lived Jesuit mission (1591–3) and then one that arrived in 1595 and remained 20 years, well beyond Akbar's reign.

Akbar, however, did not limit his exploration of the cosmos to established Asian or European cultures. Starting in 1582, Akbar experimented to resolve the long-standing philosophical debate about whether human beings have an inherent natural language and religion, from which all others diverged. He ordered 20 newborn babies purchased from their parents and isolated, attended only by absolutely silent servants. After a few years, Akbar observed that the children had no language or religion at all, concluding 'Learning to speak comes from association, otherwise men would remain inarticulate.'[37] Akbar also tried inter-breeding varieties of animals, to observe whether they could reproduce and, if so, the nature of their offspring. Further, he worked to master alchemic production of gold and esoteric means of achieving immortality.

Akbar's search to find a universal basis for all religions, and create congeniality among all his subjects' religious communities, became his policy *sulh-i kul* (translated variously as 'universal peace' or 'tolerance for all').[38] He thus respected all groups that submitted to him as the 'perfect man' and 'universal sovereign.' Since his armies continued to suppress dissidents and conquer neighbors, Akbar did not eschew warfare, however.

Rather, Akbar justified his many invasions by asserting that enemy rulers were either immoral rebels against his sovereignty or else abusers of their people, who deserved the truly impartial justice only Akbar provided. He declared in 1586 his 'cleansing of the four corners of India ... was not out of self-indulgence or selfishness, but only for comforting human beings and for exterminating their oppressors.' He continued:

> guided by the motives of the welfare of the subjects who were the covenants ... of God, he (Akbar) had tried to clear the land of India during the [last] thirty years to such an extent that difficult places under refractory Rajas had fallen into his hands. The churches and temples of the infidels and the heretics had turned into the cells of God-fearing dervishes .... All ... stiff-necked individuals have placed the rings of obedience in their ears and have enrolled in the victorious [Mughal] armies. In this way the heterogeneous people had been brought together in one stroke.

Akbar thus wanted to bring all regional rulers into his great host and to unite all people under his transcendent sovereignty.

Over Akbar's final years in Fatehpur, his policies shifted from his family's and his earlier strong identification with Sunni Islam. Instead, Akbar and his close companions created a new court culture centering on him that 'made the world his bride.' Service to Akbar would be the main—perhaps the only—way for men to reach their highest virtue. Their own households should be microcosms of his, and they themselves perfect men within them. Reorienting time, Akbar devised a new solar-based calendar, *Tarikh-i Ilahi* ('Divine Era'), that began with his own accession. This calendar also had practical administrative advantages since the annual harvest and thus the revenue cycle varied within the lunar Islamic Hijri calendar. Akbar also added 'Allah-o-Akbar' to imperial documents and coins. Critics created a popular couplet in 1584:

> The king this year has laid claim to be a Prophet,
> After the lapse of a year, please God, he will become God![39]

Indeed, among Akbar's courtiers and household, an imperial cult with him as spiritual master began to emerge.

All these trends continued to develop after Akbar suddenly left Fatehpur in 1585, taking most courtiers and officials with him. He never lived there again. Instead, he eventually made Lahore his next imperial capital.

THE LAHORE PERIOD, 1586–98

By 1585, various factors contributed to Akbar's shift from Fatehpur Sikri toward the north-west. Akbar had been curtailing his devotion to Chishti pirs, including Shaikh Salim—deeply identified with Sikri. Simultaneously, Akbar perceived political instability and also opportunities for expansion on his Empire's north-western frontier. Uzbek incursions were pressing on Badakhshan and Kabul. Yusufzai Afghans were rebelling. Additionally, Akbar saw prospects for conquest of Lower Sind, Kashmir and Qandahar. The specific precipitating factor for Akbar's move, however, was Mirza Hakim's death in Kabul (10 October 1585); Akbar began marching his massive entourage from Fatehpur a week after receiving that news. By 1586, Akbar had settled in Lahore as his new operations-base.

Unlike Sikri, Lahore was already well-established and thriving when Akbar moved his court there. The city had long remained the center for commerce and for military, administrative and political control over strategic Punjab—the major route for trade and invasion to and from Central Asia and Iran. Akbar had occasionally visited Lahore. But, in his absence, Lahore had been repeatedly attacked from Kabul and Badakhshan. In 1565, Akbar had ordered Lahore fort reinforced with brick walls and stronger gates. To secure the crucial region further, Akbar also hardened Rohtas fortress in western Punjab, guarding the upper Indus.

While Mirza Hakim lived, he posed an ongoing political and military threat to Akbar. But Hakim's rule in Kabul also buffered against Uzbek and Safavid invasions and helped control Afghans. So, at Hakim's death from alcoholism, Akbar immediately rushed Raja Man Singh and other trusted commanders to consolidate power in Kabul. Akbar considered using Hakim's young sons as nominal governors, but decided they might embody a Timurid threat to his supremacy. In 1588–9, Akbar journeyed to Kabul to supervise personally.

From Babur's reign onward, various Afghan communities resisted Mughal control. Babur's political marriage alliance with a Yusufzai chief had long ended. During the 1580s–90s, the militant millenarian Roshaniyya movement mobilized Yusufzai in Swat, which particularly threatened Mughal communication and commerce with Kabul. To suppress the Yusufzai, Akbar had sent strong forces in 1589, but

Raja Birbal's entire army met fatal ambush. Now, Raja Man Singh's forces retaliated, temporarily subduing the Yusufzai, and Akbar coordinated his armies to re-impose order.

Akbar also sent commanders to conquer southward down the Indus River to Lower Sind and northward through the mountains to Kashmir. Lower Sind controlled both the Indus delta and also the main land route to strategic Qandahar. Since about 1585, Timurid Mirza Jani Beg Tarkhan (d. *c.* 1598) had been nominally a mansabdar but effectively independent ruler of Lower Sind, based in Thatta.[40] He had often proven uncooperative and Akbar rejected his offer of a daughter as an imperial bride.

From 1590, Akbar sent Mughal forces to make Jani Beg actually submit. Eventually, Akbar's commander defeated Jani Beg, who then gave daughters as brides for the commander and the imperial family, came to court where he became a disciple in Akbar's imperial cult, and retained his mansab. However, when Akbar shifted him to be governor of Upper Sind and moved his jagir, many of his followers accompanied him, disrupting Thatta's economy. Hence, Akbar pragmatically soon returned him as governor of Lower Sindh and restored his jagir there. Thus, Jani Beg retained much of his old kingdom as his watan jagir (inherited by his son, who held it until 1611) but now as a Mughal official, not an autonomous ruler.

Akbar also ordered Mughal forces to march through Lower Sind to retake Qandahar from the Safavids, who had seized that strategic city during Mughal weakness following Humayun's death. While attacking Qandahar proved militarily unfeasible, Akbar's agents convinced the Safavid commander to defect to the Mughals, turning over the city in 1595 and receiving a high mansab. Thereby, Akbar secured this major land route into India from the west.

Northward, Kashmir stood historically distinctive in its culture and physical environment, separated from the Punjab by difficult mountain passes (impassible by armies in winter). Occasionally, Humayun's supporters had controlled Kashmir's main valley and its capital, Srinagar. Soon after moving to Lahore, Akbar sent forces that defeated Kashmir's Muslim king and annexed the region in 1586 (although various popular rebellions arose sporadically until 1622). Like his successors, Akbar found Kashmir a cool and verdant refuge from hot summers on the plain. He visited Kashmir in 1589, 1592 and 1597. During the last of these visits, Akbar remained in Kashmir for six months while the Lahore palace complex was restored following a major fire.

Akbar lived over a dozen years in Lahore. But, unlike his earlier capitals, he invested only modest resources in buildings there.[41] However, he did continue to develop his court culture. He welcomed various ambassadors and visitors from west and Central Asia and from Portugal. He recruited about 130 painters who, among many projects, produced richly illustrated editions of calligraphically exquisite Persian texts, including translations into Persian.[42]

Vastly expanding his library, Akbar ordered scholars to translate literary and religious epics, romances and morality tales from Sanskrit, Portuguese and other languages into Persian (and sometimes vice versa). Many were read aloud in court. Akbar's translators recruited experts in the original languages to assist. When nobody knew both the original language and Persian, an intermediary using yet a third bridge language (like Hindustani) helped.[43] But the translations were often far from literal. Akbar himself quizzed translators about the nuances and implications of their omissions and word choices. Occasionally, Akbar ordered a second translation to cross-check. One courtier, Badauni, detested the several Hindu texts he was ordered to translate, including the epics *Mahabharata* (called, in Persian, the *Razmnama*, 'Book of War') and *Ramayana*. Indeed, Akbar directly confronted Badauni when his interpretations were vastly shorter than the massive originals and differed from Akbar's own understanding of Hindu theology.[44] In contrast, Abu-al-Fazl and others in accord with Akbar's sentiments helped translate works from Sanskrit and Portuguese into Persian more sympathetically. After initially commissioning translations of literary and religious works, Akbar expanded to historical texts. Following the Mughal conquest of Kashmir, for instance, Akbar ordered Badauni to translate from Sanskrit into Persian Kalhana's *Rajatarangini*, a remarkable history of Kashmir's kings with similarities to Persianate and European historical genres.[45]

Abu-al-Fazl explained his (and Akbar's) major ideological and political goals for these Indic translation projects.[46] Accurate translations would inform Muslims and Hindus about the actual content of their own and each other's sacred texts. This would disempower those pretentious religious leaders who deviously misrepresented these texts.

Such cross-cultural exchanges helped Akbar locate himself in Indic traditions and, conversely, helped Hindus identify with his Persianate court culture. Akbar, his wives and some courtiers also patronized literature and musical lyrics in Braj Basha and other popular north Indian languages.[47] These translation and literary projects also fostered Akbar's other policies that created a new imperial ideology centered on him as the peerless imperial pir and universal sovereign, superior to all other human religious or political authority.

A devotional sect dedicated to Akbar developed at his court, perhaps as early as 1582. But its nature, composition and goals were controversial, then and today. This cult had secret mystical practices so only full initiates knew them. The most extensive surviving descriptions were by Badauni, an outsider and bitter opponent. Even the name was disputed. Frequently, Badauni called it *Din-i Illahi* ('Religion of God' or 'Divine Religion'), a name used by many later commentators but not the initiates. Further, recent scholars who characterize Akbar as secularist question the use of *din* ('religion').[48]

In other places, Badauni wrote 'His Majesty gave his religious system the name of *Tauhid-i-Ilāhi*'.[49] The Arabic term tauhid has a long philosophical tradition and range of meanings including: 'belief in the unity of God' and 'the fifth degree of perfection in Sūfī life, where the divine essence is contemplated as void of any attribute conceived by thought.'[50] This ideology resonated with the theology of *wahdat al-wujud* ('unity of existence'), most prominently expounded by the Arab Andalusian Sufi Ibn al-'Arabi, whom Akbar's supporters explicitly evoked.[51]

The imperial cult had an exclusively elite membership. Some contemporary texts listed only 19 members, all high mansabdars in Akbar's inner circle. But other sources suggested many of Akbar's personal bodyguard (totaling hundreds of men), or even a majority of high mansabdars were admitted.[52] The initiation reportedly involved especially deep prostration to Akbar and vowing: 'I ... voluntarily, and with sincere predilection and inclination, utterly and entirely renounce and repudiate the religion of Islám ... and do embrace the [Tauhid-i Ilahi] of Akbar Sháh, and do accept the four grades of entire devotion, *viz.*, sacrifice of Property, Life, Honour, and Religion.'[53] Initiates received from Akbar an icon of the sun, a special turban and a small portrait of him to wear on the turban or breast. Imitating Akbar, but going against orthodox Muslim custom, many disciples shaved off their beards. Further, initiates stopped using among themselves the conventional Arabic greeting *as-salam alaykum* ('peace be upon you') and response *wa alaykum-us-salam* ('and unto you peace'), instead substituting *Allah-o Akbar*, with the response *jalla jalaluhu* ('glorified be His glory'), evoking Akbar's title, Jalal-ud-Din. Akbar and his initiates periodically performed sun and light worship, presumably further development of rituals Akbar had devised in his late Fatehpur years. This imperial cult bound the initiated to him, overriding their other loyalties, including ethnicity and kinship.

But not all those invited would join. In 1587, Raja Man Singh responded that he would convert to Islam if Akbar ordered, but he would not join this new cult: 'If Discipleship means willingness to sacrifice one's life, I have already carried my life in my hand: what need is there of further proof? If, however, the term has another meaning and refers to Faith, I certainly am a Hindú. If you order me to do so, I will become a Musalmán, but I know not of the existence of any other religion than these two.'[54] While some courtiers clearly benefitted from their initiation, Man Singh's refusal did not noticeably hurt his subsequent career.

Contemporary writers, both favorable and critical, also noted that there was also a public sect of worshippers of Akbar—the *Darshaniyyah*, those who sought Akbar's darshan. Badauni wrote critically:

> [Those] not admitted into the palace, stood every morning opposite to the window ... and declared that they had made vows not to rinse their mouth, nor to eat and drink, before they had seen the blessed countenance of the Emperor. And every evening [assembled] needy Hindús and Musalmáns, all sorts of people, men and women, healthy and sick, a queer gathering and a most terrible crowd. No sooner had His Majesty ... stepped out into the balcony, than the whole crowd prostrated themselves.[55]

To some extent, Babur and, even more so, Humayun had evoked the model of the emperor as 'Shadow of God on earth.' But Akbar's publicist Abu-al-Fazl repeatedly proclaimed him 'divine light' itself: an earthly embodiment of the sacred, the millennial sovereign. Some recent scholars explain that Akbar was asserting this status above all other sovereigns to wipe out, either in his own mind or diplomatically, the shame of Babur's and Humayun's humiliating religious and political submissions to the Safavids. However, Akbar's contemporary critics, including Naqshbandi pir Shaikh Ahmad Sirhindi (d. 1624), Badauni and other orthodox Sunnis, condemned Akbar for making heretical pretensions of his own divinity.[56] Such claims affronted orthodox Sunni Islam's unqualified monotheism and absolute prohibition against worshipping any except Allah.

Another factor probably strengthening Akbar's millennial ideology was the approaching Hijri year 1000 (1591–2 CE), when many Muslims expected the Mahdi to reveal himself and lead the faithful to eternal salvation. In anticipation, in 1585 Akbar ordered seven courtiers to begin to co-author the *Tarikh-i Alfi* ('History of the First Thousand Years'), chronicling Muslim rulers from the death of the Prophet Muhammad to Akbar. He later ordered 'Era of the Thousand' minted on his coins.

Despite Akbar's decades of adulation by his courtiers and the significant expansion of his empire, he had to confront his own mortal limitations. As Akbar approached age 50, he reflected on his dynasty's place in history. He commissioned his aunt, Gulbadan Begum, and other courtiers and attendants who had personally known Babur or Humayun to write or dictate their memories of those predecessors.

The death of Mirza Hakim had ended any fraternal challenge to Akbar (as the deaths of Babur's and Humayun's brothers had for them). But Akbar's own three maturing sons were each maneuvering for independent power, encouraged by dissidents against Akbar. As Akbar aged, he faced the conflicting desires of both protecting his sons from each other and also securing the unity of his empire. Accomplishing both would have been unprecedented since none of Akbar's ancestors had done so (nor would any of his imperial descendants). Further, everyone anticipated the opportunities and dangers of the inevitable new regime.

In military and diplomatic terms, the Empire's western frontier had stabilized by the late 1590s. Kabul, Sind, Kashmir and Qandahar seemed secure. Akbar's hopes of retaking Badakhshan from the Uzbeks proved ever less plausible. However, the threat of an Uzbek invasion diminished due to a succession struggle beginning in 1598. Akbar thus shifted even more resources and attention to the last promising major frontier, the Deccan. To supervise these southern initiatives, Akbar moved his court not back to Fatehpur but rather to the Deccan and eventually to Agra, where he largely remained for the rest of his life.

IN THE FIELD IN THE DECCAN, 1598–1601, AND IN AGRA, 1601–1605

Akbar invaded any neighboring kingdom or territory that appeared promising. By 1595, Akbar had 1,823 mansabdars, with an official collective obligation to provide for imperial service an estimated 141,000 or more cavalrymen.[57] Additionally, there were considerable forces directly under Akbar's command. By 1598, Akbar clearly decided to devote much of this manpower and his other resources to advancing the Empire's southern frontier.

The Deccan had been politically unstable since the fragmentation in 1527 of the Bahmani Sultanate into rival successor states: Ahmadnagar (which annexed Berar in 1572), Bidar, Bijapur and Golkonda. Additionally, Khandesh stood between these and the Mughal Empire. Even before conquering the Deccan, the Mughal administration anticipated their potential revenue value. An early (1591) version of Abu-al-Fazl's *Ain-i Akbari* includes the estimated revenues of all the Deccan Sultanates and Khandesh, listing each city and district.[58] However, these estimates were inaccurately high, making the prospective Mughal conquest appear far more lucrative than it proved (Akbar's descendants learned this to their cost since even partial conquest would take nearly a century and never paid off financially). While the other Deccan kingdoms lay beyond Akbar's immediate scope, he had long sent diplomatic and military expeditions to Ahmadnagar and Khandesh. These imperial initiatives intensified as Akbar shifted from Lahore.

Much earlier, Akbar had made several moves southward toward Ahmadnagar, including a hunting expedition in 1576 warily watched by that Sultan as a possibly disguised invasion.[59] Then, after a disputed Ahmadnagar succession in 1588, the unsuccessful younger brother, Burhan Shah, fled to Akbar for shelter. Akbar protected this refugee and encouraged him to fight for the throne, but was not yet willing to provide military support. Nonetheless, Burhan Shah himself mounted a successful campaign for the Ahmadnagar throne in 1591.

As Sultan Burhan Nizam Shah II, however, he resisted Mughal pressures to submit, including from a diplomatic mission led by the prominent poet-courtier Shaikh Faizi in 1591–3. But on Burhan Nizam Shah's death in 1595, another disputed succession offered an opening for Akbar, now ready to commit resources to the Deccan. He sent Prince Murad to invade Ahmadnagar from neighboring Gujarat. Meanwhile, in Ahmadnagar, a royal widow, Khanzada Humayun Sultana (known popularly as Chand Bibi), had seized power as regent over the infant heir, Bahadur Nizam Shah. She defended Ahmadnagar fort against Murad until 1596, when she negotiated recognition of Akbar's supremacy and ceded Berar to the Mughals in exchange for remaining regent.

When Mirza Murad died in Berar in 1599, Akbar appointed his third son, Mirza Daniyal, to command renewed assaults on Ahmadnagar fort. In 1600, Khanzada Humayun Sultana offered to submit if the boy sultan received mansab 5,000 and she continued as regent. Instead, her rivals within the fort assassinated her and tried unsuccessfully to hold out. Finally, Mughal forces seized the fort, imprisoned the young sultan and annexed much of Ahmadnagar. But Malik Ambar, a liberated Ethiopian military-slave, led continued resistance for decades under the banner of puppet Ahmadnagar princes.[60]

Akbar had been unsuccessfully working for decades to incorporate Khandesh through military expeditions, reciprocal political marriages and other means. In 1599, Mughal forces under Mirza Daniyal seized the Khandesh capital, Burhanpur, and imprisoned the ruler, Bahadur Shah (who died in prison in 1624). Akbar himself commanded the siege of the strong fortress of Asirgarh, the last Khandesh holdout (although he did not personally take part in the fighting). Asirgarh fell in 1601 and Khandesh became a Mughal province.

Akbar then put Daniyal in command of all Mughal forces and administration in the Deccan and turned back to Agra. Mughal armies, however, did not continue their expansive assaults in the Deccan until after Akbar's death. Instead, the revolt of Mirza Salim set Mughal armies against each other, leading to five years of danger at the Mughal center.

Mirza Salim's revolt, followed by Akbar's demise after nearly half a century of rule, created apprehension and even panic among many within the Empire. While assessing popular sentiment four centuries later remains difficult, we can see the trauma—occasioned by Akbar's death and the uncertainty of the succession by the recent rebel Salim—in the personal account of Banarsidas, a Jain jewel merchant in Jaunpur. Long-reigning Akbar was the only sovereign whom Banarsidas and most others in north India had ever known. Nevertheless, painful memories of the devastation that had accompanied previous successions remained strong. Thus, on hearing the shocking news of Akbar's end, Banarsidas immediately collapsed, wounded his head, and was 'put to bed with my sobbing mother at my side.' Banarsidas continued that the whole city likewise panicked:

> People felt suddenly orphaned and insecure without their sire. Terror raged everywhere …. Everyone closed the doors of his house in panic; shop-keepers shut down their shops. Feverishly, the rich hid their jewels and costly attire underground; many of them quickly dumped their wealth … on carriages and rushed to safe, secluded places. Every householder began stocking his home with weapons and arms. Rich men took to wearing thick, rough clothes such as are worn by the poor …. Women shunned finery, dressing in shabby, lusterless clothes …. There were manifest signs of panic everywhere although there was no reason for it since there were really no thieves or robbers about.[61]

Only after a terrified ten days did news of Salim's relatively peaceful accession reach Jaunpur and life resume its normal course.

Over Akbar's long reign, he and his close advisors developed the key elements of the Mughal Empire. Subsequent emperors all built, with varying degrees of success, on those foundations. Thus, for Mirza Salim, who acceded as Emperor Jahangir, and his successors, Akbar provided standards against which they each compared themselves.

Part III

The Mughal Empire
Established, 1605–1707

7

EMPEROR JAHANGIR AND THE EFFLORESCENCE OF THE IMPERIAL COURT, 1605–27

In counsels on State affairs and government it often happens that I act according to my own judgment and prefer my own counsel to that of others.

Emperor Jahangir[1]

For nearly five years, Prince Salim ruled his self-proclaimed imperial court in Allahabad, openly rebelling against Emperor Akbar in Agra. Already in his early thirties, Prince Salim had long anticipated his own accession and had considerable experience maneuvering against his rivals. As Akbar's death approached, Salim humbly resubmitted himself to his father's authority, accepted humiliating but brief chastisement, and, with the intercession of influential Mughal women, received forgiveness just before Akbar died. Salim then selected his new imperial name, Jahangir. His own 22-year-long reign built on Akbar's extensive imperial foundations but with embellishments of his own devising.

YOUTH AND REVOLT

The Mughal dynasty never institutionalized primogeniture. Instead, virtually every emperor tried to arbitrate his own succession, although few accomplished it. Emperors rightly feared their own premature displacement by any heir whom they made too powerful. Further, emperors simultaneously dreaded both an internecine war for succession that would kill all but one son and also a division of their hard-earned empire. Babur and Humayun had followed the family's Central Asian tradition of assigning appanages to junior sons, thus seeking to protect them but also keep the Empire linked loosely together. While subsequent Mughal emperors moved to a more individualized imperial model, Akbar, Jahangir and most of their successors still tried to balance power among their sons. Conversely, almost every Mughal prince, as emperor-in-waiting but also potential casualty of the inevitable succession struggle, maneuvered ruthlessly against his brothers (often each supported by his mother, foster-mother, sisters and his wives' families).

Prince Salim, Akbar's long hoped for first surviving son, had been especially favored throughout his early youth, although Akbar had also advanced his two younger sons, each from a different mother. Having created the mansab system, Akbar awarded the eight-year-old Salim rank 10,000, double that of any other mansabdar except for seven-year-old Prince Murad at 7,000 and five-year-old Prince Daniyal at 6,000. These unmatched ranks provided each prince (guided by his experienced guardian) with vast resources to build up his own household, military forces and court faction. As each prince grew, Akbar increased their mansabs: by 1584, 15-year-old Salim ranked 12,000, Murad 9,000 and Daniyal 7,000.

Akbar kept Salim mostly at court. But there he quarreled with his younger brothers. Thus, in 1591, Akbar posted Murad as governor of Malwa, then Gujarat, reportedly 'in order to set the distance between East and West between the two brothers, and that they might remain safe.'[2] Similarly, Akbar later appointed his third son, Daniyal, governor of distant Allahabad. As their subjects bemoaned, these princely governors and their guardians asserted arbitrary and oppressive authority, amassing resources to strengthen their respective factions for the coming succession struggle.[3]

Suddenly, in 1591, courtiers noted with dismay that Akbar's 'constitution became a little deranged and he suffered from stomach-ache and colic, which could by no means be removed. In this unconscious state he uttered some words which arose from suspicions of his eldest son, and accused him of giving him poison ...'[4] Although Akbar eventually recovered, tensions between him and Salim and among the three princes intensified. Typically for emperors, Akbar determined to hold power as long as he lived and to determine his legacy.

To elevate yet another contender for accession, in 1594 Akbar awarded the high mansab 5,000 to Prince Khusrau, eldest son of Salim and his first wife (Kachhwaha Rajput Manbhawati Bai), although the boy was only seven. To strengthen Khusrau's faction, Akbar appointed powerful Raja Man Singh (Khusrau's maternal uncle) as his guardian. This made Khusrau another plausible heir, especially if Akbar lived as long as he intended.[5]

While Salim chaffed under Akbar's direct supervision, Akbar entrusted command over his concentrated forces in the Deccan to Murad during the mid-1590s. However, Murad failed to cooperate with the far more experienced Mughal commanders there and

Prince Salim Hunting (detail), by Muhammad Nasir al-Munshi, 1600–1604 (Allahabad period). Courtesy Los Angeles County Museum of Art (M.83.137) www.LACMA.org

accomplished little. When Murad died in 1599, Akbar personally went to supervise, defeating the last holdouts in Khandesh. Meanwhile, Salim marched his own forces to seize Agra but failed. Salim then moved five hundred kilometers down the Jumna River and took Allahabad, which Akbar had heavily fortified.

Over Salim's years in Allahabad, he established his own court, with escalating assertions of his own sovereignty. Using his prospects as emperor-in-waiting, and also his considerable military force, he ruthlessly compelled everyone in the region—Mughal officials and the populace—to submit to him. He extracted taxes to expand his household. He employed artists who developed a distinctive style, reflecting Salim's taste.[6] Assuming imperial trappings, Salim proclaimed himself Padshah, minted coins bearing this title and ordered the khutba recited in his name from 1602. He constructed a throne platform, inscribed with pretentious verses. Some supporters of the late Mirza Hakim had already thrown their support to Salim. With Murad's death followed by Daniyal's in 1604 (both officially of alcohol abuse but widely believed assassinated by Salim), members of those princely establishments also joined Salim. Some regional notables, especially Indian Muslims, supported Salim, as did some leading members of the 'ulama and mansabdars opposed to Akbar's administrative and religious innovations. Tensions between Akbar and Salim escalated, each marching armies threateningly against the other.

Salim also maneuvered to eliminate opponents. Abu-al-Fazl, the courtier most associated with Akbar's policies, had been appointed governor of Khandesh and promoted to high mansab 5,000. As Abu-al-Fazl returned to Agra in 1602, the Bundela Rajput ruler of Orchha, Raja Bir Singh Dev, overwhelmed his escort, decapitated him, and sent his head to Salim. Salim candidly explained:

> Shaikh Abu-l-fazl who excelled ... in wisdom and learning, had adorned himself outwardly with the jewel of sincerity, and sold it to my father at a heavy price .... Since his feelings towards me were not honest, he both publicly and privately spoke against me. At this period when, through strife-exciting intriguers, the august feelings of my royal father were entirely embittered against me, it was certain that if [Abu-al-Fazl] obtained the honour of waiting on [Akbar] it would ... preclude me from the favour of union with him. It became necessary to prevent him from

coming to Court .... I sent [Bir Singh Dev] a message that if he would stop that sedition-monger and kill him, he would receive every kindness from me.[7]

Furious, Akbar sent forces to punish Bir Singh Dev, but he retreated to the surrounding forests as had many opponents of the Empire. (On Jahangir's accession, he awarded Bir Singh Dev mansab 3,000/2,000, and later made him Maharaja with mansab 5,000/5,000. Graciously forgiving, Jahangir employed Abu-al-Fazl's son, entitling him Afzal Khan and appointing him governor of Bihar.)

As ailing Akbar weakened, Salim maneuvered from Allahabad to regain his father's favor. Salim's first wife, Manbhawati Bai, the strongest advocate of her son Khusrau's cause, committed suicide. Finally, Salim's partisans succeeded and he safely submitted to Akbar in Agra. After Akbar chastised Salim, they were reconciled, just months before Akbar's death in October 1605. Later historians sympathetic to the new emperor recounted Akbar's alleged deathbed designation of Salim as his sole heir; few accounts of the event detrimental to Salim survived.

The new emperor himself later denied any revolt had ever taken place, claiming always to have been loyal despite his traitorous advisors:

Short-sighted men in Allahabad had urged me also to rebel against my father. Their words were extremely unacceptable and disapproved by me. I know what sort of endurance a kingdom would have, the foundations of which were laid on hostility to a father, and was not moved by the evil counsels of such worthless men, but [rather] waited on my father, my guide, my qibla [Mecca-orientation], and my visible God, and as a result of this good purpose it went well with me.[8]

As emperor, Jahangir thus retrospectively condemned anyone who rebelled against imperial authority—particularly his own eldest son, Khusrau.

During his own years of struggle against Akbar, Jahangir had feared Khusrau's powerful supporters. After Jahangir's accession, he kept Khusrau confined. Jahangir distanced Khusrau's guardian, Raja Man Singh, by dispatching him as governor of Bengal with the unprecedented (for a non-prince) mansab 7,000/7,000. Jahangir also

Akbar's Tomb, Sikandara, outside Delhi, *c.* 1890[9]

offered Khusrau distant Kabul as his appanage, following family tradition. But Khusrau refused, aiming to acquire the entire Empire for himself.

In 1606, Khusrau obtained permission to show devotion to Akbar by visiting his tomb, currently under construction at Sikandara, outside Delhi. Once there, Khusrau escaped into the Punjab. When directly confronted by this senior Mughal prince and possible next emperor, many mansabdars submitted and provided funds and soldiers. Many dignitaries, including Guru Arjun (r. 1581–1606), leader of the rising Sikh movement, offered their blessing.

Jahangir immediately mobilized troops in pursuit. After Punjab's governor refused to open Lahore's gates to Khusrau, his followers were caught and defeated by Jahangir's forces. Jahangir then imprisoned Khusrau and lined the roads with hundreds of his impaled followers. Jahangir fined and then executed Guru Arjun and imprisoned for two years his son and heir, Guru Hargobind (r. 1606–44).[10] In earlier royal revolts, the gracious imperial victor customarily forgave defeated enemies and their followers who begged his pardon, so this mass execution raised the stakes for princely rebellion.

Nonetheless, from prison, Khusrau headed another plot in 1607. His supporters included an Iranian immigrant, Ghiyas Beg Tehrani (whom Jahangir had entitled I'timad-ud-Daula and made co-Wazir) and his eldest son, Muhammad Sharif. When Jahangir's third son, Khurram, revealed his eldest brother's conspiracy, Jahangir had Khusrau blinded, Muhammad Sharif and other prominent followers executed, and I'timad-ud-Daula demoted, fined and temporarily imprisoned. Despite this, Khusrau inspired later insurgences, although he remained a prisoner until he died in 1622 while in Khurram's harsh custody.

JAHANGIR'S ELABORATIONS

Jahangir determined to distinguish himself above all other monarchs, including his daunting father. Two Ottoman emperors had already used the title Salim, so he chose a new one for himself, explaining: 'the labour of the emperor is world domination so I named myself Jahangir ("World Seizer").'[11] He also enhanced many of Akbar's imperial models, especially featuring divine light, taking as his 'title of honour' Nur-al-Din ('Light of Religion') 'inasmuch as my sitting on the throne coincided with the rising and shining on the earth of the great light (the Sun).' Jahangir inherited treasuries worth roughly 150 million rupees cash (about 150 per cent of the Empire's total annual income) plus incalculable jewels and other valuables.[12] However, Jahangir's lavish acquisitions considerably reduced this vast reserve and his innovations often had unconsidered economic and political consequences.

Initially, the new emperor sought supporters, at the expense of his own income. He confirmed and enhanced the revenue grants for many Sunni 'ulama. He raised the rank and jagir incomes of many mansabdars, including both those who had supported him in Allahabad and also those he now tried to win over. While the total for all mansabs under Akbar never exceeded 200,000, Jahangir awarded nearly 800,000, although his Empire and the number of his mansabdars were not significantly greater.[13] Also from Jahangir's tenth regnal year onward, he instituted extra payments for favored mansabdars, authorizing (and paying for) double the number of cavalrymen for the same sawar: *do-aspa seh-aspa* ('two-horse three-horse' increment, hereinafter indicated 2-3h). Therefore, the share of imperial revenue that remained in khalisa—from which came most of Jahangir's own income—shrank to 5 per cent (in contrast, Akbar had maintained over 25 per cent in khalisa).[14] Jahangir also increased the salaries paid from the imperial treasury to his womenfolk and other courtiers. Making such extravagant expenditures, Jahangir (like Babur and Humayun) evidently had no planned budget and ran an annual deficit that only Akbar's well-stocked treasury enabled. Jahangir also began occasionally to practice *ijaradara* ('revenue farming'): selling entrepreneurs the right to collect imperial revenues for the coming year from designated khalisa territories. This garnered cash in advance but relinquished much imperial control over the collection process.[15]

Jahangir also personally redefined imperial standards for weights and measures, which meant recalculation of all official accounts. He ostentatiously designed the largest ever Mughal gold coin (used mainly in his elaborate ceremonies).[16] He also increased by 20 per cent the size of silver coins minted for general circulation, which disrupted the jagir economy. Indeed, even Jahangir realized that he had overreached; after six years, he restored the official coinage to Akbar's standards.

But Jahangir continued to innovate. In his thirteenth regnal year: 'it entered my mind that ... in each month that a coin was struck, the figure of [that month's astrological] constellation was to be on one face, as if the sun were emerging from it. This usage is my own, and has never been practised until now.'[17] Additionally, he had coins portraying himself holding a wineglass, offending his most orthodox Muslim subjects.

Jahangir's coins with zodiac images and bust with wineglass[18]

Jahangir's universalist self-image presented him as the embodiment of righteousness. On accession, he ordered a golden 'chain of justice' strung from his throne room to outside the fortress, so any aggrieved subject could directly evoke his imperial intervention. However, Jahangir evidently never referred to this chain again and we have no proof that it was ever installed within public reach. Nonetheless, he periodically initiated or renewed his symbolic moral authority, banning the production of alcohol and drugs (although he over-indulged in both and compelled his sons to imbibe as well).[19] He thus portrayed himself as imposing impartial justice on all.

During Jahangir's reign, courtiers composed numerous books on etiquette.[20] These instructed aspirants in the protocols and merits of approaching and pleasing the emperor, which should far outweigh all other interests. In fact, Jahangir's favor brought great honor, power and wealth.

Jahangir himself assiduously kept a Persian-language journal, *Tuzuk-i Jahangiri*, from his coronation until 1624 (when substance abuse disabled him). His journal's candid personal observations had similarities with Babur's Turki-language memoir, which Jahangir himself annotated. But, unlike Babur, Jahangir revealed his self-location in Hindustan through his vocabulary and orientation.[21] Since Jahangir evidently never revised his journal, it richly documents his changing moods, attitudes and condition: e.g., the origin of his alcohol and opium addictions, their increasingly debilitating effects (by age 26 his hands trembled excessively, so he needed someone to bring his cup to his lip), and his slow withdrawal to what was still a substantial daily consumption.[22] In addition to recording the business of empire, this journal repeatedly lauds his own masterful expertise over the arts, natural sciences and theology, and the quality of his collection of the leading human practitioners of all three.

As emperor, even more than as a prince, Jahangir patronized fine art both for its own sake and also as political propaganda. Many artists who had served him in Allahabad moved into his expanded imperial studios, while those he inherited from Akbar had to adjust to Jahangir's tastes, which valued stylistic individuality.[23] Akbar had favored narrative paintings, showing him vigorously heroic in battle and performing other dramatic actions. Jahangir preferred more naturalistic and direct representations, having himself portrayed ruling peacefully and serenely while engaged in spiritual rather than worldly concerns. Jahangir employed fewer artists and commissioned fewer paintings than had Akbar. But Jahangir's atelier featured artistic refinement and high-quality materials, using sumptuous colors and occasional gilding.[24] Jahangir also celebrated his own connoisseurship of both aesthetics and technique:

> my liking for painting and my practice in judging it have arrived at such a point that when any work is brought before me, either of deceased artists or of those of the present day, without the names being told me, I say on the spur of the moment that it is the work of such and such a man. And if there be a picture containing many portraits, and each face be the work of a different master, I can discover which face is the work of each of them. If any other person has put in the eye and eyebrow of a face, I can perceive whose work the original face is, and who has painted the eye and eyebrows.[25]

Indeed, Jahangir tested visitors, including the English ambassador Sir Thomas Roe, who (perhaps diplomatically) failed to match Jahangir's acumen.[26] Artists trained in Jahangir's atelier incapable of his high standards often found employment with his leading courtiers.[27]

Jahangir also used fine art to depict his primacy over other rulers and enemies (even if his Empire could not defeat them). Several of Jahangir's paintings show him symbolically triumphing over Malik Ambar, the Ethiopian commander of Ahmadnagar armies in the Deccan, despite (or perhaps to compensate for) setbacks and defeats Jahangir's forces suffered from fighting him. Safavid, Ottoman, English and other monarchs appear as his courtiers or inferiors, illustrating Jahangir's pronouncement: 'Although he is the king of Hindustan in outward appearance, inwardly he is the emperor of the world by right and by heritage.'[28] Jahangir's painters also featured him embodying and transmitting divine light.

A collector, Jahangir expanded his library of individual paintings and illustrated manuscripts. An authority, he sorted these by quality and subject matter: e.g., grading manuscripts into five classes based on the quality of the calligraphy, illuminations, paper and content. He also selectively patronized poets and other authors who produced literature in Persian and Indic regional languages, especially if they praised and located him in divine cosmology.

Further, throughout Jahangir's life, he acquired natural rarities, embellished by his workshops into fine objects for his pleasure. Courtiers, diplomats and other visitors learned that offering precious objects would attract Jahangir's attention and favor. For instance, Jahangir noted in 1619:

> ... out of the veined spotted tooth [walrus tusk] which my son Shah-Jahan had given me as an offering, I ordered to be cut off sufficient for two dagger-hilts [carved in] the Jahangiri fashion .... One hilt came out coloured in such a way as to create astonishment [since] the flowers looked as if a skilful painter had depicted them .... In short, it was so delicate that I never wish it to be apart from me for a moment ...[29]

When he acquired a rare flower, fruit, or animal (including a North American turkey imported via Goa), he had them documented in paintings, and sometimes physically dissected to satisfy his curiosity and enhance his knowledge of natural principles. Jahangir's possession of such works of man and nature revealed his self-proclaimed mastery over the world.[30]

Jahangir valued city building and monumental architecture less than his predecessor or successor. While Jahangir did complete, restore, or expand some forts and palaces, he preferred patronizing pleasure gardens and pavilions, hunting lodges, bridges, caravanserais and tombs. When Jahangir's favorite antelope died in his garden near Lahore, he marked the grave with an impressive tower, embellished with a sculpture and an engraved prose eulogy.[31] Jahangir's architecture displayed his aesthetic sense by ordering light and airy spaces. His buildings often used costly white marble exteriors. He adorned the interior walls of his vast encampment tents and buildings with rich textiles, murals and portraits.

Over time, Jahangir interested himself in various religious dignitaries, assembling current favorites at court. While maneuvering for accession and to strengthen his early regime, he courted the support of leading advocates for Sunni orthodoxy, including Naqshbandi pir Shaikh Ahmad Sirhindi, so critical of Akbar. But Jahangir never wanted these religious leaders to interfere in his reign. After 14 years as emperor, Jahangir noted:

> ... a *Shayyād* (a loud talker, a cheat) of the name of <u>Shaikh</u> Ahmad [Sirhindi] had spread the net of hypocrisy and deceit ... and caught in it many of the apparent worshippers without spirituality .... I considered the best thing for him would be that he should remain ... in the prison of correction until the heat of his temperament and confusion of his brain

were somewhat quenched, and the excitement of the people also should subside. He was accordingly ... imprisoned in Gwalior fort.[32]

After a year, Jahangir released Shaikh Ahmad Sirhindi and brought him to court.

Jahangir also initially developed his self-identification with Chishti pirs. Jahangir recounted that his namesake, Shaikh Salim Chishti, had prophesized his own *'urs* ('wedding' with Allah, meaning death) as soon as the infant prince memorized anything. When, at age two, the prince learned a simple couplet (from a maidservant unaware of the pir's prophesy), Shaikh Salim indeed died; but only (according to Jahangir) after designating Jahangir as his spiritual heir. Emperor Jahangir employed Shaikh Salim's male descendants, awarding them mansabs and important offices; some became Jahangir's own spiritual devotees.

Jahangir claimed in 1614 that long-deceased Shaikh Mu'in-ud-Din Chishti restored him from illness to health. Jahangir displayed this mark of spiritual blessing by piercing his earlobes for pearl earrings. Out of devotion to Jahangir, hundreds of mansabdars, both at court and in the field, imitated him; Jahangir supplied 732 pearl earrings to his devotees.[33]

Indeed, Jahangir made himself pir over many mansabdars. They received imperial initiation, symbolized by receipt of his miniature portrait which they wore on breast or turban. Jahangir also appeared in visions and dreams to his disciples, curing them of illness, often over great distances.[34]

For a time, Jahangir interested himself in a famous holy recluse, Gosain Jadrup (*c.* 1559–1638).[35] Born a wealthy Brahmin jeweler, Jadrup had left his parents, wife and children for a tiny cave near Mathura. Jahangir first met him in 1601 with Akbar. In 1617 and then four times in 1619, Jahangir visited Jadrup. Jadrup discoursed about Vedanta theology but also gave administrative advice, some of which Jahangir implemented. For instance, when a local jagirdar (Hakim Beg, a son-in-law of I'timad-ud-Daula) chastised Jadrup, Jahangir had the official dismissed (albeit temporarily). But Jahangir's attention to Jadrup was temporary.

Jahangir quizzed men from various religions, often posing provocative queries and pitting theologians against each other in evening sessions. For instance, Portuguese Jesuits (a small but constant presence at his court) recorded how Jahangir questioned their beliefs about Jesus and his miracles, evidently bemused by some responses about celibacy and the Trinity. But he permitted Jesuits in 1610 to baptize three sons of his late brother Daniyal.

While Jahangir and his court regarded as relatively marginal the growing presence in the Empire of European missionaries, merchants and diplomats, we can perceive through hindsight the significance of these early interventions. During Jahangir's reign, Portuguese naval vessels continued to capture merchant and pilgrim ships, some owned by Mughal courtiers (including imperial womenfolk). In retaliation, Jahangir in 1613 closed Catholic churches in Lahore and Agra. He stopped providing financial aid to Jesuits at court, expelling some. And he opportunistically allied with the increasingly assertive English to punish the Portuguese in Surat and Daman. After a 1615 treaty, however, these Mughal-Portuguese hostilities subsided temporarily.

The Portuguese, the English East India Company, and then (from 1616) the Dutch East India Company also affected the Empire through increasing intercontinental trade. Europeans used vast amounts of silver and gold from the Americas to purchase Indian-made textiles and other products in substantial amounts, thus lubricating and bolstering the Mughal economy. Crops from the Americas, including tobacco, maize, chilli peppers and tomatoes, were widely adopted by Indian cultivators. For instance, tobacco's production for local use and export spread rapidly. Akbar had questioned the allegedly healthful benefits of tobacco smoking. Jahangir futilely banned it for his courtiers (except for incurable addicts) because of 'the disturbance that tobacco brings about in most temperaments and constitutions.'[36]

Among other diverse attendants at Jahangir's court were leading Jain ascetics. While he reportedly mocked their celibacy, he also enquired about their beliefs, especially in total non-violence. Periodically, he himself made vows not to hunt on certain weekdays or for specific time periods.

Yet, Jahangir also prided himself on his bow- and musket-shooting, a family tradition, boasting that, by age 47, he had already successfully hunted 17,167 animals (hunts which he supervised killed another 11,365).[37] Jahangir continued other Central Asian martial traditions as well. His victorious forces erected towers of severed enemy heads. Cavalrymen, armed with bows plus swords and spears, still held primacy for mansabdars.

Simultaneously, Jahangir and his high mansabdars also increasingly integrated gunpowder weapons into imperial armies. They hired scattered Europeans and Ottomans to manufacture and fire heavy artillery. Wealthy regional rulers did so as well. Improved firelock muskets proliferated in India's military labor market. Cannon and firearms thus proved ever more decisive in battle, both for and against the Empire.

Throughout much of his reign, Jahangir traveled in procession through his domain, mainly in its dryer western half. He travelled for hunting and for aesthetic pleasure but not to engage personally in war. While he occasionally approached imperial frontiers, he never entered a battlefield, preferring distant supervision. Nonetheless, Jahangir dispatched mansabdars to both resolve campaigns Akbar left uncompleted and extend imperial frontiers. Jahangir's physical presence was not necessary for campaigns to succeed, showing the Empire's stability. However, while imperial armies achieved victories to the east, west, north, and south, many newly conquered territories were never fully integrated, producing an ever more sprawling Empire.

In the East, Bengal remained unsettled through much of Jahangir's reign, even as imperial armies struggled to subdue hilly Cooch Bihar and Kamrup. A young officer, Mirza Nathan, recorded his rise from mansab 100/50 to 900/450 during these hard-fought campaigns.[38] Son of the commander of the provincial riverine navy, Mirza Nathan detailed how imperial forces fought and negotiated with zamindars and local chiefs, battled the Ahom (a rival empire expanding from the east), and tried to fight off Portuguese and Arakanese coastal raids. Idealized administrative models produced by the imperial center contrast with Mirza Nathan's first-hand description of actual processes on the ground. He and his colleagues struggled to master the environment: excavating and breaching canals, damming streams and cutting forests. Military setbacks proliferated. Coalitions of mansabdars maneuvered, betrayed and assassinated their rivals. Imperial officials vied to produce reports of distinguished results for Jahangir's approval.

A major Mughal strategy was to co-opt enemy leaders. Mansabdars enrolled local leaders into the provincial administration. The most prominent were enticed to aspire to attend the imperial court, where they were expected to be overwhelmingly impressed. But when the

Bengal governor's son escorted some Arakanese headmen to Jahangir, he recoiled:

> Briefly they are animals in the form of men. They eat everything there is either on land or in the sea, and nothing is forbidden by their religion. They eat with anyone .... They have no proper religion or any customs that can be interpreted as religion. They are far from the Musulman faith and separated from that of the Hindus.[39]

Such alienating attitudes by the emperor and khanazad mansabdars would limit the efficacy of this coopting strategy for people from beyond Hindustan or west or Central Asia.

As prince, Jahangir had been assigned by Akbar to march westward to subdue the long-defiant Sisodia Rajputs of Mewar. But he made little progress. As emperor, Jahangir directed his second son, Parvez, to complete this campaign. When he largely failed, Jahangir replaced him with his third son, Khurram, who finally forced ruling Sisodia Rana Amar Singh (r. 1597–1620) to negotiate submission and enroll his son, Karan Singh (r. 1620–28), with mansab 5,000/5,000. Jahangir claims to have treated Karan Singh as a foster-child, training him in sophisticated imperial court culture. Jahangir also ordered full-sized marble statues of the Rana and his son put below the jharoka in Agra Fort—honoring and showing his mastery over them.

Jahangir also sent armies northward. Imperial troops finally recaptured repeatedly rebellious Kangra in the Himalayan foothills. When Jahangir visited, he ordered the fortress leveled and a mosque built to impress his supremacy upon the local population. Jahangir additionally dispatched troops beyond Kashmir into Kishtwar and Ladakh from 1616 onward. As on other frontiers, these Mughal forces proved able to overwhelm local rulers but failed to incorporate them into the Empire, thus having to face subsequent revolts.

To the South, the Deccan remained an unstable frontier, populated by hostile martial communities. Jahangir ordered his second son, Parvez, to complete the conquest of Ahmadnagar (veteran mansabdars actually commanded the imperial forces). However, stubborn resistance continued under Malik Ambar, even after a Mughal victory in 1616. Eventually, Jahangir transferred Parvez to Allahabad and sent Khurram to the Deccan. As on other imperial frontiers, defeating and coopting enemies proved difficult. Deccani

Maratha and Telugu leaders proved particularly resistant to Mughal enticements, rarely accepting mansabs during Jahangir's reign.

Among his mansabdars, Jahangir evidently balanced his personal preferences with recognition of their competence. Those whom he favored rose high. But even those he distrusted sometimes proved useful, particularly Rajputs whom his father had bound to the imperial dynasty through marriage. Although Jahangir respected his Rajput mother, he highlighted his paternal Timurid ancestry far more. Jahangir formally married at least five Rajput brides (in addition to about 14 Muslim wives) but he appointed no Rajputs or other Hindus to high offices at the imperial center and only a few as governors—Raja Man Singh being the major exception.

Man Singh was one of Jahangir's most accomplished commanders and governors, and also his maternal cousin and senior wife's brother. Yet Man Singh had supported Khusrau against him at Akbar's court. Therefore, Jahangir appointed him to high posts and awarded outward honors but candidly criticized:

> Raja Man Singh came and waited on me ... [only] after orders had been sent to him six or seven times. He ... is one of the hypocrites and old wolves of this State .... The aforesaid Raja produced as offerings 100 elephants, male and female, not one of which was fit to be included among my private elephants. As he was one of those who had been favoured by my father, I did not parade his offences before his face, but with royal condescension promoted him.[40]

Further, in 1608, Jahangir 'demanded in marriage' Man Singh's granddaughter, reiterating Mughal superiority.

In addition, Jahangir had hundreds of concubines. Shahriyar (1605–28), and other sons with concubines, held status as imperial princes and potential heirs. As Jahangir prematurely aged, factional maneuvering for control over him and the impending succession intensified.

DOMINANT INFLUENCES DURING JAHANGIR'S LATER REIGN

Distinctive of Jahangir's later reign was the rise to dominance of I'timad-ud-Daula's family. An impoverished Irani immigrant from the Safavid court, Ghiyas Beg Tehrani, had joined Akbar's service and climbed due to his administrative expertise, gaining the title I'timad-ud-Daula. Early in his career, he had married his 17-year-old daughter, Mihr-un-Nissa (born during their immigration in Qandahar), to another Irani immigrant, entitled Sher Afgan Khan. Posted with a low mansab to Bengal, Sher Afgan Khan violently quarreled with the governor, resulting in both their deaths in 1607. I'timad-ud-Daula then brought his widowed daughter and her daughter, Ladli, to join the household of a step-mother of Jahangir.[41]

Every imperial wedding required the Emperor's approval. In 1607, Jahangir engaged his 15-year-old third son, Khurram, to fourteen-year-old Arjumand Banu, another of I'timad-ud-Daula's granddaughters. Seeming far more significant at that time was Jahangir's wedding in 1610 of Khurram to the daughter of another Iranian immigrant, Mirza Muzaffar Husain, a Safavid prince.

For supporting Khusrau's attempted coup against newly enthroned Jahangir, I'timad-ud-Daula was temporarily disgraced and his eldest son executed. But I'timad-ud-Daula's submission and abilities soon restored him to Jahangir's favor. From 1611 onward, I'timad-ud-Daula rose quickly in mansab. Simultaneously, his 35-year-old widowed daughter, Mihr-un-Nissa, improbably caught 42-year-old Jahangir's eye. Within a few months he married and entitled her Nur Mahal ('Light of the Palace'), echoing his own title, Nur-al-Din. The next year, Jahangir also consented to the wedding of Khurram and her niece, Arjumand Banu, later famous as Mumtaz Mahal ('Excellence of the Palace').

Unlike Akbar's marriages, these two weddings did not advance Jahangir politically. However, they added to the increasing influence of I'timad-ud-Daula and his family, including his surviving son, Asaf Khan. Nur Mahal soon eclipsed Jahangir's many other wives, but only hints survive about how they regarded her. In his memoirs, however, she receives increasing praise from 1614 onward as devoted companion, masterful huntswoman and astute political advisor.[42]

I'timad-ud-Daula gained premier positions in Jahangir's administration, reaching by 1619 mansab 7,000/7,000. He was governor of Punjab and then Wazir and Diwan until his death.[43] Jahangir appreciated both his administrative accomplishments and also his increasingly lavish gifts and hospitality. Jahangir noted that he honored I'timad-ud-Daula 'as an intimate friend by directing the ladies of the harem not to veil their faces from him.'[44]

Indeed, I'timad-ud-Daula's family and their mostly Irani supporters so flourished that some later historians label them a 'junta.'[45] As of 1621, Iranis had risen to the plurality (28 per cent) among all mansabdars (even more among the highest ranked). In contrast, Turanis shrank from the plurality to only 20 per cent (Indian Muslims and Rajputs remained at 14 per cent each, stable since Akbar's late reign).[46] Other clans also rose, but I'timad-ud-Daula's family dominated the last half of Jahangir's reign.

Caravanserai Gateway, commissioned by Nur Jahan, Punjab, *c.* 1620[47]

Jahangir became ever more personally devoted to Nur Mahal, elevating her title in 1616 to Nur Jahan ('Light of the World'), especially unusual since they had no children. Jahangir joined her in deep mourning for her mother's death, soon followed by her father's demise in 1622. Despite both Islamic and Mughal tradition, Jahangir gave I'timad-ud-Daula's vast wealth to Nur Jahan, rather than to his eldest son, Asaf Khan, or his son-in-law, Khurram. Although Asaf Khan succeeded his father as Wazir, Nur Jahan thereafter expanded her personal power even further, with Jahangir's approval.

Like Nur Jahan, many imperial womenfolk built tombs and caravanserais.[48] But she prominently participated in public affairs, which had become unusual by this time. She awarded *khilat*s and honors and issued farmans and coins, both joined with Jahangir and independently. She conducted diplomacy, exchanging missions with the Uzbek queen mother. Further, she sought to perpetuate her power by determining the imperial succession; both Nur Jahan and her brother, Asaf Khan, allied with Jahangir's current favorite son, Khurram, against his brothers.

Silver rupee with Nur Jahan and Jahangir's names[49]

Khurram had surpassed his brothers in martial achievements, Jahangir's affections, and mansab, thus enhancing his position as heir-apparent. While one elder brother, Parvez, foundered in the Deccan, in 1620, Khurram's forces recaptured the notoriously impregnable hill fortress of Kangra after a year-long siege and gained mansab equal to Parvez. The vital strategic need for a competent princely commander in the troublesome Deccan led Jahangir to entrust Khurram with that post, giving him royal titles Shah Sultan and then Shah Jahan ('King of the World,' the title he used, and we will use, henceforth). Shah Jahan, before leaving court for the Deccan, demanded vast military and financial resources and also custody of his imprisoned eldest brother, Khusrau. Jahangir granted these demands and wrote 'my consideration for this son is so unbounded that I would do anything to please him ... in his early youth [he] has accomplished to my satisfaction, everything that he has set his hand to.'[50]

Among shifting factional alliances, each of Jahangir's surviving sons, as well as Nur Jahan and Asaf Khan, maneuvered to gain allies and control over the emperor and imperial resources. Shah Jahan initially showed success, reconquering resurgent Ahmadnagar, subduing Malik Ambar (albeit temporarily), and forcing tributes from Golkonda and Bijapur. Jahangir traveled to Mandu, distantly supervising the Deccan campaigns. There, in 1617, he welcomed victorious Shah Jahan, standing to receive him and awarding him the unprecedented rank 30,000/20,000 (10,000 2-3h) and the unique privilege to sit adjacent to the throne. Nur Jahan hosted the victory feast for him.

Jahangir's capacity further weakened from illnesses exacerbated by long-standing alcohol and drug addictions. From 1620 onward, he traveled almost every springtime to Kashmir, where he spent the summer savoring its cool climate, far removed from the heat and politics of north India. Nur Jahan nursed Jahangir devotedly. A contemporary criticized: 'she gradually acquired such unbounded influence over His Majesty's mind that she seized the reins of government and abrogated to herself the supreme civil and financial administration of the realm, ruling with absolute authority till the conclusion of his reign.'[51]

Further, Nur Jahan began to regard Shah Jahan as a rival and raised a new claimant to the throne: Shahriyar, son of one of Jahangir's concubines. She married teenage Shahriyar to Ladli Begum, her daughter from her first marriage. Shahriyar soon rose to mansab 30,000/8,000 (his high zat showing his elevated personal rank, but his significantly lower sawar showing his limited military role).

Hitherto, Jahangir's relations with the Safavids had largely continued through competitive diplomacy rather than warfare. For example, Jahangir commissioned paintings displaying his superiority. Additionally, the Mughal Empire still retained disputed possession of commercially, strategically and symbolically significant Qandahar. However, ailing Jahangir's complacency was shattered in June 1622 when a powerful Safavid expedition threatened to seize Qandahar from the inadequate Mughal garrison.

Jahangir immediately ordered almost all his imperial forces diverted from their current deployments for a massive expedition to defend and then, when the city fell, retake Qandahar. Jahangir also dreamed of retaliating by capturing the Safavid capital, Isfahan. Jahangir demanded that Shah Jahan bring his armies from the Deccan to lead this expedition: 'wait on me with all possible speed with a victorious host, and elephants of mountain hugeness, and the numerous artillery ... in order that he (the king of Persia) might discover the result of breaking faith and of wrong-doing.'[52] Instead, Shah Jahan delayed complying, unwilling to abandon the Deccan and journey to distant Qandahar. But his non-compliance antagonized Jahangir who, encouraged by Shah Jahan's rivals, discerned disloyalty.

Then, Shah Jahan seized some jagirs assigned to Nur Jahan and Shahriyar, killing their agents. This convinced Jahangir that '[Shah Jahan] was unworthy of all the favours and cherishing I had bestowed on him, and that his brain had gone wrong ... henceforth they should call him *Bī-daulat* (wretch).'[53] Jahangir executed courtiers he suspected were Shah Jahan's partisans. So overcome was Jahangir by physical frailty and these disturbing events that he could no longer write his own journal, instead dictating it to a trusted courtier.

To punish Shah Jahan further, Jahangir spitefully repudiated his five-year-old vow against hunting (taken to ensure the recovery of Shah Jahan's son from illness). More materially, Jahangir appointed Shahriyar to command the futile and abortive expedition to retake Qandahar. Additionally, Jahangir appointed Parvez to resume the Deccan command with mansab 40,000/30,000, thereby replacing and outranking Shah Jahan.

Despite Shah Jahan's superior military reputation, once openly rebellious against the Emperor, he lost repeatedly against stronger imperial armies. Each time, his status as imperial prince and possible next emperor enabled him to gather more forces, only to be defeated again. He fled to Golkonda, Orissa, Bengal, Bihar, Allahabad, then temporarily received refuge from Malik Ambar in Ahmadnagar. Finally, Shah Jahan negotiated a submissive truce, sending his sons to Nur Jahan as hostages and agreeing to stay in the Deccan, away from the imperial court. So harried was Shah Jahan that, in 1626, he decided to seek shelter in Iran with the Safavid Shah (as had two of his ancestors). But the Mughal governor in Sind blocked his passage and the Iranian Shah offered no aid.[54]

Meanwhile, veteran general Mahabat Khan, who supported Parvez, emerged as another rival for control over the Emperor. This Afghan warrior had fought up the ranks, serving Jahangir from his Allahabad days onward, with much experience and success on the battlefield. By 1623, he had reached mansab 7,000/7,000 with the commanding titles Khan-i Khanan and *Sipahsalar* ('Army Commander'). In March 1626, Mahabat Khan staged a coup, capturing Jahangir from Nur Jahan and Asaf Khan. Mahabat Khan kept anxious Jahangir in custody, successfully repulsing armed attempts to recapture the Emperor. Mahabat Khan could have executed Jahangir, and perhaps ended the Mughal dynasty, or he could have enthroned his own favored candidate, Parvez. Instead, as would happen repeatedly during the next century, Mahabat Khan respected the incumbent Emperor's sovereignty; he escorted Jahangir to Kabul in a fruitless attempt to retake Qandahar and then back to the Punjab.

After a few months, Nur Jahan mobilized enough military force for a successful counter-coup. Her loyalists forced Mahabat Khan to relinquish custody of Jahangir. Mahabat Khan then joined his former opponent, Shah Jahan. Further, Parvez died from alcoholism, eliminating that claimant. The succession, however, remained uncertain.

Jahangir's health continued to decline. After his final visit to Kashmir, he died back in Punjab in October 1627. This deprived Nur Jahan of her strongest claim to imperial authority: acting in Jahangir's name. Asaf Khan ousted his sister and, to forestall an interregnum, enthroned Dawar Bakhsh (r. 1627–8), Khusrau's eldest surviving son. Meanwhile, Asaf Khan summoned his real candidate (and son-in-law), Shah Jahan, from the distant Deccan. Asaf Khan and Shah Jahan defeated, imprisoned, blinded and then executed Shahriyar, along with his younger brother. Asaf Khan then executed the temporary emperor, Dawar Bakhsh, plus two sons of Daniyal (both converts to Catholicism), and many of their followers.

This bloody elimination of unsuccessful potential claimants to the throne became typical of Mughal successions henceforth, as the ideology of a single, imperial incumbent overlay the earlier Central Asian-based Mughal tradition of familial shared sovereignty (although the latter remained a potential model until the dynasty's end).[55] This ideology made succession struggles desperate affairs for each prince: accede to the throne or die. Many scholars regard these contested Mughal successions as an inherent weakness since they squandered lives and resources; others see the deadly struggles by princes for supremacy as rigorous testing of their abilities to mobilize constituencies, thus ultimately strengthening the imperial dynasty as a whole.[56]

Instead of execution, Nur Jahan was allowed by triumphant Shah Jahan to withdraw quietly from imperial politics. She completed her parents' artistically innovative and expensive tomb near Agra. This had a white marble-clad exterior with particularly intricate stone carving. Much of the interior and exterior surfaces were decorated with flowers, cypresses, vases and wine jugs, all Iranian motifs in a technique Europeans call *pietra dura* (inlaid semi-precious stones). These features thereafter all became prominent in Mughal imperial architecture. Nur Jahan also constructed a more simple tomb for herself and her widowed daughter, Ladli, near Jahangir's grave at Lahore.[57]

Tomb of I'timad-ud-Daula and Asmat Begum and interior, commissioned by Nur Jahan[58]

When Shah Jahan reached Agra, Asaf Khan installed him as Emperor in 1628 with himself as chief minister holding mansab 8,000/8,000. Shah Jahan proceeded to reshape the imperial court over his three-decade-long rule. However, many of the tensions that marked Jahangir's reign persisted even as Shah Jahan added to the splendor of the Mughal Empire.

8

EMPEROR SHAH JAHAN AND BUILDING UP THE MUGHAL EMPIRE, 1628–58/66

> ...many valuable gems had come into the Imperial jewel-house, each one of which might serve as an ear-drop for Venus or would adorn the girdle of the Sun. Upon the accession of the Emperor, it occurred to his mind that ... the acquisition of such rare jewels ... can only render one service, that of adorning the throne of empire ... [so] that beholders might share in and benefit from their splendor, and that Majesty might shine with increased brilliance.
>
> Shaikh 'Abd-al-Hamid Lahori, court historian about Shah Jahan[1]

After six years fleeing imperial armies, Shah Jahan succeeded dramatically as emperor. He then commanded the production of manifestations of his imperial splendor, including the Peacock Throne, the Taj Mahal and his entirely new capital, Shahjahanabad. He fought for years to subdue residual opposition from mansabdars and regional rulers and to extend his Empire's frontiers, especially south and north-west. To fund all these projects, he decreased the real income of mansabdars, even as their nominal ranks rose. But he exceeded the limits of imperial power and his own. After two decades, Shah Jahan had weakened politically and physically. His four sons fought a bloody civil war; the victor seized Shah Jahan's throne, imprisoning him for eight years until his death.

ACCESSION AND THE DECCAN WARS, 1628–36

When 36-year-old Prince Shah Jahan reached Agra early in 1628, he was installed as Emperor by Asaf Khan, the most powerful mansabdar. Then, on an especially auspicious day in August, they repeated the coronation with even more pomp. Ritualized representations of imperial power remained essential to the new Emperor and his close supporters as they sought to contrast the new regime from the previous decade under increasingly enfeebled Jahangir.

Despite Jahangir's draining of the imperial treasury, Shah Jahan nevertheless determined to lavishly display his own imperial glory. He soon commissioned the uniquely brilliant golden Peacock Throne: a raised 6.3-square-meter platform under a 4.6-meter-high canopy surmounted by ornamental peacocks, everything thickly gem-encrusted. It took seven years, until 1635, to accumulate the vast amounts of bullion and precious stones (worth about ten million rupees) and to craft the throne that Shah Jahan considered worthy of his reign. From when he first occupied his Peacock Throne, over the next century, all who saw or heard of it were awed with Mughal magnificence (indicating the Empire's security, this throne remained intact until 1739, even when emperors were long distant; it remains legendary today).

He retained the royal title, Shah Jahan, bestowed by his father. But he added others, including Sahib-i Qiran-i Sani, 'Second Lord of the [Astrological] Conjunction,' evoking his ancestor Timur ('Lord of the Conjunction') with status as millennial sovereign.[2] From his youth, Shah Jahan wore a full beard, breaking with Akbar's and Jahangir's practice of shaving all but a mustache, but emulating Timur and also many religiously observant Sunnis.

Shah Jahan identified strongly with his Sunni Central Asian ancestors. His grandfather, Akbar, had entrusted his upbringing to his Turani grandmother, Ruqaiya Sultana Begum. Indeed, Shah Jahan always devoutly performed the required five daily prayers and Ramadan-month fast. He reinstated imperial sponsorship of Hajj pilgrims, sending nine missions to Mecca with generous donations. Although Jahangir had compelled him to start drinking alcohol at age 24, he repudiated this at 30 (distinguishing himself from his many alcoholic relatives). The proportion of Sunni Turanis among high mansabdars rose during his reign. He favored orthodox Sunni

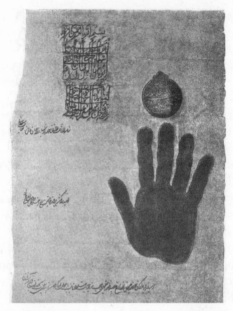

Imperial Farman with Shah Jahan's Handprint[3]

'ulama and generally enforced the Sharia more than his predecessors. Additionally, he associated with orthodox Sunni Naqshbandis.

Shah Jahan also patronized the India-based Chishti and Shattari Sunni Sufi orders. Approaching his accession, Shah Jahan devotedly attended Mu'in-ud-Din Chishti's shrine at Ajmer. There, he constructed an impressive white marble mosque (completed 1637–8) plus an imperial palace; he would revisit thrice more (1636, 1643, 1654) often approaching on foot.[4] He also respected the Shi'ism of his favorite wife, Mumtaz Mahal, her father, Asaf Khan, and his numerous other Irani mansabdars.

Shah Jahan's biological mother was a Hindu Rathor Rajput of Marwar. Among Rajputs, Shah Jahan favored Rathors. But he also employed other Rajputs extensively as warriors, including on several imperial expeditions into distant Central Asia. However, he gave Rajputs no high appointments in his central administration and only one governorship. Further, he strongly condemned marriages in which either spouse left Islam for Hinduism. While his armies destroyed the Hindu temples of defeated enemies and, in 1633, he

Canopied Jharoka, Lahore

forbade the construction of new Hindu temples, these were largely punitive political policies rather than religiously motivated ones.

Overall, Shah Jahan made his court more gloriously stately. His demeanor remained grave, solemn and elevated (in contrast to Akbar's sincere questioning of diverse visitors and to Jahangir's quizzing them). Shah Jahan had his jharoka made into a raised, vaulted loggia, removing him spatially and symbolically from those assembled below. He replaced the temporary canopy over assembled courtiers (which allowed intrusive rain) with more formal pillared halls, first of wood then of stone.[5] These halls were also used for the formal distribution of imperial charity. Shah Jahan ended the deep prostrations of *sijdah* ('forehead to the ground') and *zamin-bos* ('kiss the ground')—used for Akbar and Jahangir, who centered imperial cults on themselves—which some orthodox Muslims considered ungodly worship of the emperor. Instead, Shah Jahan directed that courtiers and others approaching him should use the more dignified but still respectful triple *taslim* (thrice raising from the ground the back of one's right hand to touch palm to forehead).[6] Thus, Shah Jahan sought to bind mansabdars to him not through discipleship but rather through formal court rituals and life-long loyal service (epitomized by khanazad mansabdars).

Shah Jahan also asserted control over his reign's official histories. Unlike Babur and Jahangir who personally wrote their own memoirs, Shah Jahan instead closely supervised the series of historians he commissioned to compile his massive official regnal chronicle, the *Padshahnama*.[7] Shah Jahan had drafts regularly read out for his correction or elaboration. After reigning ten years, Shah Jahan changed from solar to lunar dating (thus conforming to the Islamic calendar), requiring retroactive rewriting of the manuscript by the latest new author (and confusing revenue and other official record systems).

Similarly under Shah Jahan's close supervision, his atelier reflected his formalistic taste for polished, static scenes elaborately displaying his imperial power.[8] His commissioned portraits present

Emperor Shah Jahan (detail), attributed to Bichitr, *c.* 1650. Courtesy Los Angeles County Museum of Art (M.78.9.15) www.LACMA.org

him in majestic full profile with halo. Non-imperial paintings during his reign showed much innovation, but imperial artists emphasised the stability and gravity of events, even festivities like royal wedding celebrations. War scenes showed not Shah Jahan fighting but rather his generals enacting the ever-victorious orders of their distant but commanding emperor (closer to Jahangir's style than Akbar's). In court scenes, Shah Jahan had each man accurately painted as an individual in profile, but not interacting with each other. Rather, all courtiers appeared focused on him on the Peacock Throne. This reflected his court's heightened decorum: courtiers stood for hours, not speaking or moving without permission—many carried elegant canes to lean on during these prolonged twice-daily formal audiences. Imperial artists also widely incorporated select European motifs and techniques, thereby suggesting his lofty power over Christian iconography.

Also adorning his court were many diplomatic missions, from Safavid, Uzbek, Ottoman and other rulers. They presented and received rich presents in culturally significant ritual interactions, and gathered and disseminated much political information. Further, Shah Jahan's court was also attended by various defeated or tributary Indian rajas and zamindars who came personally or sent sons or emissaries to submit and receive forgiveness (or, more rarely, punishment). Despite its grave decorum, his court was also the site of an assassination by one courtier of another, and even a frustrated attempt on Shah Jahan himself, suggesting tensions below the serene surface.

When Asaf Khan outmaneuvered Shah Jahan's rivals and enthroned him, other high mansabdars remained discontented, particularly those whom Jahangir had favored or who had supported a defeated imperial claimant. Further, to save money, Shah Jahan did not lavishly raise the zat for most mansabdars as had his father, although he pragmatically did not reduce their sawar since martial force remained vital for the regime.[9] Simultaneously, Shah Jahan shifted resources from mansabdars into his own treasury (nearly empty at his accession but after 20 years worth about 37 million rupees, even after his vast expenditures on the Peacock Throne, imperial buildings and wars).[10]

As the extended aftershock of Shah Jahan's own princely rebellion (and also revealing resistance to his policies), various revolts marked his early reign. One arose in the central Indian forested shatter zone of small, semi-autonomous kingdoms, some quite wealthy. Maharaja Bir Singh Dev of Orchha had served Jahangir—from assassinating Abu-al-Fazl onward—reaching mansab 5,000/5,000. He died in 1627, late in Jahangir's reign. Bir Singh's son, Jujhar Singh, came to court for confirmation of his inheritance, receiving mansab 4,000/4,000 and the title Raja. But, doubting his prospects under the new emperor and hopeful he could repel imperial interventions into his densely forested kingdom, he soon fled, even before Shah Jahan's formal coronation. Shah Jahan, rather than permit such a blatant early rejection of his authority, sent three strong imperial armies to subdue Jujhar Singh. As a further weapon, they brought a rival claimant for the Orchha throne. Shah Jahan regarded this test of his new regime so seriously that he left Agra for Gwalior to supervise the campaign. Fearing destruction, Jujhar Singh negotiated his resubmission: appealing for imperial forgiveness and paying a punitive tribute. He then rejoined Shah Jahan's service, fighting for him in the Deccan and obtaining promotion after a year to his father's rank 5,000/5,000.

Like many local rulers, however, Jujhar Singh also retained his own acquisitive ambitions. He seized the treasury, lands and family of a neighboring ruler and Mughal tributary. Jujhar Singh rejected Shah Jahan's order to give his gains to the Empire as the price of again being forgiven. Retaliating, Shah Jahan sent yet another expedition, nominally under his young third son, Aurangzeb, which captured Jujhar Singh's strongholds and drove him into the surrounding forests. There, his Gond and Bhil rivals killed him in 1635. The Mughal commanders recovered Jujhar Singh's head and 10 million rupees from his treasury, both sent to Shah Jahan. They also punitively leveled Orchha's main temple and reportedly converted Jujhar Singh's grandsons to Islam. Shah Jahan personally visited Orchha to celebrate. As frequently occurred, however, once the overwhelming imperial forces left the recently subdued region, other local rulers and chieftains resumed resistance. Such rebellions along external and internal imperial frontiers punctuated Shah Jahan's entire reign.

Additionally, Shah Jahan struggled for years against leading mansabdars who anticipated more self-advantage in rebellion than in serving him. One early challenger had been among Jahangir's highest commanders, a Lodi-clan Indo-Afghan entitled Khan-i Jahan with mansab 6,000/6,000 who commanded the imperial armies with the title Sipahsalar, and had held several sequential governorships. However, late in Jahangir's reign, Khan-i Jahan as Deccan governor had transferred imperial territories to Ahmadnagar Sultanate, reportedly receiving a massive bribe. Then, during the succession wars, Khan-i Jahan had backed Shah Jahan's rivals. To win his submission, Shah Jahan promoted him to 7,000/7,000 (7,000 2-3h). But the new emperor also transferred his office of Sipahsalar to Mahabat Khan (a proven supporter) and shifted Khan-i Jahan from the strategic Deccan to the lesser governorship of Malwa. Khan-i Jahan rebelled in 1629. Fighting desperately against pursuing imperial armies, he fled with his followers to the Ahmadnagar Sultan, while simultaneously asserting his own imperial pretensions.

During the Delhi Sultanate and then during the later period of Mughal decline, such strong military commanders occasionally split off successfully to create effectively independent dynasties. These differed from local uprisings because these rebel commanders had military force but no roots in the regions they seized. Further, although Khan-i Jahan rallied many fellow Afghans around him, not all Afghans joined him; indeed some fought against him, so this was not an ethnic movement. Nonetheless, Shah Jahan regarded this rebellion very seriously, personally moving south to Burhanpur to supervise the year-long campaign that finally defeated and executed Khan-i Jahan in 1631.

Shah Jahan (like other emperors) had to decide where and when to deploy his massive (but not infinite) military resources. During major campaigns elsewhere, some disobedience and provocation by subordinate rulers or communities was necessarily tolerated. But Shah Jahan deployed imperial forces to inflict exemplary punishment on particularly prominent local rebellions. For instance, the Portuguese had held a commercial and military base at Hugli since 1579. When they egregiously provoked the Bengal governor in 1631, he mobilized his soldiers, reinforced with imperial troops sent by Shah Jahan. In a relatively short but bloody land and riverine campaign, Mughal forces crushed the Portuguese and their Arakanese allies. Four hundred prisoners—European men and also men and women of mixed European-Asian biological or cultural ancestry—reached Shah Jahan's court in 1633. He released those who converted to Islam but he imprisoned or distributed the rest as slaves to his courtiers.[11] His actions, however, were apparently punishment for their resistance rather than anti-Christian.

As prince, Shah Jahan had spent much time fighting in the Deccan, so he knew that dangerous region well. As emperor, he determined as his first major military initiative to concentrate his forces and complete the subordination of the three remaining Sultanates: Ahmadnagar and then Bijapur and Golkonda. To supervise, Shah Jahan remained in Burhanpur for two years (1630–32). He entrusted actual command to his most proven mansabdars, Asaf Khan (1631–2) and then Mahabat Khan (1633), although he gave his second son, Shah Shuja', nominal charge. Mughal expeditions captured Ahmadnagar's major fortified cities and also attempted—with less success—to co-opt opposing Maratha and other Deccani commanders and chiefs by offering high mansabs. For example, around 1630, Maratha commander Shahuji Bhonsle accepted mansab 5,000/5,000. But many newcomers were alienated by the condescension of the khanazad. Thus, after a year, Shahuji fled Shah Jahan's court to resume fighting for autonomy.

Gradually, the more powerful imperial armies won victories in the Deccan. They captured and imprisoned the Ahmadnagar Sultan in 1632, annexing much of his territory. In 1636, Shah Jahan returned to the Deccan to approve treaties of subordination by the Bijapur and Golkonda Sultans. Both agreed to cease their political relations with the Safavids, curtail Shi'i practices in their courts, recognize Mughal sovereignty and pay substantial annual tribute. With Mughal concurrence, both Sultans then redirected their armies southward, away from the Mughals. This precarious peace lasted two decades, enabling Shah Jahan to concentrate his military resources elsewhere. He also used his accumulating wealth to make vast material assertions of his magnificence.

MANIFESTING IMPERIAL POWER IN STONE AND IN CENTRAL ASIA, 1636–53

Advancing Shah Jahan's deep commitment to glorifying his reign, he personally supervised most major imperial building projects and periodically inspected their progress. A courtier noted:

the superintendents of construction of royal buildings, in consultation with the wonder-working architects, lay before the critical royal eye designs of proposed edifices. The royal mind, which is illustrious like the sun, pays full attention to the planning and construction of these lofty and substantial buildings, which ... for ages to come will serve as memorials of his abiding love of constructiveness, ornamentation, and beauty. The majority of the buildings he designs himself; and on the plans prepared by the skillful architects, after long consideration he makes appropriate alterations and emendations.[12]

While Shah Jahan apparently did not design the mausoleum of Jahangir near Lahore (completed 1635), he deeply engaged himself in both the tomb in Agra of his favorite wife, Mumtaz Mahal, and also his entirely new capital city in Delhi, named after himself.

Shah Jahan had daughters by his first and third wives, and he gave these womenfolk honored places in his imperial harem. But he remained devoted to his second wife, Mumtaz Mahal, from their marriage until her death, and after. When he acceded as Emperor, Mumtaz Mahal had already borne him 11 children—four sons and two daughters were still living. In 1631, only three years into his reign, Mumtaz Mahal died at age 38 while giving birth to her fourteenth child. She had joined him in Burhanpur for the Deccan campaign. Shah Jahan eventually sent her body the 800 km. to Agra for burial in the Rauza-i Munauwara ('Illuminated Tomb')—a personal tribute and also a stone manifestation of his imperial power. This tomb has been celebrated globally as the Taj Mahal.

Selecting a site on the Jumna just downstream from Agra Fort, Shah Jahan ordered his builders to construct this most distinctive of all Mughal garden-tombs. Unlike many Mughal mausoleum-mosques, which centered the garden, this tomb stood at the north end, overlooking the river (as was customary in Agra). Many architectural elements designed by Nur Jahan for the tomb of her parents (Mumtaz Mahal's grandparents) were developed five years later by Shah Jahan's builders to their highest degree and on much vaster scale. Both used fully white marble exteriors (earlier generally reserved for holy men's shrines) instead of red sandstone (hitherto customary in tombs for the Mughal family and high mansabdars). Both also expansively used inlaid semi-precious stones.

Shah Jahan commissioned a far larger mausoleum on a quite different plan, with a dome and four detached minarets. He selected the Qur'anic verses inscribed extensively in elegant calligraphy on its interior and exterior walls. He supervised closely, attending most years during the decade of its construction to commemorate Mumtaz Mahal's death anniversary and to inspect progress. By the time of its completion, this tomb-garden had cost about 5 million rupees (a vast amount, but only half the Peacock Throne's cost). For nearly four centuries, the Taj Mahal has stood as an architectural masterpiece, famous world-wide for the technology of its construction, and, even more, for the quality of its workmanship and the exquisite balance and proportion of its forms.[13]

The 'Illuminated Tomb,' known as the 'Taj Mahal,' today and transection[14]

After this tomb's construction, Shah Jahan ordered the skilled builders and workmen to migrate to Delhi in 1639, where he commissioned his imperial city, Shahjahanabad.[15] In contrast with Akbar's Fatehpur, this new capital had an imposing red-sandstone-walled citadel, the Qila-i Mu'alla ('Exalted Fort,' popularly known as the Red Fort) costing six million rupees. Like the Agra Fort, this new fortress overlooked the Jumna River, designed for defense and also to enclose the imperial palace complex. Perfumed water canals extended through the complex and cascaded over illuminated falls. The separate structures for dwelling, administration and pleasure were mostly constructed with interior and exterior walls of white marble (or stucco burnished to appear marble), often with highly ornate, semi-precious stone inlays. Some glazed tiles depicted European-style images of jointly Qur'anic-Biblical people and angels. During Shah Jahan's rebellion, he had observed the Bengali regional style of deeply curved sloping roofs which he thereafter

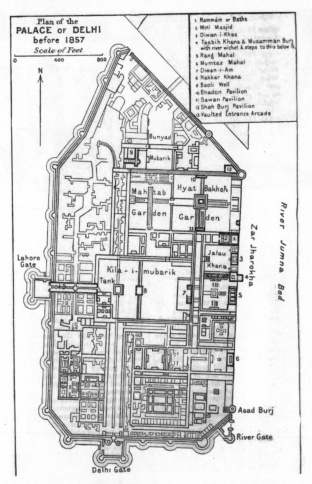

Map 7: Plan of 'Exalted Fort,' known as 'Red Fort'[16]

occasionally used, sometimes with gilded metal coverings. He was also the first emperor to use extensively baluster columns (bulbous pillars emerging from a pot, perhaps inspired by European prints); these were generally reserved for imperial buildings. Near the Red Fort, and also of red sandstone, Shah Jahan constructed the Jami' Mosque (1650–56), the largest in India at that time, costing another million rupees. In 1653, he faced Shahjahanabad's city walls (initially brick and mud) with red sandstone.

Cascading perfumed water (left panel) and glazed tiles (right panel) adorned
Shahjahanabad Palace complex

Jami' mosque, Shahjahanabad, *c.* 1891[17]

Within the city walls, high mansabdars built mansions
surrounded by their workshops and their attendants' homes,
forming a distinctive neighborhood. Courtiers and leading imperial
women sponsored additional mosques and pleasure gardens within
and without the city. The main market boulevard, Chandni Chawk,
ran from the Red Fort west to the city's Lahore gateway, with shops

lining both sides and a canal running down its center. Throughout the citadel and city, imperial hydraulic engineers constructed elaborate and efficient water-supply and sewage systems. Plentiful potable water came from wells in each neighborhood or from the Jumna either raised by Persian water-wheels or channeled from upstream by canals. This system also provided for wet-carriage sewage into the Jumna downstream. Since most waste was organic and the city's human population was only in the tens of thousands, the river healthfully absorbed it. Further, surrounding market gardens received human and animal dry-carriage sewage and produced vegetables for the city.

In building Shahjahanabad, Shah Jahan sought to combine a newer model of an omnipotent monarch ruling from a stable capital with the Central Asian tradition of imperial mobility. During the next nine years following the Red Fort's completion in 1648, he lived there a total of five-and-a-half years (during six visits). In between, he traveled: supervising his domain and military campaigns and visiting Lahore and thrice Kashmir (1634, 1645, 1651).[18]

Meanwhile, the Empire faced challenges. Especially along the Empire's external and internal frontiers, various local rulers and landholders only paid tribute or taxes under compulsion. Larger rebellions erupted when imperial armies were committed elsewhere. Prominent rebels were eventually punished by superior imperial force, but most who begged forgiveness were graciously pardoned and reinstated by Shah Jahan. This often produced moral hazard: a recurring pattern of revived rebellions alternating with repeated subjugations. For example, while a prince, Shah Jahan had gained prestige when his subordinates recaptured repeatedly rebellious Kangra in 1620. But as emperor, he had to order suppression of that Himalayan kingdom's current ruler, Raja Jagat Singh. Jagat Singh had long served the Mughals, reaching mansab 3,000/2,000. However, seeking more autonomy, he rebelled (1640–42). Despite stubborn resistance, he was eventually defeated by imperial forces. He then humbly submitted in person to Shah Jahan, received generous forgiveness and restoration of his kingdom and mansab, and later died fighting for the Empire against Uzbeks in Central Asia.[19] But his heirs only awaited the opportunity to renew their fight for autonomy.

Shah Jahan oriented himself culturally and politically toward Central Asia. As emperor, he remained within his domain's western half (although as prince he had fled throughout Bengal). Thus, after negotiating relative peace with Bijapur and Golkonda in 1636, Shah Jahan turned his attention to the north-west. While Central Asia's economic value never justified the vast expense of his campaigns there, he was motivated by the potential prestige of defeating the Safavids and Uzbeks and recovering Timur's homeland.

From his accession onward, there had been conflicts around Kabul. The earliest came when Uzbeks, during the tumultuous succession struggle, captured Kabul, albeit briefly before Mughal reinforcements expelled them. Periodically thereafter, various Afghans asserted their autonomy, only to be sequentially suppressed. In 1636, Shah Jahan proposed to Ottoman Sultan Murad IV and the Uzbeks a triple attack on the Safavids, but nothing eventuated. Shah Jahan himself traveled to Kabul five times (1639, 1646, 1647, 1649, 1652), combining hunting trips with preparations for war.

Strategic Qandahar caused repeated clashes between the Mughal and Safavid Empires. In 1638, Safavid governor Ali Mardan Khan defected and gave Qandahar to Shah Jahan. Shah Jahan welcomed him with mansab 5,000/5,000 and prominent appointments.[20] Incensed, Safavid Shah Safi (r. 1629–42) launched an expedition to retake Qandahar in 1642. Shah Jahan sent his eldest and favorite son, Dara Shukoh, to reinforce Qandahar, but Shah Safi's death halted this war.

Simultaneously, Shah Jahan intervened to protect Muslims from alleged oppression by Uzbeks, with Naqshbandi pirs sometimes supporting him.[21] In 1646, he sent substantial forces under his second son, Murad Bakhsh, capturing Badakhshan and Balkh, which Shah Jahan considered 'properly his hereditary domains.'[22] Shah Jahan improbably aspired to seize Samarkand, Timur's capital. However, the harsh terrain and local population were uncongenial for this generation of Mughal soldiers, especially for the many Rajput and Hindustani troops among them. Abruptly, Murad insisted on withdrawing, angering Shah Jahan, who demoted him. Shah Jahan then entrusted command to his third son, Aurangzeb. He negotiated nominally honorable withdrawal in 1647, with Uzbek symbolic submission. These expeditions gained the Empire virtually nothing but cost a vast 40 million rupees, plus substantial loss of life and prestige.

Further, resurgent Safavid forces retook Qandahar during the 1648–9 winter. Insistently, Shah Jahan sent futile expeditions to recover Qandahar: two under Aurangzeb (1649, 1652), then the largest under Dara (1653). These achieved nothing but expended 35 million rupees, many lives and much morale. Stubbornly, Shah Jahan planned (but could not implement) yet another recovery expedition (1656).

These huge but unproductive campaigns intensified long-standing strains within the mansab-jagir system. These expeditions cost more than double Shah Jahan's massive building projects (which totaled 29 million rupees).[23] The gap between most mansabdars' official jagir income and their actual expenses had widened, making many unable to support the military contingent specified by their sawar. The imperial administration thus could not strictly enforce the dagh system of inspection, and so permitted maintaining only a proportion of their sawar. In 1642, this deviation was institutionalized: e.g., mansabdars with jagirs in Hindustan only needed to provide one-third of their sawar number when serving there, only one-quarter when serving in other provinces, and only one-fifth when on the north-west campaigns.[24] In addition, Shah Jahan also encouraged lower mansabdars dispatched to Central Asia by temporarily increasing their sawar and giving a substantial cash subsidy for each soldier actually there.

By 1647, Shah Jahan's total assessed revenue was 220 million rupees: a quarter more than Jahangir's peak and more than double Akbar's.[25] This increase came from a combination of newly conquered territories in the Deccan and elsewhere, growth in the overall economy, but also inflation (especially from the continuing substantial influx of silver via European merchants). Simultaneously, the gap widened between the official assessed revenue and the actual amount collected. To recognize the mansabdars' loss of purchasing power while not embarrassingly lowering their nominal income, each jagir's official worth was recalculated on a sliding monthly scale (from eleven-twelfths of the nominal revenue down to four-twelfths, with most set between six- and eight-twelfths). Nonetheless, these stresses intensified, especially by persistent imperial commitments of resources to the Deccan, from the last phase of Shah Jahan's reign onward.

DECCAN AND SUCCESSION WARS, 1653–8

For two decades following the 1636 treaties of submission by Bijapur and Golkonda, the Empire's Deccan frontier remained relatively stabilized. Under diplomatic supervision by Shah Jahan's governors of his Deccan provinces, these two remaining sultanates seized agriculturally and commercially rich territories further south and struggled against the expansive Marathas. Simultaneously, imperial governors enticed Deccani commanders and officials with mansabs.

Most prominently, Golkonda's powerful Irani-immigrant chief minister, entitled Mir Jumla, defected in 1655. Such was Mir Jumla's reputation that Shah Jahan appointed him Diwan-i Kul (chief imperial revenue officer) with mansab 5,000/5,000 and additional honors. When Golkonda's Sultan Qutb-al-Mulk punitively seized Mir Jumla's property and son, the imperial viceroy in the Deccan, Aurangzeb, besieged Golkonda. Aurangzeb only partially relented after Golkonda's Queen Mother personally begged for mercy and Qutb-al-Mulk gave his daughter as a bride to Aurangzeb's son, paid 2 million rupees in indemnity, and promised substantial annual tribute.[26]

In 1657, Aurangzeb pressed hard against Bijapur during a succession. He forced the new sultan to cede Bidar and other territories and pay 10 million rupees tribute. Aurangzeb's triumphs in the Deccan considerably strengthened him militarily and in prestige, particularly contrasted with his three lackluster brothers.

Shah Jahan, like his predecessors, wanted (but failed) to delay the succession struggle until after his own death, but also control his legacy. He tried to will the Empire intact to his eldest son, Dara, but also to protect his three other sons. While he occasionally deputed Dara as governor (Allahabad, Gujarat and Lahore) or as commander of especially substantial campaigns, Shah Jahan mostly kept him close at court. Shah Jahan awarded Dara escalating dignities: the title Buland Iqbal ('High Fortune') in 1642 and then Shah Buland Iqbal in 1655, and seated him adjacent to the imperial throne. Shah Jahan included among Dara's jagirs Hissar Firoza, customarily assigned to the heir apparent. By 1658, Shah Jahan had raised Dara to the unprecedented mansab 60,000/40,000 (30,000 2-3h).[27]

Shah Jahan also kept his eldest child and favorite daughter, Jahanara Begum, near him.[28] At the death of her mother, Mumtaz

Mahal, Shah Jahan gave half her 10 million rupee estate to 17-year-old Jahanara (the other half divided among her siblings). Jahanara remained unmarried, led the harem and managed the imperial household, although Shah Jahan had two living wives. In 1644, Jahanara's delicate, perfumed clothing accidently caught fire. Two of her maids died extinguishing the blaze and Jahanara received life-threatening burns. Shah Jahan personally tended her and, upon her recovery, weighed her in gold that was then distributed in charity.[29] With her own funds, she bestowed much patronage, commissioning gardens and mosques in Shahjahanabad and Kashmir. Combining her religious and literary commitments, she had herself initiated into the Qadri Sufi order and wrote an account of Qadri pir Shah Badakhshi, entitled *Risala-i Sahabiyya*, which included a dozen of her own verses. Similarly, she was deeply devoted to the Chishti order, writing a biography of Khwaja Mu'in-ud-Din, entitled *Mu'nis-al-Arwah*. Further, like Shah Jahan, she strongly supported Dara, her nearest younger full-brother, who shared many of her inclinations.

Dara similarly had himself initiated into the Qadri order in 1640 by Shah Badakhshi and wrote five works on Sufism (1640–53). Dara sought the universal truth of Islam, including through esoteric Indic religions.[30] He wrote a comparative study of Islamic and Indic esotericism, entitled *Majma'-al-Bahrayn* ('Meeting-place of the Oceans'). Further, he gathered fellow seekers into his household and supervised their translations into Persian of over 50 major Indic religious works, including the *Bhagavad Gita* and some Brahminic texts, collected as *Sirr-i Akbar* ('The Greatest Mystery'). From this title and Dara's sincere spiritual searching beyond the Islamic tradition alone, many commentators identify him with his great-grandfather, Akbar. But neither Shah Jahan nor Dara could secure his succession in the deadly competition against his brothers.

In contrast to Shah Jahan's treatment of Dara, the Emperor deployed his three other sons as governors and commanders throughout his Empire. This gave them administrative and military experience and enabled them to build their own factions. The second eldest, Shah Shuja', received his first mansab (10,000/5,000) at 17, rising gradually thereafter. From 1638 onward, he spent much of his career as governor of Bengal and Orissa, building a power base in one of the Empire's richest agricultural and commercial regions, with a long history of autonomy.

The fourth son, Murad Bakhsh, received his first mansab (10,000/5,000) even earlier, at 14. Shah Jahan posted him briefly in a series of governorships (Multan, Kashmir, Deccan, Kabul, Malwa, Gujarat) and military commands but repeatedly chastised Murad for repeated misjudgments and proven inadequacies. Nonetheless, despite his disappointing record, as an imperial prince, he received yet other high appointments.

Over time, Shah Jahan's third son, Aurangzeb, proved the most successful governing and commanding forces in the Deccan and northwest. Despite his better record, however, he received less recognition; his highest mansab was 20,000/15,000, only a fraction of Dara's. Still, while governing the Deccan, Aurangzeb assembled and commanded the Empire's most powerful and battle-hardened armies.

The actual succession crisis began prematurely, when Shah Jahan suffered a serious intestinal disorder in September 1657. While disabled, he entrusted rule to Dara. Although Shah Jahan recovered by November, the three younger sons had already agreed to combine against Dara. Only a plurality of high mansabdars supported Dara and the imperial cause, so his brothers could collectively overwhelm them.

Prince Shuja' declared himself Emperor and advanced up the Ganges from his long-established Bengal base. Near Banaras, the eastern imperial army under Dara defeated him in 1658. While Shuja' fled back to Bengal, Dara's western army faced the forces mobilized by Murad and Aurangzeb.

Murad, based in Malwa and Gujarat, also declared himself Emperor and marched toward Agra, with support from Aurangzeb and his forces from the Deccan. This time Dara's imperial army lost badly. Driving onward, Aurangzeb imprisoned Shah Jahan in Agra. Aurangzeb then claimed the whole Empire at a hurried imperial coronation in July 1658. Desperate, Shah Jahan proposed ending the war by dividing his Empire among his four sons. Instead, Aurangzeb's army swelled. He seized Murad (executing him in 1661).

Early in 1659, Aurangzeb crushed advancing Shuja'. Shuja' fled to Bengal and then beyond (eventually, the Arakanese king assassinated him and most followers). Aurangzeb even imprisoned his own eldest son, Muhammad Sultan, who had supported his father-in-law, Shuja'.

Meanwhile, defeated Dara escaped to the Punjab, Sind, Gujarat, and Rajasthan, where Aurangzeb's forces again triumphed. Desperate,

Dara fled back into Sind, hoping to seek refuge in the Safavid court. Instead, Aurangzeb's men captured him. After a show trial for *kufr* ('heresy'), Dara was executed in 1659 on Aurangzeb's orders, as was Dara's eldest son, Sulaiman Shikoh, in 1662. Thus, the pattern begun with Shah Jahan's accession—only one prince survived the bloody succession war—recurred at his reign's end. However, this time, the former emperor remained alive.

For nearly eight years Aurangzeb kept Shah Jahan closely imprisoned in Agra Fort, bereft of any significant support among mansabdars or his subjects. Jahanara Begum remained his sole prominent attendant until his death from natural causes in January 1666. Even then, Aurangzeb allowed little ceremony for his interment next to Mumtaz Mahal. Aurangzeb, already firmly enthroned and in control, would rule five decades until his death during his ninetieth year in 1707.

9

EXPANDING THE FRONTIERS AND FACING CHALLENGES UNDER EMPEROR 'ALAMGIR, 1658–1707

The only benefit which we kings derive from our position in the world is the gaining of fame. I had wished that one of my sons would gain it; but it is not to be. I therefore, wish to go (in person)...

Emperor 'Alamgir[1]

Prince Aurangzeb proved himself the best commander among Shah Jahan's four sons, sequentially defeating and eliminating the others. After an unprecedented coup against his father, Emperor 'Alamgir reformed the regime according his own beliefs, often more rigorous than those of his predecessors. He constantly campaigned, asserting his imperial authority over opponents across almost the entire subcontinent. While he did not spare himself, he often saw his subordinates fail to accomplish his goals. Under his direction, the Empire reached its territorial limits, but vital imperial processes were overstrained. In many ways, his nearly half-century reign marked the Empire's peak and also its significant deterioration.

ACCESSION, IDEOLOGY, COURT CULTURE AND WARS OF SUPPRESSION, 1658–79

Rushing north from the Deccan, Prince Aurangzeb conducted lightning military campaigns (1658–9) that gained him the throne. A courtier lauded this momentous achievement:

> ... few kings had to fight so many royal battles and lordly encounters ...
> through God's grace he achieved victory everywhere by dint of his strong
> arm and sharp sword. But ... so great was his humility that he never
> ascribed these victories to his own powers, but always spoke of them as
> miracles wrought by God, and ever rendered his thanks to the Creator
> for this great good fortune by adoration of Allah, the establishment of
> the Holy Law of the Prophet, and the extinction of all traces of illegal
> and prohibited practices .... Not for a moment did he yield up his body
> to repose or slackness.[2]

Indeed, his proven record of military victories and personal piety
impressed many mansabdars. But omitted in this glorifying account
are both that his victories were over his brothers and also that he
deposed and imprisoned his father, reigning Emperor Shah Jahan.

Many members of the Mughal imperial family had previously
rebelled against the incumbent emperor, including Jahangir and Shah
Jahan himself. But none before had actually deposed and imprisoned
the sovereign. Thus, Aurangzeb's legitimacy was questionable from
his rushed initial coronation in 1658 throughout Shah Jahan's
rigorous confinement until his death in 1666.

During the succession war and thereafter, Aurangzeb sought
to convince mansabdars that their careers and the Empire would
improve under him, compared to his less competent brothers or
enfeebled father. The new emperor largely succeeded in this: most
mansabdars eventually supported him and none seriously tried to
restore his father. Holding a second, full ceremonial installation on
the Peacock Throne in June 1659, he suggested his political goal
by selecting his imperial name—'Alamgir ('Seizer of the World').
(Although he is commonly known even as emperor by his princely
name, Aurangzeb, we will use his chosen title, 'Alamgir, hereafter.)

'Alamgir mobilized public support from leading Sunni 'ulama and
Naqshbandi pirs throughout his reign. For instance, the Chief Qazi
issued a fatwa validating 'Alamgir's unfilial and otherwise illegal
usurpation as necessary for Islam and the Empire. 'Alamgir soon
appointed a *Muhtasib* with a staff to enforce Islamic moral standards.

'Alamgir himself consistently sought to behave and govern according
to strongly orthodox Sunni beliefs. His personal piety would secure
God's blessing on his Empire and assure its triumphs over its enemies

and those of Islam, he believed. Even as a prince, he was known for strictly observing the devotional, dietary and sartorial practices of a sincere Muslim, even pausing amidst heated battle to perform the requisite prayers on time. He kept the Ramadan-month fast and never indulged in drink or opium (which had debilitated so many relatives). As a 26-year-old prince, he had displeased his father by resigning his governorship of the Deccan and begging permission to devote his life to religious devotion; after six months, Shah Jahan ordered him to resume his imperial duties. When companions or loyal servants died, 'Alamgir personally led commemorative prayers as imam and followed the bier, even while Emperor.[3] Late in 'Alamgir's life, he sewed prayer caps and copied the Qur'an for sale, with the proceeds going toward his modest personal expenses.

After 'Alamgir's formal enthronement, he began to purify his court's culture and protocols of his predecessors' alleged unorthodox and un-Islamic practices. An early reform ended the solar *Nauroz* ('New Year') festivities—a pre-Islamic Iranian tradition celebrated since Akbar's reign which differed from the lunar Hijri calendar. To protect the Islamic creed from possible disrespect, 'Alamgir removed it from imperial coins. He sent a richly laden embassy to the Sharif of Mecca seeking validation for his reign; when this first mission failed, he sent a second, eventually gaining the Sharif's sanction.[4]

'Alamgir also exchanged embassies with the rulers of Abyssinia, Balkh, Bukhara and Persia, each vying for advantage. In 1666, for instance, Safavid Shah Abbas II sent a condescending missive which 'Alamgir found insulting and threatening invasion. Although 'Alamgir prepared for the expected Persian offensive, internal politics there precluded one.

Since the succession war devastated much of north India, compounded by famines and repeated failures of the vital monsoons, 'Alamgir officially suspended or abolished some taxes. Further, he performed his charitable obligation as sovereign by increasing food distribution from imperial alms houses. This temporarily aided his exceptionally needy subjects, but 'Alamgir did not invest in infrastructure for long-term improvements in their condition. Indeed, he evidently never gained the affection of many among his subjects. Perhaps indicative of popular sentiment, throughout his reign, disrespectful insults, sticks and other projectiles were launched toward him as he passed in procession, which even official historians

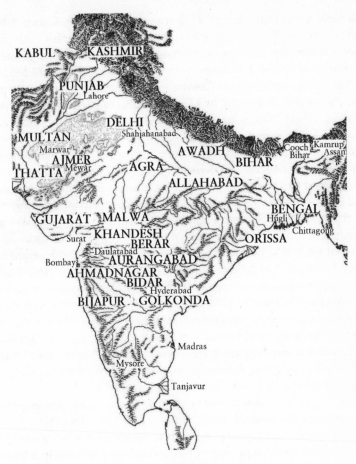

Map 8: Major States and Regions, 'Alamgir's Reign

noted (denigrating the perpetrators as insignificant ruffians, disaffected wretches, or 'mad').[5]

From his accession onward, 'Alamgir sought to demonstrate his regime's power by controlling the Empire's long-troublesome frontiers and conquering beyond them. For instance, in 1661, he ordered Bihar's governor to end the persistent resistance of Raja Medini Rai (r. 1662–74), the Charo chieftain in heavily forested south Bihar. Medini Rai had briefly served Shah Jahan, but had revolted. Mughal forces drove him into the jungle and annexed his state. Simultaneously,

'Alamgir commanded Bengal's governor to annex hilly Cooch Bihar and Kamrup. After seven years of costly campaigning, Mughal armies forced the Ahom ruler in Assam to submit, cede his western territories and send a daughter to wed 'Alamgir's third son, 'Azam. In 1663, 'Alamgir ordered Gujarat's governor to annex Navanagar and Ramnagar kingdoms. In 1665, he directed Kashmir's governor to force Tibet's 'zamindar Dalai' to submit tribute.[6] The next year, Mughal forces seized Chittagong from Portuguese and Arakanese 'pirates'.[7] These early hard-won successes, however, were unexpectedly expensive in financial and human resources. Further, almost every gain proved temporary: imperial administration there soon weakened and many of these rulers regained their territory and independence.

After long-imprisoned Shah Jahan's death at age 74, 'Alamgir sought control over official and public memory of his father. He ordered Shah Jahan's body be transported by boat without ceremony from his Agra Fort prison to his Taj Mahal grave. In later years, 'Alamgir instructed his own sons that Shah Jahan was a model of rectitude and himself was the embodiment of filial devotion. Indeed, 'Alamgir rhetorically questioned one rebellious son: 'In the race of the Emperors of India which son ever fought against his father ... and, with the aim of gaining the crown and the throne, has uplifted the sword in his hand against his own father?'[8] 'Alamgir thus denied any precedent for his sons' disobedience against him.

'Alamgir's household contrasts with those of his predecessors, where imperial women held more public prominence, political influence and artistic patronage (albeit customarily from within the harem).[9] While 'Alamgir had various wives, he particularly honored his unmarried sisters and eldest daughter. His nearest elder sister, Roshanara Begum, lobbied on his behalf during the succession and thereafter held influence over him. However, he later shunted her aside when he felt she overreached. He next appointed his eldest sister, Jahanara Begum, to head the harem; he particularly respected her piety. He also favored his eldest daughter, Zeb-un-Nissa. But when she encouraged her brother, Akbar, in revolt, 'Alamgir confined her for 20 years until her death. During 'Alamgir's last decades, he kept his wives distant and directed his second daughter, Zinat-un-Nissa, and a humble consort, Udaipuri Mahal, to attend him.

Additionally, 'Alamgir manifested his personal piety by relinquishing his predecessors' putatively impious pretensions.

Considering immoral the near deification of earlier emperors, 'Alamgir stopped courtiers from prostrating before him. He no longer bestowed an anointing *tilak* on the forehead of acceding Rajput rulers. He ordered to be removed the two life-size stone elephants ornamenting Agra Fort's main gate, like a Hindu temple. He also ceased displaying himself for daily darshan by the public.

To impose more Islamic decorum, 'Alamgir reduced his court's pomp. He forbade courtiers from wearing ostentatious garments, including gold or red cloth, considered improper by many devout Muslims. Mansabdars were forbidden 'ribbon frills in the European style' on their palanquins or boats.[10] Earlier emperors had weighed themselves against gold and other precious substances on the solar and lunar anniversaries of their coronations and births. By 1668, 'Alamgir ended this practice in his court (although he allowed favored sons to perform this ritual occasionally on recovery from illness, with the wealth distributed charitably). Later, he further reduced the gift-giving and other ceremonies of even his own coronation anniversary. 'Alamgir also terminated the disputations among advocates of various religious traditions that his predecessors had patronized. Instead, 'Alamgir listened to orthodox Sunni 'ulama and Naqshbandi pirs almost exclusively.

'Alamgir had commissioned the official history of his reign, *'Alamgirnama*. But in his tenth regnal year, he ordered this halted (although he did not object to scholars unofficially writing chronicles or compiling biographical dictionaries of notables).[11] Similarly, he initially tolerated astrological almanacs, but in 1675 ordered them banned as un-Islamic. Instead, 'Alamgir ordered his best Sunni 'ulama to edit in Persian the most authoritative Hanafi legal judgments into the still widely consulted *Fatawa-i 'Alamgiri*. Thus, Islamic sciences always received his patronage.

As a pious Muslim and emperor, 'Alamgir renounced his own earlier personal pleasures that diverted him from sober fulfilment of his religious and imperial duties. He had frequently indulged in hunting, but he relinquished that pastime. As he advised a son, 'Hunting is the business of idle persons. It is very reprehensible for one to be absorbed in worldly affairs, and to disregard religious matters.'[12] Although 'Alamgir had been a connoisseur of music, he came to believe music excited emotions, so he eschewed it for himself. He ordered his chief singers, dancers and instrumentalists to cease performing in his court and household, while he continued their salaries. However, he did not ban music for his courtiers and officials; indeed, significant theoretical texts on Hindustani music emerged during his reign under such sub-imperial patronage.[13] He even curtailed the *naubat* (drum ensemble), played to announce imperial arrivals and court rituals. Similarly, he closed the imperial painting atelier and stopped much poetry recitation in court, although courtiers and women in his household, especially his daughter Zeb-un-Nissa, patronized and savored these arts.

THE PEARL MOSQUE, DELHI.

The Moti Mosque, Red Fort, Shahjahanabad, 1890[14]

In strong contrast with his father, 'Alamgir commissioned little monumental architecture, although he built, restored or enlarged many mosques. His early, delicately ornamented Moti ('Pearl') Mosque (1658–63) within Shahjahanabad's Red Fort was exclusively for his household and court. His most prominent construction project was the huge Padshahi Mosque (1673–4) adjacent to the Lahore Fort (which he rarely visited).[15]

Nor did 'Alamgir erect grand mausoleums. The tomb in Aurangabad for his first wife, Dilras Banu (d. 1657), was built when he was a prince and not under his direction; indeed, this proved the

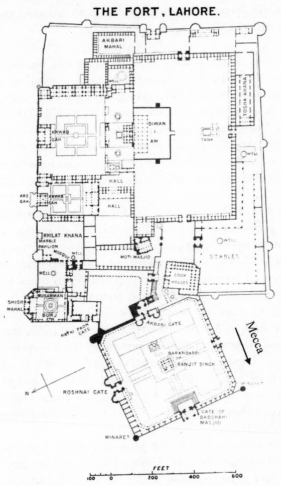

Map 9: Padshahi Mosque and Lahore Fort Palace Complex[16]

last major imperial mausoleum.[17] 'Alamgir made his own grave a simple structure open to the sky, in the courtyard of the fourteenth-century tomb of Chishti Shaikh Zain-ud-Din near Daulatabad. Thus, 'Alamgir withdrew from the long-established role of emperor as chief taste-setter and art patron; instead, mansabdars and regional rulers developed their own aesthetic styles.

Part of 'Alamgir's constraint on ostentation also arose from worsening imperial budget imbalances. Personally scrutinizing the accounts, he devoted particular attention to reducing expenses. In 1670, he ordered:

> the diwani [financial] officers ... should report to the Emperor the income and expenditure at the end of the year and should bring to the ghusalkhana (every) Wednesday the registers .... Since the reign of Shah Jahan the public expenditure has exceeded the income by [14,000,000] rupees. It was ordered that the privy purse (*khalisa*) income should be fixed at [40,000,000] rupees, and the expenditure the same. After looking over the accounts of disbursements, His Majesty retrenched many items of the expenditure of the Emperor, the Princes, and the begams.[18]

'Alamgir tried not to increase zat for the mansabdars collectively. But, the pressures of continued warfare led to increases in sawar (occasionally unconventionally raising it above zat), with extensive use of the 2-3 horse supplement for mansabdars on campaigns.

Substantial popular uprisings punctuated his reign. In reaction, 'Alamgir deputed imperial forces, sometimes under his personal direction, to support provincial officials in suppressing them. Extensive Afghan revolts recurred. Starting in 1667, the Yusufzai, Afridi and Khatak Afghan communities each expelled Mughal authorities. Imperial armies sent to crush them instead suffered major defeats (1674, 1675). Only after 'Alamgir himself went to supervise were these risings suppressed by combining force and subsidy-payments (protection money), thus securing the vital route to Kabul (by 1676).

Peasant communities in the Mughal heartland also persistently rebelled. Through the late 1660s, Hindu Jats around Mathura rallied under their popular leader, Gokula. Eventually in 1670, Mughal troops subdued this insurrection (albeit temporarily) and captured Gokula's children. 'Alamgir renamed Mathura 'Islamabad' and ordered the demolition of the major temple there built by Bir Singh Dev (recycling its stonework into a mosque in nearby Agra). 'Alamgir also had Gokula's son and daughter converted to Islam, made respectively a Qur'an reciter and a wife of an imperial servant. Yet, Jat uprisings re-emerged in the late 1680s.

In 1672, members of the Satnami religious movement in eastern Punjab revolted. Imperial accounts disparaged them as a 'rebellious horde of low people like goldsmiths, carpenters, scavengers, tanners and members of other menial professions.'[19] But 'Alamgir personally oversaw the imperial forces that gradually repressed them.

In the Punjab, another popular religious movement, the Sikhs under their Gurus, revolted repeatedly against Mughal rule and repulsed several imperial suppression campaigns.[20] After the death of the seventh Guru, Hari Rai (r. 1644–61), who had aided Dara Shukoh against 'Alamgir, he tried to arbitrate this succession—as Mughal emperors had done for many other dynasties. Instead, the Sikh community chose Guru Har Krishnan (r. 1661–4), who died very young in Delhi. Then, Sikhs recognized Guru Tegh Bahadur (r. 1665–75), who proselytized widely, especially among Jats in the Punjab. 'Alamgir had him arrested and executed. Nonetheless, the tenth Guru, Gobind Singh (r. 1675–98), mobilized increasingly militant resistance against Mughal authorities for decades. Other uprisings by various Jats and other regionally based groups would persist well beyond 'Alamgir's reign.

The Marathas of the western Deccan were the community on the Mughal frontier most powerfully resistant to both imperial arms and also enticements. Many Marathas had rallied under their charismatic leader, Shivaji (1627–80), as he maneuvered against Deccan sultans and Mughal governors. 'Alamgir sent some of his best commanders and troops against Shivaji, but they repeatedly failed. In a daring, lucrative and politically significant expedition, Shivaji sacked the rich strategic port of Surat in 1664, which Mughal authorities proved incompetent to defend. Unable to stop Shivaji, Mughal commanders allied with him against Bijapur (1665–6), but with limited imperial gains. In 1666, 'Alamgir sought to incorporate Shivaji by investing his seven-year-old son, Sambhaji, with mansab 5,000 and by summoning them both to the imperial court at Agra.

Like many outsiders to the court, Shivaji was alienated rather than assimilated. One courtier reflected their condescending attitude toward Shivaji (and other newcomers):

> ... this wild animal of the wilderness of ignorance, who knew not the etiquette of the imperial court, went into a corner and made improper expressions of dissatisfaction and complaint .... His brainless head led him to make a tumult. The Emperor ordered that he should return to his lodging ... in view of the fraud and satanic trickery of this arch-deceiver.[21]

Shivaji deceived his guards, dramatically escaped back to his homeland and rallied his followers there.

As Bijapur, Golkonda, various other rulers and rival factions within the Mughal administration all engaged in multi-sided conflicts in the Deccan, Shivaji intermittently supported or opposed each of them. In 1670, Shivaji plundered Surat again, adding to his own wealth and fame and humiliating its imperial defenders. In 1674, Shivaji further enhanced his status through an elaborate Brahminical enthronement as *Maharaja Chatrapati* (Sanskritic 'Universal Emperor'). Shivaji had made the Maratha coalition the most expansive force in the Deccan, mobilized around potent Hindu cultural symbols—like so many other rebellions against 'Alamgir's regime and policies.

After Shah Jahan's death, 'Alamgir implemented his own programs even more forcefully. He expressed his deep commitment to Sunni Islam by particularly favoring mansabdars, other officials and subjects who did likewise, including converts. But 'Alamgir increasingly resented rival international leaders of Sunni Islam. After sending several missions with gifts to the Sharif of Mecca, and after receiving even more missions seeking more presents, 'Alamgir expressed his frustration in a letter to the Sharif: 'Having heard about the great wealth of India, Sharif-i-Mecca, for taking an advantage for himself, sends me every year an envoy. This sum of money which I sent is for the needy. We should take care whether the money is distributed among the poor or is wasted by the Sharif...'[22] In his 1690 mission to the other most powerful Sunni ruler, the Ottoman Sultan, 'Alamgir recognized him only as Caesar of Rome, not Caliph (although the Ottoman sultans had claimed the Caliphate since 1517 and had long governed Mecca). Further, 'Alamgir gave high mansabs to successive Ottoman governors of Basra who defected and immigrated.[23]

'Alamgir increasingly ordered constraints on non-Muslims. He was both offended by the non-Muslim ideologies that motivated many opponents and also swayed by his own self-identification as leader of the Muslim community. Among other policies, he reinstated the pilgrim tax for non-Muslim religious festivals and tried to curtail them. While 'Alamgir gave financial support to some Hindu temples, he also cancelled revenue grants and directed the destruction of others, especially those belonging to rebels. In 1679, 'Alamgir re-imposed the long-abolished *jizya*, sparking popular demonstrations against him even in Shahjahanabad's streets. Shivaji reportedly wrote 'Alamgir, protesting the re-imposition of *jizya* as an unjust burden on non-Muslims. Theoretically, this tax was payment for the privilege of living under Muslim rule while not serving it, so many Rajputs and other Hindus working for the Empire were still exempt.

During the succession war, far more Rajput mansabdars had supported 'Alamgir than Dara or their brothers.[24] Nonetheless, 'Alamgir imposed policies that especially burdened Rajputs. To help alleviate the overstressed jagir system, he largely limited Rajput mansabdars to jagirs in their homelands, reducing their effective income. Rajputs also tended to receive less prestigious postings. By 1678, the proportion of Rajputs with mansab 1,000 or above was 15 per cent and declining; indeed, Rajputs comprised an even smaller proportion of high mansabdars than immigrants to India.[25]

Overall, despite 'Alamgir's considerable expenditures of manpower and financial resources, his reign's first dozen years proved disappointing to him and to many khanazad mansabdars, who formed the imperial core. Many also resented the appointment to high mansabs of former enemies, particularly those considered culturally inferior. This resentment intensified since there were insufficient available jagirs and since even those jagirs usually failed to produce their nominal income. As 'Alamgir admitted, 'We have a small sum of money and many have a demand for it.'[26] All this led many inside and outside the imperial establishment to question 'Alamgir's authority and act in their own interests.

THE RAJASTHAN WAR AND EARLY DECCAN CAMPAIGNS, 1679–89

In 1679, 'Alamgir left Shahjahanabad, never to return to that city or Hindustan. Until then, he had largely reigned from Shahjahanabad, travelling out relatively rarely: supervising campaigns in Afghanistan, visiting Agra and Allahabad and once (severely exhausted) resting in Kashmir. His 1679 departure initiated the pattern that would dominate his remaining four decades: 'Alamgir moving among military encampments and provisional capitals to deal personally with imperial crises, sometimes himself commanding battles.

Ever since Emperor Akbar had incorporated Rajputs into the Mughal core—receiving brides and service in exchange for advancement—they had provided much of the Empire's military manpower. Imperial armies almost all had significant Rajput contingents. But 'Alamgir's policies alienated many Rajputs. For example, Maharaja Jaswant Singh Rathor of Marwar had risen under Shah Jahan to mansab 7,000/7,000 (5,000 2-3h). During the succession war he had repeatedly backed 'Alamgir's brothers, intermittently forgiven each time he rejoined 'Alamgir. In 1678, Jaswant Singh died serving at the distant Khyber Pass, leaving no living sons but two pregnant wives (only one newborn survived). 'Alamgir determined to decide the Marwar succession, as emperors customarily did for such subordinated dynasties. However, 'Alamgir uncustomarily took into the imperial household a newborn, allegedly Jaswant Singh's son (converting him to Islam as Muhammadi Raj). Further, 'Alamgir selected as Marwar's ruler an unpopular but compliant nephew of Jaswant Singh.[27]

Many Rathors objected to such blatant interference. Some rebelled, claiming they had Jaswant Singh's real newborn son. To suppress this uprising, 'Alamgir himself oversaw the annexation of Marwar, converting long-standing Rajput watan jagirs into much needed khalisa. The Sisodia Rana of neighboring Mewar, fearing a similar intrusion into his territories and rights, joined the rebellion. To break the economy and spirit of these Rajputs, 'Alamgir supervised as Mughal armies devastated both Marwar and Mewar—seizing crops, looting cities and destroying temples.

'Alamgir entrusted direct imperial military command to his fourth and currently favorite son, Akbar. After initial victories, however, Akbar suddenly switched in 1681 to the Marwar side, proclaiming himself emperor. He nearly captured 'Alamgir, who only saved himself by deceiving Akbar's Rathor allies into deserting him. Akbar refused to surrender and beg his father's forgiveness. Instead, Akbar fled south for refuge with the current Maratha leader, Maharaja Sambhaji (the late Shivaji's eldest son and main heir). 'Alamgir confined for life his own eldest daughter and former favorite, Zeb-un-Nissa, for allegedly encouraging her traitorous brother.

After the Sisodia Rana of Mewar died, 'Alamgir forced the newly enthroned successor into ceding territories in lieu of *jizya*. However, in Marwar the guerilla war continued for decades (until 1709, after 'Alamgir's death). These struggles deeply damaged the long-standing and mutually advantageous alliance between the Mughal dynasty and many Rathor and Sisodia Rajputs. Further developments in the

Deccan would also weaken 'Alamgir's relationship with many other Rajput mansabdars.

In 1681, 'Alamgir returned to the Deccan which he had governed as a prince for 15 years (1636–44, 1652–8). He had three main objectives: punish errant Akbar; complete his conquests of Bijapur and Golkonda (interrupted by the succession war); and suppress Akbar's Maratha hosts. During 'Alamgir's first decade there, he apparently accomplished all three.

While 'Alamgir offered his rebellious son forgiveness if he would submit, Akbar instead continued to challenge his father's regime. Akbar launched ineffective raids into Hindustan. He sent his father scolding letters:

> in your Majesty's reign the ministers have no power, the nobles enjoy no trust, the soldiers are wretchedly poor, the writers are without employment, the traders are without means, the peasantry are downtrodden .... Men of high extraction and pure breeding belonging to ancient families have disappeared, and the offices and departments ... are in the hands of mechanics, low people and rascals,—like weavers, soap-venders and tailors ... buying posts with gold and selling them for shameful consideration.[28]

He urged 'Alamgir to retire and make the Hajj, taunting 'Alamgir about overthrowing his father.

But Akbar could not mobilize sufficient support from Deccanis or mansabdars. In 1683, he fled to the Safavid court, emulating several of his Mughal predecessors. Unlike Babur and Humayun, however, Akbar never returned as triumphant conqueror of India. Instead, he died in exile there, predeceasing his father.

'Alamgir's presence in the Deccan strengthened the resolve and resources of his soldiers fighting against Bijapur, Golkonda, the Marathas and kingdoms further south. 'Alamgir first concentrated his armies against Bijapur, the weaker sultanate (which he had fought when a prince). Imperial forces under his third son, 'Azam, besieged Bijapur. 'Alamgir went in 1686 to command the final victory personally. Triumphant, 'Alamgir imprisoned the youthful Sultan for life and annexed Bijapur into the Empire, recruiting as mansabdars select courtiers and commanders from the conquered regime.

Next, 'Alamgir focused his forces against still wealthy Golkonda Sultanate. His second son, Mu'azzam, had captured Hyderabad

THE GREAT HOWITZER CALLED MALIK-I MAIDAN.

Cannon from Bijapur Fort, *c.* 1688[29]

city in 1685 but the Sultan had withdrawn to nearby Golkonda Fort, which seemed impregnable. 'Alamgir took command himself. Convinced that the Sultan had bribed Mu'azzam, 'Alamgir had Mu'azzam, his wife and sons imprisoned in 1687 (and not released until 1695). Finally, after a costly eight-month siege, the fortress fell. 'Alamgir seized the 60 million rupee treasury, imprisoned the Sultan forever, and annexed the Sultanate. 'Alamgir appointed as mansabdars select members of the Golkonda court—24 Muslims, including the ex-king's adopted son, received mansab 1000 or more. But 'Alamgir gave mansabs to only two Hindus: a Brahmin and a Telugu Nayak, although these communities had been especially prominent in Golkonda's administration. For the next 15 years, most of Golkonda's local officials remained in place so links between zamindars and imperial officials were consequently weak.[30] Additionally, the eastern Deccan had suffered devastating war, famines and plague. Consequently, many mansabdars assigned jagirs there could not collect their full revenues. Further, the relatively few imperial troops, based in scattered forts, struggled to suppress local uprisings and Maratha raids.

'Alamgir next committed most of his troops against Marathas in the western Deccan. Shivaji's main heir, Sambhaji, had lived at the imperial court and received mansab 5,000, later 7,000. But Sambhaji had not assimilated well into the Empire and now led Marathas against it. As 'Alamgir had moved his troops against Bijapur and Golkonda, light, mobile Maratha troops harassed them, seizing people and property. In 1689, however, a rapid raid by a former Golkonda commander who had joined 'Alamgir captured Sambhaji. 'Alamgir had him publicly humiliated, blinded and executed. 'Alamgir also seized his capital, Raigarh. Many Marathas next recognized Shivaji's younger son, Rajaram, as their leader against the Empire. However, 'Alamgir tried to determine the Maratha succession by recognizing instead Sambhaji's nine-year-old son, Shahu, as Raja, awarding him mansab 7,000/7,000, and raising him within the imperial household.

Indeed, 'Alamgir awarded mansabs to many Marathas, until they outnumbered Rajputs. This raised the proportion of Hindu mansabdars (suggesting 'Alamgir did not exclude Hindus per se). But these new Maratha mansabdars rarely received prominent administrative posts and, largely alienated by the imperial culture, lacked commitment to the Empire. Nonetheless, by 1689, 'Alamgir had seemingly succeeded in his three main objectives in the Deccan and his regime superficially appeared stable everywhere.

EXTENDED DECCAN WARS AND IMPERIAL DETERIORATION, 1689–1707

Below the surface, the Empire was losing effectiveness due to structural stresses from financial imbalances, over-expansion and conflicting interests among 'Alamgir, mansabdari factions, his diverse subjects, rival powers and his own heirs. The Empire had always needed to expand in order to capture enemy treasuries and gain productive territories. This income paid for its armies that enabled the expansion and for its administration that collected the revenues. But over 'Alamgir's final two decades, the costs of empire came to outweigh the benefits for many mansabdars and subjects. Neither the imperial center nor its armies nor its administration had the policies, technology or manpower to control such a vast territorial expanse and array of regionally based rulers and communities.

As 'Alamgir passed through his seventies and eighties, he struggled to manage the Empire as a whole. Imperial commanders raided kingdoms as far south as Tanjavur during the early 1690s, making those rulers nominal tributaries. But the imperial administration exerted little control there, or even over earlier captured Deccani

Emperor 'Alamgir, As Remembered (detail), *c.* 1725. Courtesy Los Angeles County Museum of Art (M.72.88.1). www.LACMA.org

territories.[31] Seeing few of his goals accomplished unless he directed them personally, 'Alamgir concentrated imperial revenues and manpower in his own hands. He doled out resources only temporarily to his mansabdars and distrusted sons, instead ensuring that the most productive lands were designated khalisa, funneling their revenues into his own establishment.

Throughout his reign, 'Alamgir never spared himself. While he occasionally visited the capitals of defeated Deccani rulers, he did not live in their luxurious palaces. Instead, from 1699 to 1706, 'Alamgir stubbornly moved his vast imperial encampment around the western Deccan countryside, assaulting a dozen hill-forts held by Marathas and their allies. He eventually captured each fort after long and costly sieges, but often had to negotiate their surrender with little benefit to him and little cost to their defenders. Further, overstretched imperial forces could retain only transient possession of these forts and the territories they controlled; most soon reverted into Maratha hands. One imperial official lamented: "'Alamgir, who is not in want of anything, has been seized with such a longing and passion for some heaps of stone [i.e., hill forts].'[32]

During the decades before 'Alamgir's death, leading mansabdars were divided into particularly strong and antagonistic factions, each seeking advantage, often at the Empire's expense. While these factions contained various ethnicities, the two strongest were respectively headed by Shi'i Irani and Sunni Turani mansabdars. Many mansabdars needed powerful patrons to protect their interests, since their expenses often far outweighed the actual income from their jagir—if they were influential or fortunate enough to receive a jagir. Some had to wait five years for any jagir. Consequently, many mansabdars left their soldiers and retainers long unpaid, which fostered disloyalty. Many mansabdars also extracted as much licit and illicit revenue as possible from jagirs they obtained, and resisted relinquishing them to the next assignee. Several mansabdars eventually turned their jagirs into hereditary kingdoms, since the imperial center was losing control over provincial administrations.

Overall, the Empire began to segment as revenue flows and communication links between North and South were periodically interrupted *en route* due to predations by bandits, warlords and even intermediate imperial officials. Most mansabdars in north India faced regional uprisings without the prospect of military reinforcement or financial support from 'Alamgir in the Deccan. Further, distant mansabdars did not bond to the emperor through recurrent direct personal exchanges of nazr and *khilat* as they had earlier. Conversely, most governors remained unchecked by effective supervision from the imperial center, and were able to retain provincial revenues for themselves. By the time of 'Alamgir's death, no north Indian province was sending substantial revenues to him—except for prosperous Bengal where an especially effective Diwan (later Subadar), Murshid Quli Khan, managed an expanding agricultural base, developing artisanal production and increasing exports.

In the Deccan, many mansabdars who originated in north India— including Rajputs and many long-settled Muslims—had been serving far from home through decades of frustrating harassment by local insurgents, especially Marathas. One official lamented the frustrating and interminable Deccan campaigns: 'Ever since His Majesty had ... adopted all these wars and hardships of travel, ... the inmates of his camp, sick of long separation, summoned their families ...

and ... a new generation was thus born (in the camp).'[33] Imperial commanders often saw little prospect of defeating these insurgents or particular benefit to the Empire or themselves from doing so. Instead, many imperial generals preserved their own financial and manpower resources by negotiating private settlements with those enemies, despite 'Alamgir's repeated, explicit orders forbidding this. On their part, many new Deccani mansabdars, whose submission had been thus purchased, had little loyalty to the Empire. They often saw better prospects in repudiating imperial service in order to carve out kingdoms for themselves or to join leaders from their own community who were doing so. These included various Marathas and other regionally rooted warlords.

In both north India and the Deccan, many tributary rulers, landholders and other subjects—including peasants, artisans, merchants and bankers—faced revenue demands from the Empire but increasingly doubted the value of paying. Imperial officials had diminished capacity to provide justice, law and order and also to compel tax payments. In contrast, local rajas and zamindars often had bonds with the local population and retained more revenues, which they used to bolster their own power. Particularly in the Deccan, much of the economy had been devastated by decades of warfare and disrupted commerce. Expanding areas were subject to annual levies by Maratha-led war bands: *chauth* (payment of a 'quarter' of the assessed revenue) plus other tribute in exchange for relief from even more costly depredations. Imperial officials often acquiesced in these exactions, often unable to resist them.

While European assertions in India would not appear prominently until long after 'Alamgir's death, their effects were already significant. Parts of the Indian economy were engaging more extensively in exporting cloth, saltpeter, spices and other goods aboard European ships. The more expansive English, Dutch and French East India Companies were replacing the Portuguese as controllers of the Indian Ocean trade and passage to Mecca. These joint-stock corporations also established trading enclaves along India's west and east coasts and inland, seeking profits and negotiating with local officials and with 'Alamgir himself for tax concessions. When negotiations broke down, violence sometimes ensued, for example in skirmishes between imperial officials and the English at Hugli (1686–90), Bombay (1688–9), Surat (1695–9) and Madras (1702).

Further, various independent European sea-captains also preyed upon merchant shipping as pirates and privateers, which imperial officials could not prevent. 'Alamgir scolded his son, 'Azam, Gujarat's current governor:

> ... ships cannot sail without the permit of the *Firangi*s [Europeans]. The Muslim community has become so impuissant that even the imperial vessels are unable to cruise. For the last twenty years, the ships of the Surat merchants and those destined for the Holy Land are being plundered on the high seas. Steps taken by [mansabdars] to combat the problem have proved fruitless. Negligence, indolence, and indifference towards this matter are contrary to the Islamic sense of honour .... Concession and favour to the *Firangi*s have been shown beyond measure. Moderation will not work. Severity and harshness are required.[34]

'Alamgir himself futilely tried to force English and Dutch ambassadors to make their Companies protect Indian shipping, or even cease seizing it.[35] But the lack of a Mughal imperial seagoing navy and also pragmatic and self-serving collaboration in port cities between imperial officials and Europeans meant continued insecurity for Indian ships, their cargoes and pilgrim passengers.

'Alamgir also feared for his dynasty, not perceiving much capacity in any of his potential heirs. Each son aspired to succeed him but each lost his confidence and suffered accordingly. 'Alamgir tried to keep them and his already maturing grandsons dependent on his cash grants and loaned military and administrative manpower; he had them assigned less productive or inadequate jagirs. To economize, several princes reduced their military contingents, which weakened them in fulfilling their assigned duties, even as the inevitable succession war approached. Hence, by 'Alamgir's death, none of his sons was particularly strong, especially relative to powerful imperial commanders and governors. Two sons, Sultan and Akbar, had already died, the former in imperial prison, the other exiled in Iran.

Of the three remaining sons, Mu'azzam was already aged sixty-three at 'Alamgir's death. Mu'azzam and his family had for seven years been imprisoned by 'Alamgir for treachery. Even after Mu'azzam's release, he remained in disfavor, posted from 1700 onward far from court, as governor of Kabul and Lahore. However, he gathered supporters among mansabdars there for the coming succession war.

Prince 'Azam, aged 54, had also occasionally incurred 'Alamgir's displeasure, notably in 1692 for reportedly taking a large bribe from a besieged local chief in exchange for lifting the siege. Despite 'Azam's objections, he had been posted by 'Alamgir away from court, as governor of Malwa, then Gujarat (1701–5). After finally gaining permission to return to dying 'Alamgir, he was again expelled. But 'Azam delayed his departure, intending to seize the imperial treasury and establishment immediately on 'Alamgir's death, as the first step toward securing the entire Empire.

'Alamgir's youngest son, Kam Bakhsh, was the child of Udaipuri Mahal, the low-born concubine who attended 'Alamgir in his old age. 'Alamgir always kept Kam Bakhsh nearby, only once entrusting him with a military command. That ended badly, however, when, in 1693, veteran imperial commanders arrested him for conspiring with Rajaram, the Maratha ruler. In 'Alamgir's last years, he appointed Kam Bakhsh nominal governor of Golconda, hoping to protect him from his higher-born half-brothers. 'Alamgir wrote him regretfully '... I pity you for your want of intelligence and ability; but now of what use?'[36] 'Alamgir, thus finding no son worthy, began to favor his nine grandsons, the eldest already age 46 when 'Alamgir finally died.

By 1705, illnesses and the intensifying infirmities of old age forced Aurangzeb to withdraw from his hitherto continuous campaigns and rest in Ahmadnagar. As with each Mughal predecessor, 'Alamgir struggled to balance leaving a strong Empire intact against preserving all his sons' lives. His purportedly last written will partitioned his Empire after his death.[37] He had long allotted Golconda and Bijapur to Kam Bakhsh, and he directed his other two surviving sons to respect that. But he unrealistically willed the division of the rest of the Empire between 'Azam and Mu'azzam, one receiving the title Padshah and the contiguous provinces of Agra, Ajmer, Aurangabad, Berar, Bidar, Gujarat, Khandesh and Malwa while the other should hold Delhi and the widely separated provinces of Allahabad, Awadh, Bengal, Bihar, Kabul, Kashmir, Multan, Orissa, Punjab and Thatta. But 'Alamgir's dying testament, evoking the earlier Central Asian tradition of appanages, could not control events: the Empire soon fragmented under a long series of weak emperors.

Part IV

The Fragmentation and Memory of the Mughal Empire, 1707–the Present

10

THE THINNING OF THE EMPIRE, 1707–1857

The skies have fallen down upon us,
I can no longer rest or sleep.
Only my final departure is now certain,
Whether it comes in the morning, or night.

Bahadur Shah II (r. 1837–57), penname 'Zafar'[1]

Over the Empire's last 150 years (1707–1857), a series of weak emperors reigned but rarely ruled. While no emperor held much control over events, many strove to recover power and participate in the surrounding political and cultural worlds. Further, the image of Mughal sovereignty proved so enduring that warlords, regional rulers and many others (Indian and European) still recognized the dynasty, albeit nominally. The final imperial cataclysm of 1857–8 showed the Empire's continued significance but also ended it.

LATE SUCCESSION IN ESTABLISHED AND NEW PATTERNS, 1707–13

Retrospectively, some historians define the Mughal Empire as ending in 1707 with 'Alamgir's death.[2] Yet, the ensuing succession struggle appeared superficially similar to previous ones. Each surviving son—Mu'azzam, 'Azam and Kam Bakhsh—rallied his supporters, declared himself emperor and sought to defeat and execute his brothers. For the first time, however, no imperial prince controlled much military

Prince Mu'azzam, *c.* 1675 (detail). Courtesy Los Angeles County
Museum of Art (M.74.123.5). www.LACMA.org

force of his own, largely due to 'Alamgir's policies of awarding them
inflated mansabs but insufficient jagirs. Instead, the most powerful
mansabdars, while accepting the legitimacy of the imperial house and
avoiding acts of direct disobedience, protected their own interests by
not fighting for any of these self-proclaimed emperors. Additionally,
the claimants were aging and many of their sons were already active
politically and militarily, which rightly portended extended struggles,
not a secure, long-lasting reign.

'Alamgir's contending sons each launched into action on learning
of their father's long-expected death in Ahmadnagar. The youngest and

weakest claimant, Kam Bakhsh, tried to fortify himself in Golkonda, which 'Alamgir had assigned to him. More aggressively, the middle brother, 'Azam, who had strategically camped near Ahmadnagar, forcibly secured 'Alamgir's corpse, household, immediate wealth, courtiers and Deccan army, and then marched north to try to seize Shahjahanabad and Agra, which still contained the bulk of the dynasty's coins, jewels and other treasures. The eldest brother, Mu'azzam, recruited mansabdars in the north-west where he was governor, and then rushed across the Punjab, reaching Shahjahanabad and Agra first, taking the regnal title Emperor Bahadur Shah (r. 1707– 12). He reportedly offered 'Azam the Deccan, Gujarat and Ajmer as appanages if he would submit. Instead, just months after 'Alamgir's death, these two brothers battled near Agra, resulting in the deaths of 'Azam, two of his sons and many supporters. Then, early in 1709, Bahadur Shah attacked and killed Kam Bakhsh in the Deccan.

At Bahadur Shah's accession, he was already elderly. Seeking support from prominent mansabdars who commanded imperial armies and governed its provinces, he lavishly awarded promotions, titles and offices. But many mansabdars anticipated the impending next succession war and conserved their resources. Several entrenched themselves in the provinces they administered, including Nizam-al-Mulk in the Deccan and Murshid Quli Khan in Bengal.[3] Increasingly, local rulers and communities ceased regarding the Emperor as the source of stable and just rule.

Bahadur Shah needed money. To raise immediate cash, he practiced revenue farming far more extensively than his predecessors. He distributed much of the remaining lands he controlled as jagirs to reward mansabdars who held real power. He himself remained almost constantly campaigning to subdue stubborn resistance even within the Empire's core provinces, particularly against Rajputs in Rajasthan and Sikhs in the Punjab. Bahadur Shah thus spent his four-year reign struggling to restore bonds among the Emperor, his mansabdars, and his subjects—the beginning of a long 'crisis of empire.'[4]

Bahadur Shah's anticipated death in 1712 loosed a destructive, multi-round war among his male descendants, each desperately seeking support from mansabdars and others with military, financial and other resources. His four sons each proclaimed himself Emperor. At first, three sons warily conspired to divide the Empire among themselves, as soon as they defeated and killed the fourth, Azim-ush-

Shan—the leading contender, since he had accumulated substantial treasure during a decade as governor of Bengal. But when these three brothers killed Azim-ush-Shan, they turned on each other. After a three-way melee, the eldest, Jahandar Shah (r. 1713), seized the throne and executed his remaining brothers, many of their sons and their major commanders. Rather than consolidate his reign, however, Jahandar celebrated his accession, prominently featuring his concubine-consort, Lal Kunwar. Many khanazad resented the Emperor's feckless behavior and promotion to high office of Lal Kunwar's family of court entertainers.

Within months, the late Azim-ush-Shan's 29-year-old second son, Farrukh-siyar (r. 1713–19), marched up the Ganges from Bengal, rallying diverse discontented commanders against his newly enthroned uncle. Farrukh-siyar defeated the ill-prepared, dispirited and weakly led imperial army near Agra. He seized the throne, executed fleeing Jahandar and many of his supporters, and blinded three imperial princes who were possible rivals. However, Farrukh-siyar, like all his successors until the end of the dynasty, struggled futilely to hold together the fragmenting Empire.

FROM SALATIN TO EMPERORS UNDER REGENCIES, 1713–59

While nominal authority remained with the incumbent Emperor, effective military and political power had shifted into the contending hands of powerful courtiers, imperial commanders and governors and rising regionally based communities mobilized by charismatic leaders. Nonetheless, such was the ideological force of Mughal sovereignty that the Emperor's decrees, appointments and awards of elevated titles could often have effect, even when obviously dictated by the current regent. Further, the residual prestige of the Mughal house meant that no regent ascended the throne himself nor ended the dynasty, even if he terminated individual emperors.[5]

Farrukh-siyar had improbably attained the throne largely due to the martial skills of Sayyid Hasan Ali Khan and his brother, Sayyid Husain Ali Khan, current governors of Allahabad and Bihar respectively. They led the Sayyid clan long settled in Barha (today in western Uttar Pradesh) which for generations had provided famously brave contingents to imperial armies. Even as Emperor, Farrukh-siyar lacked revenues to fund his own forces, so he could not confront the Sayyid brothers. Further, they threatened to enthrone another imperial family member whenever Farrukh-siyar proved too demanding. Hence, throughout his six-year reign, Farrukh-siyar schemed to offset the Sayyid brothers by favoring other mansabdars. Most notably Farrukh-siyar turned to the head of the Turani khanazad family, best known by his hereditary title Nizam-al-Mulk, with his own power-base in the Deccan, where he was periodically governor.

On Farrukh-siyar's accession, he also sought support from Rajput and other Hindu mansabdars and regional rulers (including by abolishing *jizya*). Nonetheless, Raja Ajit Singh Rathor soon rebelled, expelling imperial officials from Marwar and Ajmer, aided by the Rajput rulers of Mewar and Amber.[6] After Sayyid Husain Ali Khan compelled Ajit Singh's submission and restored imperial authority in Rajasthan, Farrukh-siyar took Ajit Singh's daughter, Bai Indra Kunwar, as a bride in 1715.[7] Unlike Emperor Akbar, who bound leading Rajput houses to his dynasty through mutually respectful marriages, Farrukh-siyar converted her to Islam. Further, under pressure from strongly orthodox Muslim courtiers, Farrukh-siyar re-imposed *jizya* in 1717. When Bai Indar Kunwar was later widowed, she repudiated Islam, undertook a purification ceremony and returned to Hinduism and her family— all unprecedented for an empress and revealing rising Rajput resistance to Mughal culture.

In several core provinces, Farrukh-siyar and the Sayyid regents battled Jat communities climbing to local dominance. Concentrated imperial armies under strong commanders could still subdue such peasant uprisings, but these communities no longer routinely accepted Mughal authority. In the strategic Punjab, many Jats were Sikhs, an ever more militant movement. For years, imperial forces campaigned hard to defeat the current Sikh leader, Banda Bahadur, eventually capturing and executing him and many of his followers in 1716. Sikh insurrections recurred, however.

In the upper Gangetic region around Mathura, most Jats were Hindu. They had also periodically repulsed the Empire. Eventually, mansabdars compelled the current Jat leader, Raja Churaman, to submit. But this pacification also proved temporary; by the mid-eighteenth century, rising Jat leaders had made Bharatpur their major power base.

In the Deccan, various leaders of a similar community of independent farmers, the Marathas, had long been alternately fighting and allying with the Empire. During the eighteenth century, various powerful Maratha commanders repeatedly led armies northward into Gujarat, Malwa, Rajasthan and the Punjab—occasionally seizing Shahjahanabad. They also marched eastward into the Deccan provinces governed by Nizam-al-Mulk's dynasty and beyond, into Orissa, southern Bihar and southwestern Bengal. In each region, Maratha chiefs negotiated or simply collected chauth, *sardeshmukhi* ('headman's fees') and other exactions.[8] Maratha forces also conquered south to Tanjavur and Mysore. But, periodic internecine conflicts among the Maratha ruling dynasty, their *Peshwa*s ('chief ministers'), other courtiers and semi-independent generals, as well as occasional battlefield defeats, led to temporary withdrawals. This pattern of Maratha conquest and occasional retreat persisted throughout the reigns of Farrukh-siyar and his weak successors until the early nineteenth century.

Farrukh-siyar made ineffective efforts to regain fiscal and political control. He allocated to potential supporters those few territories still paying imperial revenues. But this reduced even further the little remaining khalisa land that supported his own court and forces.[9] Lacking power to manage events, Farrukh-siyar spent much time hunting, writing poetry and futilely conspiring to free himself either from the Sayyid brothers or their powerful rivals. Unable to dismiss his potent mansabdars, the Emperor reportedly tried to poison various of them; he also awarded the same office to two men, hoping one would destroy the other and be weakened in the process.[10]

Finally, in April 1719, the Sayyid brothers took the decisive step of replacing Farrukh-siyar with an even more compliant emperor. They had him dragged from his harem, blinded, harshly imprisoned and assassinated. They enthroned his short-lived paternal first cousin, Rafi-ud-Darjat (r. 1719). Never before had an established emperor been deposed by mansabdars.

This precedent shattered the concept of individual Mughal sovereignty, and would be repeated seven times in the next 40 years by various other regents. Nonetheless, the concept of corporate sovereignty possessed exclusively by males of the Mughal house would persist. The Sayyid brothers—having temporarily united by their actions many diverse opponents—were themselves sequentially each assassinated soon thereafter. A series of other regents followed who drew puppet emperors out of the pool of hitherto passed-over male descendants of 'Alamgir, known collectively as the *salatin* ('imperial princes').

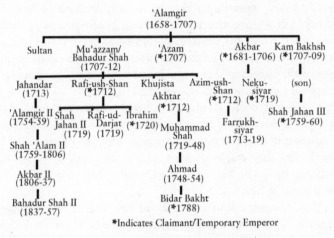

'Alamgir
(1658-1707)

Sultan	Mu'azzam/	'Azam	Akbar	Kam Bakhsh
	Bahadur Shah	(*1707)	(*1681-1706)	(*1707-09)
	(1707-12)			

Jahandar   Rafi-ush-Shan   Khujista   Azim-ush-   Neku-   (son)
(1713)   (*1712)   Akhtar   Shan   siyar
                             (*1712)   (*1712)   (*1719)

'Alamgir II Shah   Rafi-ud- Ibrahim   Shah Jahan III
(1754-59)   Jahan II Darjat   (*1720) Muhammad   Farrukh-   (*1759-60)
             (1719) (1719)   Shah   siyar
Shah 'Alam II   (1719-48)   (1713-19)
(1759-1806)

Akbar II   Ahmad
(1806-37)   (1748-54)

Bahadur Shah II   Bidar Bakht
(1837-57)   (*1788)

*Indicates Claimant/Temporary Emperor

Chart 2: Later Mughal emperors (with reign)

Over the decades following Farrukh-siyar's assassination, these salatin, confined in various degrees of impoverishment within the Shahjahanabad or Agra forts, remained fearful whether they were about to be executed or enthroned. Occasionally, rival would-be kingmakers simultaneously crowned different princes. Of the ten emperors taken from among the salatin by regents over the next half-century, three were assassinated while on the throne and another four were eventually returned to the pool of salatin, grateful to have escaped alive. Half these emperors reigned only a few months but one remained weakly on the throne for nearly three decades: Muhammad Shah (r. 1719–48). Almost all these emperors reached the throne having no experience in administration or warfare, being chosen and controlled by regents.

Each regent who clawed his way to power found staying alive and in control as perilous as being emperor. Some regents were imperial governors who had entrenched themselves in the province where they had been posted, with no particular connection to the local population. Such rulers of 'successor states' sometimes achieved hereditary de facto kingship. Nominally subordinate to the emperor, they were known by their imperial title—most prominently the Turani Sunni Nizam-al-Mulk dynasty in Hyderabad and the Irani Shi'a Nawab-Wazir dynasty in Awadh. Other regents led a dominant regionally based community, like the Rohilla Afghans or Marathas. Yet other regents negotiated ever-shifting coalitions, with custody of the emperor and his residual authority as their major resource. Several regents looted the imperial treasury and palace, even stripping women of the harem of their valuables and chastity; one gouged out the emperor's eyes.

The imperial center had lost control over most borderlands, including the north-west frontier. There, mansabdars lacked funds and manpower to resist either insurgent Afghans or invaders from the west. The first major invader was Nadir Shah (r. 1736–47), a Persianized Turk who had risen from humble beginnings to establish his own reign in Iran.

Like the Mughal Empire, the Safavid Empire had been fragmented by various contending warlords. Nadir Shah had attracted Central Asian and Iranian warriors seeking plunder. He led his predatory forces westward against the Ottoman Empire and also eastward. In 1738, he seized poorly defended Kabul, which had remained in Mughal hands since Babur captured it in 1519. Nadir Shah's several diplomatic envoys to the current Emperor, Muhammad Shah, received promises but no effective action. Advancing, Nadir Shah led his overpowering forces across the Punjab toward Shahjahanabad.

Belatedly moving to confront Nadir Shah, various rival imperial commanders finally assembled their separate armies at Karnal (30 kilometers from Panipat) under Muhammad Shah's nominal leadership. But their vast, unwieldy encampment was encircled by Nadir Shah's battle-tried cavalry. As Babur and Humayun had proven two centuries earlier, highly mobile Central Asian horsemen could sever the supply lines of a massive but immobile Indian force. A late arriving army under the governor of Awadh, Sa'adat Khan (himself a recent Irani immigrant who had rapidly risen in imperial service), plunged prematurely into battle. Facing superior light artillery and muskets, and also ineffectively supported by other imperial commanders, this force was slaughtered and Sa'adat Khan captured.

Negotiations followed about how much tribute Nadir Shah would accept to spare Delhi and withdraw. But, on the imperial side, Sa'adat Khan and his Turani-faction rival, Nizam-al-Mulk, worked at cross-purposes until the former died suddenly. Imperiously, Nadir Shah summoned Muhammad Shah and confined him, nominally as an honored fellow emperor, but effectively a hostage. After they entered Shahjahanabad together, Nadir Shah triumphantly had the khutba and coinage feature himself as sovereign.

In the following tense days, Nadir Shah's avaricious troops clashed with Shahjahanabad's resentful inhabitants. In retaliation, Nadir Shah declared a six-hour general massacre. Nadir Shah's officers then assessed the ransom of each neighborhood and surviving notable, collecting tens of millions of rupees. On his part, Muhammad Shah surrendered an imperial princess as a bride for Nadir Shah's son, the Peacock Throne, the Koh-i Nur diamond, over a hundred million rupees, Kashmir, the territories west of the Indus and substantial annual tribute from the Punjab. Like Timur, but unlike Babur and Humayun, Nadir Shah declined to establish his own regime in India. Instead, after two months, he restored the hapless Muhammad Shah and returned to Iran laden with plunder stripped from Shahjahanabad and the imperial treasury.

Nonetheless, enough wealth remained in Shahjahanabad to attract even more looting by various Indian regents and warlords. While Muhammad Shah reigned until his natural death in 1748, he held little actual power outside of his capital and environs. His penname Rangila ('Colorful One') reflected his often-frantic search for pleasure.[11]

The fragmentation of the old imperial order opened new opportunities for the enterprising and fortunate. Some scribal service elites (mostly Hindu Khatris and Kayasthas) used their administrative expertise to attain positions of power.[12] The Maratha confederacy and the English and other European East India Companies, with their allied elements in Indian society, also fought and bargained their way upward, as did a few ex-slaves, Asian and European mercenaries, and warlords.[13]

An Afghan, Ahmad Shah Durrani (r. 1747–72), rose in Nadir Shah's service. Like his late master, he regarded north India as a source of plunder for his rapacious soldiers, but not somewhere he wished to rule.[14] From 1747, Ahmad Shah launched a series of almost

Emperor Muhammad Shah (detail), Presiding over Spring Festival of Colors (Holi), *c.* 1725–50. Courtesy Los Angeles Museum of Art (M.76.149.2). www.LACMA.org

annual raids, ransoming or sacking cities in the Punjab and Kashmir. In 1757, he seized Shahjahanabad itself. Since accumulated treasure was already pillaged, Ahmad Shah grabbed whatever he could in the Red Fort, including imperial princesses for himself and his son, while his soldiers pillaged Shahjahanabad.

Seeking yet more, Ahmad Shah invaded again in 1759–60, retaking Shahjahanabad. After Maratha forces recovered the city, the two armies fought at Panipat in 1760—one of the bloodiest battles in Indian history. The shattered Marathas withdrew from north India for a decade. Ahmad Shah's damaged army managed to re-enter Shahjahanabad and snatch more booty before withdrawing to Afghanistan, although he would launch another decade of attenuated incursions into the Punjab.[15] The incumbent emperor, Shah 'Alam II (r. 1759–1806), however, was in the east, seeking to reconstitute his imperial regime starting there.

THE FINAL GENERATIONS OF MUGHAL EMPERORS, 1759–1857

The long, peripatetic reign of Shah 'Alam II reflected many transitions in the Empire, now a multi-sided conflict zone. Unlike other Mughal princes, he had escaped impoverished confinement within Shahjahanabad's Red Fort. Despite occasional aid from Maratha generals, his early efforts near Delhi failed to restore imperial authority. So the prince ventured east down the Ganges. By 1758, he had found refuge with Nawab-Wazir Shuja'-ud-Daula, hereditary governor over Awadh and nominal chief minister of the Empire. In 1759, the current regent in Shahjahanabad assassinated the prince's imperial father and enthroned the prince's second cousin once removed as Shah Jahan III (r. 1759–60). Immediately, Shah 'Alam II declared himself the true Emperor, with support from Shuja'-ud-Daula. Just before the devastating 1760 battle of Panipat, Maratha forces recovered Shahjahanabad, executed the hapless incumbent, Shah Jahan III, and recognized Shah 'Alam as Emperor.

Simultaneously, Shah 'Alam attempted to establish his rule over Bihar and Bengal by constructing a coalition headed by Shuja'-ud-Daula. In 1759, he launched his imperial 'tour,' ordering the submission of his nominal subordinates—the puppet governor of Bengal and his current keeper, the English East India Company.[16] When they resisted, his imperial army of some 30,000 soldiers (mostly supplied by Shuja'-ud-Daula) thrice entered Bihar but narrowly failed to conquer it. Unable to dislodge the English, in 1760 the Emperor entrusted himself to them.

The English East India Company was expanding from a joint-stock commercial corporation to make itself the conqueror and ruler of ever more Indian territories. Its Court of Directors in London was elected by shareholders to manage its business and generate annual dividends. But, its British employees in India hired *sepoy*s (European-style disciplined and equipped Indian infantry) to fight under their command. Sepoy regiments were likewise recruited by French East India Company employees; European mercenaries were hired by perceptive Indian rulers. Such sepoy regiments, along with European-commanded, technologically advanced artillery, became the core of the new model armies that triumphed over much larger forces composed of Mughal-style cavalry and motley footsoldiers. Gradually, the better funded and

A sepoy matchlock infantryman, by W. Hodges, 1793[17]

supplied English pushed out the more isolated French. In 1757 at Plassey, the English Company's merchant-turned-officer, Robert Clive, led a sepoy army that defeated the bigger but divided army of the young imperial governor of Bengal. Using indirect rule, the English Company placed a series of puppet governors in office, but retained for its own advantage real military, economic and political power over still prosperous Bengal and Bihar. Taking custody over the Emperor in 1760 gave more legitimacy to English de facto rule.

But, in 1764, Shah 'Alam ambitiously left the confining protection of the English. He rejoined Shuja'-ud-Daula, who once again invaded Bihar. These imperial forces, however, lost to the English Company's sepoy army at Buxar in 1764 and then at Kora in 1765. Thereupon, the Emperor again accepted the English Company as his regent, negotiating a settlement: the English turned over Allahabad province to the Emperor, officially submitted to his sovereignty and promised 2,600,000 rupees (about £40 million in today's purchasing power) in annual tribute. In exchange, the Emperor graciously authorized the English Company's puppet to continue as governor of Bengal and Bihar. More significantly, the Emperor appointed the Company as his Diwan there. (Company agents soon started collecting and retaining revenues in Bengal and Bihar, although the Court of Directors formally accepted this imperial appointment only in 1772.)

To bring the English King into the Empire, in 1765 Shah 'Alam deployed a diplomatic mission to London. Along with 100,000 rupees and various other gifts, he sent a letter to George III:

> your Majesty will send to Calcutta 5 or 6,000 young men practiced in war [who] ... may carry me to Shahjehanabad, my capital, and firmly seat me on the throne of the Hindostan Empire, which is my undoubted right .... Your Majesty's restoring me to my right will cause your name to be celebrated till the destruction of the world in every part of the habitable earth, and I shall be obliged to you as long as I live ...[18]

To head this embassy, Shah 'Alam appointed Captain Archibald Swinton (who retired from the East India Company Army), with an Indian expert in Persianate diplomacy, Mirza Shaikh I'tisam-ud-Din, as second-in-command.

The East India Company—amidst complex negotiations with the British Parliament over its own contradictory status as a commercial corporation and ruler of Indian territories—effectively thwarted this imperial embassy to the British monarch. After many travails in Britain, I'tisam-ud-Din returned in 1769 with little accomplished politically but with much first-hand information about Britain. In addition to his oral report for the Emperor, he wrote in 1784 the earliest written account by an Indian about Britain—an extensive Persian-language travel narrative: *Shigrifnama-i Wilayat* ['Wonder-book of Foreign Lands/Europe'].[19]

Meanwhile, Shah 'Alam remained in Allahabad under uneasy English protection. The English Company shirked its tribute obligations (paying just 18 per cent of the specified amount in 1770 and 23 per cent in 1772, for example).[20] Further, the Emperor tussled with the British resident political agent over ceremonial precedence.

Nonetheless, these payments and Allahabad's revenues gave Shah 'Alam more income than emperors had received in decades, while the British treated him relatively more respectfully than many other regents, past and future.

Since the English Company evaded Shah 'Alam's commands to recapture Shahjahanabad (where much of his court and household remained) and restore his Empire, he sought other backers. In 1771, he paid Maratha generals 4,000,000 rupees and promised the future revenues from Allahabad and most other territories under imperial control in exchange for their successfully restoring him to his throne in Shahjahanabad. From there, as campaigns raged across north India, he struggled for three more decades to manage shifting coalitions of regents, warlords and regional powers, while they used him for their purposes. One regent, Ghulam Qadr Rohilla, enraged at how little was left to loot, deposed Shah 'Alam in 1788, personally dug out his eyes, imprisoned him and enthroned a distant cousin from among the salatin, Bidar Bakht (r. 1788–9). But, five months later, Maratha-led forces recaptured Shahjahanabad and restored blind Shah 'Alam to the throne. Strikingly, Mughal sovereignty nominally survived such blatant degradations and absence of actual power.

Indeed, when the English East India Company captured Shahjahanabad and the surrounding region in 1803, it still officially recognized Shah 'Alam as sovereign. Further, the Company granted him a pension of 1,150,000 Rupees annually from revenues it collected from the small 'assigned territories' nearby (a vestige of the imperial domain). However, the Company also barred aging and blind Shah 'Alam from further active participation in politics and even arbitrated his succession.

On Shah 'Alam's death in 1806, his son Akbar II (r. 1806–37) acceded. But he remained confined to Shahjahanabad and closely supervised by the Company's resident political agent. Nonetheless, the Emperor's bestowal of imperial titles, *khilat*s and even access to his court remained highly attractive to many Indians and Britons.[21]

Nonetheless, Shahjahanabad still shone as a major center of Persianate high culture. The last three Mughal Emperors were respected poets, with some of the greatest Persian and Hindustani poets valuing their appointments as imperial tutors or invited performers. Imperial princes, emulating Shah 'Alam II, toured north

Emperor Shah 'Alam II (detail), blinded but on reconstructed Peacock Throne,
by Khair Ullah Musawir, 1801. Courtesy Los Angeles County Museum of Art
(M.77.78). www.LACMA.org

Shahjahanabad, last Mughal domain, *c.* 1857[22]

India and received deferential welcome almost everywhere.[23] Even many prominent Indian progressives recognized Mughal authority: the leading Bengali social reformer, Rammohun Roy, for example, accepted the title 'Raja' from the Emperor and traveled to London as his ambassador (1831–3), negotiating with the Company's Directors for a larger imperial pension.[24] The English Company itself continued ceremonially to display its recognition of Mughal sovereignty by minting specimen coins in the Emperor's name, officially presenting nazr and receiving *khilat*s (until 1843).

But many Britons and Indians also recognized how much the Mughal dynasty had decayed. The Company's resident political agent openly held the power to scrutinize imperial orders and policies, manage the 'assigned territories' and control the emperor's movements. In 1819, the nominal Wazir of the Mughal Emperor and imperial governor of Awadh (with British encouragement) declared himself independent 'Emperor of the World.'[25] Other regional rulers who presented nazr to visiting imperial princes also privately regarded these as 'begging expeditions.'[26] For many British tourists, visiting the Emperor was an exotic thrill, but one which highlighted his tawdry decadence in contrast to 'modern' British government, still dynamically expanding its rule.

When Akbar II died, the British enthroned his eldest surviving son, Bahadur Shah II (r. 1837–58), who was already 62 and largely reconciled to remaining aloof from active politics. By the 1850s, British policymakers determined that he would be the last Emperor. They planned to recognize his heir only as a princely pensioner and force the dynasty to vacate Shahjahanabad for a rural retreat. At age 82, however, events beyond Bahadur Shah's control thrust him into the center of a massive uprising against British rule.

In May 1857, a variety of causes inspired diverse north Indians—including sepoys, deposed rulers and landholders, and Muslim and Hindu opponents of Christian British rule—to revolt. Contingents of anti-British fighters, concentrated around reluctant Bahadur Shah, proclaimed his restored Mughal imperial rule and drove the British from Shahjahanabad and much of north India. After four months of bloody fighting, however, Britons and those Indian soldiers who obeyed them recaptured Shahjahanabad and imprisoned Bahadur Shah. Vengeful British officers executed many of his sons and put him on trial for treason against the British. They

HALL OF PRIVATE AUDIENCE, DELHI.

Empty Diwan-i Khas, Shahjahanabad, *c.* 1890[27]

also forced almost all Indians out of Shahjahanabad, desecrated the Jami' Mosque, garrisoned and held Christian thanksgiving services in the Red Fort and leveled the surrounding neighborhood to create a clear-fire zone. Further, the British finally ended the Mughal Empire by exiling Bahadur Shah to Burma, where he died in 1862. Yet, many historians and other commentators have highlighted the significance of the Mughal Empire, from its origins until today.

11

CONTESTED MEANINGS OF THE MUGHAL EMPIRE INTO THE TWENTY-FIRST CENTURY

... the Great Mogul ...is allowed £120,000 a year ... a most heavy charge upon a people living on rice, and deprived of the first necessaries of life .... His authority does not extend beyond the walls of his palace, within which the Royal idiotic race, left to itself, propagates as freely as rabbits ... There he sits on his throne, a little shriveled yellow old man, trimmed in a theatrical dress ... much like that of the dancing girls of Hindostan. On certain State occasions, the tinsel-covered puppet issues forth .... Strangers have to pay a fee ... as to any other saltimbanque [street performer] exhibiting himself in public; while he, in his turn, presents them with turbans, diamonds, etc. [But] the Royal diamonds are ... ordinary glass, grossly painted [and] break in the hand like gingerbread.

Karl Marx (1853)[1]

History writing often reflects the ideological and personal perspectives of the historian and also of the major sources used. More than in any previous state in South Asia, the Mughal Empire's emperors and officials themselves produced both substantial and often highly contested historical writing and also rich primary sources, including written, artistic, architectural and numismatic. Further, so significant has been the Empire for South Asia, the Islamic world and the West that diverse historians from each have written extensively about it, from its earliest years to the present. Each historian explicitly or implicitly locates the Empire in larger contexts, informed by his or her particular methodology. We can consider the most prominent of these histories, arranged by broad chronological period: the Mughal Empire's rise; its fragmentation; the British high colonial period; and post-independence India, Pakistan and Bangladesh (all three nations lying within the Empire's territories).

RISE THROUGH THE LATE SEVENTEENTH CENTURY

Mughal Emperors and their courtiers created extensive representations of their significance in human history. Indeed, they crafted and proclaimed—on paper, in stone and in metal—Mughal sovereignty descending from Chingiz Khan and Timur, with a proven record of conquests and other achievements. Official publicists also embedded the Empire in the cosmologies of their subjects. These historical validations helped convince many diverse Indians to support and serve the Mughal dynasty.

Emperors commissioned and supervised official court historians who produced year-by-year records and narratives. Three emperors personally penned their own detailed memoirs, with varying degrees of candor and objectivity. Even illiterate Emperor Akbar directed anyone from his court or household who had personally known his ancestors to write or dictate a factual account of them. Many contemporary, non-official historians also recorded and analysed imperial events of their time.

Mughal historians often built on long-established Persianate historio-graphical traditions. In particular, they used the genres *waqai'* and *tarikh*.[2] Waqai' favored events presented in dated chronological sequence. Authors using the more interpretive tarikh genre accepted that God's will directed outcomes, but they narrated the deeds of humans on earth, usually with precisely dated events arranged sequentially, like today's conventional political histories. Distinctively, an imperial tarikh usually begins by invoking Allah, often followed by a political genealogy from the Prophet Muhammad directly (or from important earlier Muslim rulers) via Timur down to the main subject, the current emperor. Some genealogies also incorporated the Mughal dynasty's descent from the foremother of the Mongols, who was impregnated by divine light. An innovation during Akbar's reign was to transcend this Islamic framework by identifying him as the culmination of all humanity that began with Adam or Hindu deities.[3] Out of respect, deceased Mughal emperors had posthumous names, indicating their continued existence in heaven. Like many European historians of that time, Mughal authors presupposed that history's purpose was to teach moral lessons from past events. Some historians wrote about events specific to their province or personal experience, but dedicated their narrative to the emperor, evidently intending it to bring their own accomplishments to his august attention.[4]

So rich was the Empire's historiographical activity that its own historians often generated contradictory accounts. Most famously, the laudatory account of Emperor Akbar's reign by his accomplished amanuensis, Abu-al-Fazl, often clashed in fact and analysis with the generally critical account of Akbar by rival courtier, Badauni, in his 'Secret History' (not revealed until Akbar was safely dead).[5] Most Mughal imperial histories describe every decision and crucial action as done intentionally—or misguidedly—by the all-powerful emperor himself. Hence, these make the Empire appear highly centralized.

The Mughal dynasty sponsored the acquisition and production of manuscripts from many traditions. By commissioning Arabic- and Persian-language collections of fatwas and other Islamic religious texts, emperors located themselves in the lineage of exemplary Muslim rulers. Emperors, especially but not exclusively Akbar, also directed courtiers to translate works from the Sanskrit genres of *itihasa* (a largely chronological narrative of 'history,' mainly the actions on earth of humans, including gods incarnated as humans) and *purana* (a sequential account ranging over eons, from the origin of the universe through its cosmic cycles of creation and destruction, the lives of deities, down to human dynasties). When Portuguese and later other Europeans reached the imperial court, Akbar directed them to write a biography of Christ in Persian and to help translate parts of the Christian Bible.[6] When emperors conquered a region, they collected its local histories. Emperors and princes also patronized works in popular regional languages. Ever eclectic in buttressing their own sovereignty, Mughal emperors incorporated motifs and images from Islamic, Hindu and Christian sacred histories, including through visual arts.

Emperors also valued the imperial library which, in addition to chronicles, contained religious tracts, high literature, 'mirrors' [guiding manuals] for princes and courtiers, extensive albums and collections of fine paintings (most with historical or documentary purpose). The imperial court also used architecture, court newsletters, coins and other media to publicize widely the reigning emperor's titles and ideology. Further, the extensive central and provincial secretariats produced and archived the vast bodies of written records of daily events at court and across the Empire, copies of orders and judicial judgments and receipts of payments to and from the treasury. All these provide primary sources for Mughal historians, and subsequent historians ever since.

Additionally, many imperial subjects, people living adjacent to the Mughal Empire and also foreign visitors produced their own accounts, using a range of historical genres and languages. For example, the fascinating Hindi verse autobiography by Jain jewelry merchant Banarsidas described his life, feelings and relations with Mughal officials and emperors.[7] Afghan, Maratha, Rajput, Sikh and other rulers and landholders across north and central India patronized oral and written historical accounts of their sometimes antagonistic relationship with the Empire, using imperial and also regional genres and concepts of authority.[8] The Deccan sultanates and also west and Central Asian visitors generated their own histories that showed their perspectives, often following Persianate genres.[9] Other regional accounts reflect their own conceptions of the nature and purpose of history-writing.[10]

For instance, Rajput rajas had long sponsored their own historians using oral or written narratives in Sanskrit, Rajasthani, Braj Basha and other language traditions. Their goal was to highlight the origin and accomplishments of their patron's clan. Such Rajput dynastic histories shifted as their authors emulated Mughal imperial histories—highlighting human rather than divine ancestry and their patron's individual achievements.[11] When the patron joined the Empire, his historians incorporated the emperor: the greater the emperor, the greater the Rajput patron who now served him. Elided was the willing or forced provision of Rajput princesses as the emperor's wives.

Those who viewed the Empire from the outside also produced variant images of it. Safavid, Uzbek, Ottoman and other Muslim officials and historians related the Mughal Empire and its origin to their own states, often judging theirs superior. Some Muslim Asian visitors wrote about their travels and adventures within the Empire; their accounts often differed from imperial representations of the same events.[12]

From early after the foundation of the Empire onward, European Christians—including missionaries, merchants, diplomats and adventurers—compiled extensive accounts of it, either from first- or second-hand evidence. Many European views were informed by Christian Europe's long and often antagonistic relationships with Muslims in Eastern Europe and the Mediterranean. Hence, in their writings, the Muslim character of the Empire, as well as the Hinduism of most of its subjects, often appeared in critical contrast to Christianity (although some European Catholics and Protestants favored Islam or Indic religions over each other). Missionary accounts especially struggled to refute Islam and deprecate Hinduism, with the goal of converting South Asians and also convincing Christians of their own superiority.[13]

Another recurrent motif in early European accounts of the Empire was its exoticism, with attractive features like overwhelming wealth in natural and human resources. India appeared a land of fabulous wealth, with vast territories producing spices, grain, and minerals beyond the scale of Europe. Imperial armies of soldiers and artisans dwarfed those of European rulers. Further, the vast majority of Europeans who ventured to the Empire were young men, often perceiving it in hyper-sexual ways: the emperor's imagined unlimited sexual license and the contradictory fantasy of huge harems of unloved women (and the clever ways that the European author allegedly caught sight of them). Further, the relatively scanty clothing (as judged by Europeans) worn by some Indian women in public produced shock or titillation or both. Europeans also noted alleged abuses of Indian women by Indian men, particularly sati, inspiring varying degrees of wonder, repugnance and horror. In Europe, many playwrights, poets and other writers of fiction or other social commentary created powerful visions of the Empire, often based on a loose reading of European travelers' accounts.

However, predominant European attitudes toward the Empire became more deprecatory over the seventeenth century, especially as European economic, military and political power rose in relative terms in India and globally. Concepts of Oriental despotism and moral corruption increasingly informed European accounts, especially when these authors used their image of the Mughal Empire to comment on conditions or policies in their contemporary

European kingdom. For instance, in the early seventeenth century, Frenchman François Bernier sought to influence his government to cease revenue farming and also royal confiscation of private property, both policies he attributed to the injudicious Mughal Empire.[14] Some European writers came from countries with no realistic political ambitions in India, like the early-seventeenth-century Venetian adventurer Niccolao Manucci; such authors often featured their own adventures.[15] But English, French and Dutch writers, in particular, often sought information about the Empire for profit and political advantage.[16] As these European travelers' accounts became widely known through print, stereotypes about the Orient proliferated and more European men desired to venture there.[17] From the early eighteenth century onward, the historiography produced by the Mughal Empire and by those in and around it broadly shifted due to the Empire's own fragmentation and the rise of rival powers, both South Asian and European.

THE EIGHTEENTH CENTURY THROUGH THE MUGHAL DYNASTY'S END

Increasingly over the eighteenth century, people oriented toward the Mughal court used history and other literature to explain their declining condition and advocate responses to it. An entire genre of Indo-Persian and Hindustani literature, called *Shahr ashob* ('urban misfortune'), bemoaned the evident and accelerating decay experienced in Shahjahanabad and other former imperial centers. These authors, often from courtier or service-elite families, savored the past in contrast to the degraded present. However, some who still received incomes from the imperial court and its remnant administration highlighted compensating cultural achievements.[18] Leading Muslim theologians, most notably Shah Wali Ullah, attributed contemporary problems in the Mughal Empire (as well as in the Safavid and Uzbek Empires) to deviations from Islam. Such reformers and scholars thus sought a deeper understanding of the moral history of the Muslim community— globally and particularly within the Mughal Empire—in order to recover Islamic strengths through purification.[19] More progressively, Syed Ahmad Khan in 1846–7 adopted European-style scientific archaeological methods in order to document systematically, for his fellow Muslims and British employers, the architectural achievements of his fellow Muslims in Delhi.[20]

Indian authors patronized by a regional successor state recounted its history as it effectively broke away from the Empire, but still nominally belonged to it.[21] Some of these Indian historians partly incorporated European historiography to diagnose the causes for British rule's rapid expansion. Highlighting European military and other technological advances while seeking to preserve their own society's moral core, they moved their readers toward a synthesis of Indic, Islamic and Christian European cultures.[22] Increasingly, Indian historians were directly sponsored by British officials seeking an insider's knowledge about the rulers and society they confronted and conquered.[23]

By the late eighteenth century, some Indian writers began to incorporate Europe into Indian history, either from hearsay or based on the author's personal experience in Europe. As soon as European ships created a direct sea-link with India, travelers from India ventured to Europe. For the first two-and-a-half centuries, those who returned to India brought back only oral reports of European history, geography and society. Following imperial envoy I'tisam-ud-Din's 1784 autobiographical travel narrative about Britain, dozens of Indian authors wrote in Persian, Arabic, English, or Hindustani about their personal experiences in Europe.[24] Some followed the Persian-language *rihla* genre of autobiographical travel narrative with inclusion of moral lessons and poetic quotations. Others adapted English-style journalistic genres. Each author chose the language and genre he felt was appropriate for his intended audience, with some writing dissimilar accounts for different readerships.[25]

Conversely, early British Orientalists, in both India and Britain, studied Persian, Sanskrit and other Indian language texts (and employed Indian scholars to guide and translate for them) with the aim of gaining mastery over the Empire and over Indic and Islamic cultures more broadly. Some Europeans wrote with insights from their own participation in contemporary politics and wars.[26] Other Orientalists projected their Euro-centric views onto their representations of India and its history. James Mill—who never visited India—highlighted in his *History of British India* (1803–18) the disorder of the eighteenth century that compelled British rule.[27] This influential work reinforced the pattern that would become institutionalized of partitioning Indian history into the 'Hindu Ancient,' 'Muslim Medieval' and 'British Modern' periods. (Even today, leading universities in India teach 'Medieval History,' meaning the Mughal Empire and Delhi Sultanate.)

The Emperor and his court, even while confined to Shahjahanabad, remained for many Europeans a fascinating combination of the exotic and the decadent. Numerous European tourists observed the Emperor (women tourists also visited his harem), making gifts of nazr and obtaining *khilat*s as a curious 'Oriental' experience, without valuing these rituals' political significance. Increasingly, however, for British colonial authorities, the worth of the Emperor—as a 'decadent relic' contrasting with 'modernizing' British rule—declined, while the expense of pensioning him and his family remained high.

In 1853, Karl Marx himself deprecated the Emperor in colorful language for American newspaper readers as an effeminate and decadent parasite, preserved by the British government, thus stifling India's progress (see epigram).[28] More expansively, Marx identified the 'Asiatic mode of production' as a stagnant stage needing replacement by capitalism before India could enter world history. Thus, Marx condemned the British for preserving this imperial relic, and also for imperialistically annexing its various provinces into the British Empire.

Many Anglophone historians regarded the expanding British regime as the morally and technologically worthier successor to the Mughal dynasty. Studying the Empire would provide salutary lessons on how the British could build on it, while avoiding its faults. For example, in 1854, William Erskine explained his motivation for studying Mughal history: 'a nation possessing such an empire as that of the British in India ought to have some ampler record of the transactions of the different dynasties which preceded their own …. The House of Taimur [is] a natural foundation for the modern history of India.'[29] During the Empire's last year and thereafter, a wide range of people appreciated its significance, for a variety of often conflicting reasons.

THE BRITISH RAJ, 1857–1947

In 1857, many north Indians rose up against the British, with the Mughal Emperor as the most visible focal point for collective action. The bloody conflict nearly drove the British from Hindustan and was punctuated by brutal massacres by all sides, deeply affecting British and Indian accounts of each other. Long known by its British description as the 'Sepoy Mutiny,' instead some early twentieth-century Indian nationalists demanded it be called 'The First War for Indian Independence.'[30] Significantly, while these events terminated the Mughal dynasty, they also reinforced the Empire's powerful cultural significance. Given the Empire's extent and complexity, and the vast available evidence about it, diverse people have subsequently interpreted and represented the Empire according to their own understandings and interests.

During 1857 and soon thereafter, most Britons rallied together and envisioned the Emperor at the center of dark conspiracies. They wondered how a man they had dismissed as a decrepit octogenarian had been so inspiring to his allegedly frenzied followers. Many Britons concluded that analysis of the history of his Empire would reveal the deep Indian racial fanaticism and cultural need for Oriental despotism. This interpretation of Mughal history seemed to show that only the imperial state was active and the ruled society eternally stagnant. Hence many Britons believed that the British 'Raj' (which replaced the East India Company in 1858) should rule but its Indian subjects remain passive.

British colonial officials studied and adapted Mughal imperial protocols for many pompous ceremonies, especially when dealing with the hundreds of remaining 'feudal' Indian princes under British indirect rule. For instance, in 1877, Victoria proclaimed herself *Qaisar-i Hind* ('Caesar/Empress of India')—although she was still only Queen in the United Kingdom where emperors were considered archaic.[31] Her Viceroy in India staged an elaborate Mughal-British-style imperial coronation, as did some of her successors who travelled to India. The British intentionally created their imperial capital, New Delhi (built 1911–31), adjacent to Mughal Shahjahanabad. Thus, many Britons saw themselves as the Mughal Empire's more modern heir.

Further, the 1857 anti-British movement that centered on the Emperor mobilized Muslims and Hindus together. Hence, the British Raj determined to prevent the recurrence of such collective action through 'divide and rule' policies, especially protecting the Muslim minority against the Hindu majority. These British policies deepened with the emergence of Indian nationalism whose leaders were predominantly middle-class but high-caste Hindus.

Various British colonial officials devoted themselves to translating original Mughal sources into English and publishing them, thus making their implicit lessons for the British Empire more widely available, with a teleology toward the British Raj.[32] Prominent is Elliot's massive, eight-volume collection of excerpted translations from Persian texts, *The History of India as Told by Its Own Historians*.[33] Over half of the volumes are dedicated to the Mughal period, with the selections emphasizing the Empire's Islamic identity and highlighting endemic Muslim versus Hindu conflicts. Such works tried to make the British Raj seem necessary in order to limit religious violence. But these British scholar-officials largely presented these sources without considering their production conventions and authorial goals. This Positivist approach reflected Rankian historical methodology: 'giving a faithful statement of facts, to let them speak for themselves,' according to Erskine in his biography of Babur and Humayun.[34] Other European scholars, including Karl Marx and Max Weber, drew upon such work to incorporate this image of Mughal India in their universalist models.

Especially from the late nineteenth century onward, Indian nationalists increasingly recognized that writing Indian history should not be an exclusively British enterprise. Hence, growing numbers of Indian scholars committed themselves to researching and writing their own pre-colonial history, with the Mughal Empire as a major subject. Some sought to understand why the Empire had weakened and succumbed to British colonialism. This approach often highlights disorders and communal antagonisms from 'Alamgir onward. Especially influential was Sir Jadunath Sarkar who used extensive primary sources to develop his own analysis of the Empire, especially during its final stages, with the rise of the Hindu Maratha confederacy.

On their part, many Muslim nationalists followed Sir Syed Ahmad Khan in emphasizing Muslims as a community loyal to the British but separate from Hindus (this developed into the 'two nation' model). In 1877, he founded the Muhammadan-Anglo Oriental College at Aligarh (now Aligarh Muslim University) to advance his Muslim community through Anglicization and also preservation of its distinctive history in South Asia. Aligarh scholars collected and analysed Persian-language sources that demonstrated how the Mughal Empire functioned. Some argued the imperial core was strong when unified but weak when factionalized, with lessons for the current Muslim community.[35]

Liberal-nationalist Indian historians also studied the Empire for its contemporary implications. Many studied in Britain and shared British presuppositions, but reversed the valance—their teleology led to the Indian nation. Among the most widely read and influential was Jawaharlal Nehru (independent India's first prime minister, 1947–64) but professional historians also had important voices in public discourse by providing a congenial model of the Empire as a centralized Indian state with a composite Indian culture.[36] Many highlighted Akbar's Indian synthesis as admirably secularist—contrasted with 'Alamgir's religious divisiveness—but regarded the Empire as feudal, hence an obstacle to India's national reunification.

Contrasting representations of the Empire aided Muslim nationalists. They argued that heretic Akbar—by adopting Hindu customs—created fatal weakness in the Empire by divorcing it from Islam, which 'Alamgir's later countermeasures could not fully reverse. Hence, these historians and politicians advocated restored rule by the Muslim community, temporarily lost by the Empire's collapse, in the separate nation of Pakistan, created through Partition in 1947.

POST-INDEPENDENCE

The extensive violence of the Partition of Pakistan from India in 1947 reinforced and reconfigured various approaches to Mughal imperial history. During Partition, millions died and more than 10 million became refugees—most Hindus and Sikhs fleeing Pakistan and many Muslims fleeing India. Prominent issues that emerged after independence include how distinctively Muslim or else Indian the Empire was and how the perspectives of all who comprised it could be recovered.

The prime ideological claims for the creation of Pakistan were the historically distinct identity of the Muslim community and its long dominance in the subcontinent. Hence, many Pakistani scholarly and popular histories and government-sponsored textbooks present their nation as the successor to the Sunni Muslim-ruled Mughal Empire: the eastern bastion of Islamic states that extended west across north Africa.[37] Further, Christians and Hindus had worked to bring down that Muslim Empire, with lessons for today's Pakistan. The counterpart for

Bangladesh—formerly East Pakistan before its 1971 secession—was de facto independent Mughal Bengal that also succumbed to treacherous British imperialism in the late eighteenth century.[38]

In India, the Mughal Empire remains the subject of extensive popular debate and also scholarly research from a number of perspectives. The politically motivated Hindutva ('Hindu-ness') movement—led by the Rashtriya Swayamsevak Sangh (RSS) and its cultural wing, the Vishva Hindu Parishad (VHP)—regards undivided India as the Hindu homeland, with Mughal invaders as predatory and oppressive foreigners. Hindutva slogans characterize all Muslims in India today as alien 'sons of Babur,' regardless of their actual ancestry. In Ayodhya, multiple VHP assaults finally managed in 1992 to destroy the 'Baburi mosque' (erected in 1527 on the alleged site of the birthplace of divine Lord Ram). In contrast, Maratha Emperor Shivaji appears as a champion of Hindu-based Indian nationalism who fought off Mughal imperialism. During periods when the RSS-supported Bharatiya Janata Party has been in office, its administration has revised government-approved textbooks and other official histories to advance its representation of the Mughal Empire.

Indian prime ministers celiver the Independence Day address to the nation from the Lahore Gate of Shahjahanabad's Red Fort

In contrast, secularist Indian politicians and cultural leaders have worked to incorporate the Mughal Empire as a vital part of the nation's history. During the first decades after independence, progressive cultural critics who sought an indigenous (but not a Hindu-revivalist) line for the new nation drew on Mughal art and architecture to provide the spirit, but not exact models or motifs, for 'modern' India.[39] Jawaharlal Nehru began the tradition of the Prime Minister delivering the annual Independence Day address from the ramparts of Shahjahanabad's Red Fort. Other Mughal-built forts, tombs, mosques and other structures still stand as integral parts of life across the Indian nation.[40] The Archaeological Survey of India, Indian National Archive and National Museum all professionally preserve materials from the Empire as India's heritage.

Much scholarly research and writing on the Empire has emerged from India's leading universities. Among them, Aligarh Muslim University's Centre of Advanced Study in History has produced many justly influential historians with mastery of Persian sources, most prominently Irfan Habib.[41] Often Aligarh-trained scholars use Marxist-influenced analysis that features economics rather than religious identity. For example, class struggle between overburdened peasants and the oppressive imperial administration plus declines in agricultural productivity feature as prime causes of Mughal weakness. Scholars who draw primarily on Persian-language texts and documents produced by the imperial court tend to highlight the agency of the Mughal center and its institutions and ideologies.

Other important scholars in South Asia and internationally have also contributed to ongoing research and analysis about the Empire using a range of primary sources and historiographical approaches and methodologies, often stressing different factors or disagreeing over interpretation.[42] Economic historians highlight issues ranging from local market price trends to larger global trade and flows of bullion. Art and architecture historians read the paintings, buildings and ornamentation commissioned by various emperors, courtiers, noblewomen and others to decipher the influences and goals of patron and producer. Some scholars use Persian-language sources to reveal continued trade, cultural and migration links with other Asian Muslim empires, especially the Uzbeks and Safavids; this helps explain why Mughal emperors welcomed Turani immigrants and their descendants as a substantial proportion of mansabdars and continued to launch costly (and futile) military expeditions to recover their dynastic homeland. Similarly, diplomatic and military rivalry with the Safavids continued as long as both dynasties could sustain it, while Irani immigrants were always a major component among the high mansabdars.

Many social and cultural scholars concentrate on the people and ideologies interacting within the Empire. Some highlight how the uneven assimilation of indigenous Indians determined the Empire's trajectory: Rajputs and a few other elite, high-caste Hindus were initially amalgamated into the inner core; however, few lower-caste Hindus or lower-class Muslims were ever incorporated, and many Deccanis remained alienated.[43] Other scholars feature the Empire's periodic anti-Hindu discriminatory policies.[44] In contrast, yet other historians emphasize the Empire as Indian, including through imperial Rajput marriages, evolving court rituals and imperial ideologies, and the vast number of Indians who entered the imperial household, administration and army.[45] Moving below the conventional focus on emperors and mansabdars, the vital roles of Indian scribes and merchants become visible and the Empire appears more porous, as various people and ideas flowed into and out of it.[46]

Drawing on provincial or local sources, including those in regional languages, produces more decentralized models of the Empire. Scholars concentrating at these levels show the Empire as an arena for pragmatic compromises and collaborations among lower-level officials and local magnates, merchants and other power-holders.[47] From this perspective, localities collectively composed the Mughal state, but they also existed outside it, with their own on-going histories. Some scholars especially analyse popular oral and vernacular accounts to focus on those whom the Empire ruled, featuring their agency and perspectives.[48] While the influential Subaltern Studies school of neo-Marxist Gramscian interpretation overwhelmingly concentrates on the British colonial period, Gautam Bhadra has shown how to recover popular perspectives through reading imperial texts against the grain.[49] Cultural historians have deconstructed even elite texts to recover the texts' own histories, considering how and why each was produced, the presuppositions inherent in its genre, what its author could or could not express, and how it was consumed by being acquired, preserved, and read silently or aloud—alone or in communal settings.[50]

Scholars working on the British colonial period tend to regard the Empire retrospectively. They show how most parts of the world began connecting into increasingly integrated economic, political and cultural networks from the arrival of Vasco da Gama in 1498 (predating Babur) onward. Various scholars concentrating on British colonialism find different degrees of continuity and change from the Mughal Empire, with the eighteenth century as the time of major transitions as diverse Indians reoriented from the Empire toward the incoming Europeans.[51] Further, comparative perspectives raise questions about the 'modernity' of Mughal Empire (versus its contemporary states in Europe and Asia) and also about why European and Asian economies underwent dramatically diverging developments.[52]

Significantly, scholars have increasingly come together globally to form discourse communities, exchanging ideas and engaging in debates over shared engagement with Mughal history. Especially since World War II, U.S.-based scholars have increasingly participated, in part initiated by people who served in India and in part by growing awareness of the economic, political and cultural significance of South Asia on the world stage.[53] A substantial number of leading scholars from South Asia have moved to universities in Europe or America. The rich and extensive source material available from and about the Empire has attracted international scholars who specialize in the exciting new fields of environmental, gender, cultural, new military, technological and world history. New insights from all these fields are continuing to revise and deepen our understanding of what the Mughal Empire meant and currently means.

Specialist historians will recognize how this book has benefited from a vast range of contributions from a variety of approaches. The reference notes and bibliography will indicate how readers can explore specific topics in far more depth than an introductory survey like this could include. This dynamic field of history will continue to be enriched by new approaches and further new innovative historical research. Ideally, readers of this *Short History* will be intrigued and contribute their own studies of the Mughal Empire.

Notes

Introduction: The Mughal Empire's Dynamic Composition in Time and Space

1 Maddison: *Contours*, Appendix I-A.
2 Moin: *Millennial*.
3 Subrahmanyam: 'Mughal.'
4 Abu'l-Fazl: *Makatabat*, letter (3 September 1586), p. 33.

Chapter 1: Babur until His Conquest of North India in 1526

1 Babur: *Baburnama*, p. 332.
2 Ibid., p. 279.
3 For biographies, see Anooshahr: 'Author'; Dale: *Garden*; Erskine: *History*; Mohibbul Hasan: *Babur*; Moin: *Millennial*, 'Peering'; Williams: *Empire*.
4 Babur: *Baburnama*, p. 102.
5 Ibid., p. 59.
6 See: Balabanlilar: 'Begims'; Gulbadan: *History*; Lal: *Domesticity*, 'Historicizing.'
7 Babur: *Baburnama*, p. 35.
8 Ibid., p. 39.
9 Ibid., p. 93.
10 Dale: 'Poetry.'
11 Babur: *Baburnama*, p. 138.
12 Ibid., pp. 169, 180.
13 Ibid., p. 414.
14 Ibid., pp. 62, 414; Gulbadan: *History*, p. 89.
15 Babur: *Baburnama*, pp. 54, 239, 257, 263; Gulbadan: *History*, pp. 90, 276.
16 Babur: *Baburnama*, p. 273; Gulbadan: *History*, pp. 9, 266–7.
17 Gulbadan: *History*, p. 97.
18 Babur: *Baburnama*, p. 302.
19 Streusand: *Islamic*.
20 Babur: *Baburnama*, p. 372.
21 Ibid., p. 186.
22 Ibid., p. 329.
23 Ibid., p. 320.
24 Ibid., p. 324.

25 Ibid., pp. 314, 323.
26 Ibid., p. 322.
27 Ibid., p. 327.
28 Ibid., p. 328.
29 Ibid., p. 353; Gulbadan: *History*, pp. 95–6.
30 Satyal: *Mughal*, p. 50.
31 Babur: *Baburnama*, pp. 353–4.

Chapter 2: Indians and Emperor Babur Create the Mughal Empire, 1526–30

1 Jahangir: *Tuzuk*, vol. 2, p. 141.
2 Talbot: 'Becoming.'
3 Oberoi: *Construction*, p.174.
4 Chetan Singh: 'Forests.'
5 Babur: *Baburnama*, p. 334.
6 Ibid., pp. 373–80, 383; Williams: *Empire*, p. 152.
7 Babur: *Baburnama*, pp. 387, 397; Dale: *Garden*, p. 351.
8 Anooshahr: 'King.'
9 Jahangir: *Tuzuk*, vol. 1, p. 55.
10 Babur: *Baburnama*, pp. 363, 372.
11 Ibid., pp. 395, 397.
12 Ibid., p. 396.
13 Ibid., p. 409.
14 Eaton: 'Kiss.'
15 Babur: *Baburnama*, pp. 410, 425; Dale and Paynd: 'Ahrari'; Foltz: 'Central'; Moin: 'Peering.'
16 Asher: *Architecture*, p. 37; Babur: *Baburnama*, pp. 359–60, 416–18; Dale: *Garden*, pp. 426–7.
17 Babur: *Baburnama*, p. 351.
18 Dale: 'Steppe,' p. 49.
19 Dale: *Garden*, pp. 426–7, 431.
20 Babur: *Baburnama*, p. 351.
21 Masson: *Narrative*, vol. 2, p. 238.

Chapter 3: Emperor Humayun and Indians, 1530–40, 1555–6

1 Dughlat: *Tarikh*, p. 283b.
2 Gulbadan: *History*; Lal: *Domesticity*; Mukhia: *Mughals*, pp. 113–55.
3 Moin: 'Peering.'
4 Abu-l-Fazl: *Akbar*, vol. 1, pp. 314, 644–51.
5 Khwandamir: *Qanun*.
6 Ishwari Prasad: *Life*, pp. 52–3.
7 Babur: *Baburnama*, p. 362.
8 Desoulières: 'Mughal.'
9 Dughlat: *Tarikh*, p. 284a.
10 Aftabachi: *Tazkirat*, p. 81.
11 Ibid.; Ishwari Prasad: *Life*, p. 177.

12 Dughlat: *Tarikh*, pp. 286b–287b.
13 Ibid., pp. 283b–284a; Mushtaqi: *Waqʻiat*, p. 73.
14 Jahangir: *Tuzuk*, vol. 2, pp. 62–3.
15 Abbas Khan: *Tarikh*, pp. 331–2; Babur: *Baburnama*, pp. 427, 430.
16 Abbas Khan: *Tarikh*, p. 330; Ahmad: *Tabaqat*, vol. 2, pp. 150–52.
17 Husain: *Nobility*, pp. 11–44; Sukumar Roy: *Bairam*.
18 Gulbadan: *History*, pp. 149–51.
19 Bayat: *Tarikh*, pp. 50–51; Gulbadan: *History*, p. 168; Monshi: *History*, vol. 1, p. 162.
20 Monshi: *History*, vol. 1, p. 163.
21 Sukumar Roy: *Humayun*.
22 Abbas Khan: *Tarikh*; Kolff: *Naukar*.
23 Abu-l-Fazl: *Akbar*, vol. 1, pp. 642–4.

Chapter 4: Emperor Akbar Makes Himself the Center of the Mughal Empire

1   Jahangir: *Tuzuk*, vol. 1, pp. 33–4.
2   Abu-l-Fazl: *Akbar*, vol. 2, pp. 70–72.
3   Iqtidar Alam Khan: 'Nobility,' Appendix I; Naqvi: *Urbanisation*, pp. 160–86.
4   Reis: *Travels*, pp. 55–7.
5   Faruqui: 'Forgotten.'
6   Abu al-Fazl: *Ain*, vol. 3, p. 383.
7   Bayat: *Tarikh*, vol. 2, pp. 95–101.
8   Ahmad: *Tabaqat*, pp. 198, 204; Vincent Smith: 'Death.'
9   Vincent Smith: 'Death.'
10 Siddiqui: *Mughal*, pp. 90–105.
11 Nizami: *Akbar*, p. 185; O'Hanlon: 'Kingdom'; Pandian: 'Predatory.'
12 Abu-l-Fazl: *Akbar*, vol. 2, pp. 253–4.
13 Husain: *Nobility*, Chapter 2.
14 Badauni: *Muntakhab*, vol. 2, pp. 29–30.
15 Ibn Hasan: *Central*, pp. 350–51; Gauri Sharma: *Prime*, pp. 30–33.
16 Abu-l-Fazl: *Akbar*, vol. 2, p. 307.
17 Taft: 'Honor'; Ziegler: 'Marvari,' 'Some.'
18 Abu-l-Fazl: *Akbar*, vol. 2, p. 242.
19 Badauni: *Muntakhab*, vol. 2, p. 352.
20 Ahsan Raza Khan: *Chieftains*, p. 207.
21 Busch: 'Portrait,' p. 294. See also Pauwels: 'Saint'; Talbot: 'Becoming,' 'Justifying'; Vanina: 'Madhavanala.'
22 Busch: 'Portrait,' p. 310.
23 Asher: 'Architecture'; Ziegler: 'Some.'
24 Taft: 'Honor,' pp. 223, 235n6.
25 Jahangir: *Tuzuk*, vol. 2, p. 181.
26 Bilgrami: 'Mughal'; Zaidi: 'Akbar's.'

Chapter 5: Emperor Akbar and His Core Courtiers Build the Mughal Administration and Army

1   Abu-l-Fazl: *Akbar*, vol. 2, p. 198.
2   Fox: *Kin*; Grover: *Collected*; S. Nurul Hasan: 'Position.'
3   Naqvi: *Urbanisation*, pp. 160–86.
4   Badaoni: *Muntakhab*, vol. 2, pp. 193–4. See also Ahmad: *Tabaqat*, p. 456; Qandhari: *Tarikh*, p. 231; Siddiqi: 'Classification.'
5   Banarsidasa: *Ardhakathanaka*, pp. 48, 177n.
6   Shivram: *Jagirdars*, p. 15.
7   Moosvi: 'Share,' 'Zamindars"; Siddiqi: 'Classification'; Wee: 'Semi-Imperial.'
8   Bayly: *Empire*, Chapter 1.
9   Raychaudhuri: *Bengal*; Siddiqi: *'Faujdar'*.
10 Badaoni: *Muntakhab*, vol. 2, p. 388.
11 Richards: *Document*.
12 Alam: *Languages*; Guha: 'Serving.'
13 Richards: *Mughal Empire*, p. 284.
14 Blake: 'Patrimonial.' C.f., Subrahmanyam: 'Mughal.'
15 Gordon: *Robes and*; *Robes of*; O'Hanlon: 'Manliness.'
16 Shivram: *Jagirdars*, pp. 57–8.
17 Badaoni: *Muntakhab*, vol. 2, pp. 190–91.
18 Koch: *Complete*; Dale: *Muslim*.
19 Abu al-Fazl: *Ain*, vol. 3, p. 399.
20 Abu-l-Fazl, *Akbar*, vol. 2, p. 282.
21 Sinha: *Raja*.
22 Kumudrajan Das: *Raja*.
23 Chandra: 'Some'; Subrahmanyam: 'Mughal'; Subrahmanyam and Bayly: 'Portfolio.'
24 Badaoni: *Muntakhab,* vol. 2, p. 65.
25 Banarsidasa: *Ardhakathanaka*, pp. 7–10.
26 Satyal: *Mughal*, pp. 69–70.

Chapter 6: Emperor Akbar's Courts, Ideologies, and Wars, by Main Capital

1   Monserrate: *Commentary*, p. 132.
2   Ansari: *Social*; Blake: *Shahjahanabad*; Rezavi: *Fatehpur*, pp. 29ff.
3   Hodges: *Travels*, facing p. 114.
4   Naqvi: *Urbanisation*, pp. 160–86, 286.
5   Delvoye: 'Image'; Wade: *Imaging*.
6   Abu-l-Fazl: *Akbar*, vol. 2, p. 445.
7   Beach: *Early*; Seyller: 'Workshop'; Verma: *Aspects*, vol. 1, pp. 50ff.
8   Badauni: *Muntakhab*, vol. 2, p. 165.
9   Brand and Lowry: *Fatehpur*; Nath: *Fatehpur*; Rezavi: *Fatehpur*; Rizvi: *Fathpur*; D.V. Sharma: *Archaeology*.
10 Badauni: *Muntakhab*, vol. 2, pp. 168–9.
11 Havell: *Handbook*, p. 156.
12 Farooqi: 'Moguls,' 'Six.'
13 Edmund Smith: *Moghul*, p. 112.

14 Haidar: 'Prices,' pp. 1–3.
15 Abu al-Fazl: *Ain*, vol.1, p. 165.
16 Ibid., p. 242.
17 Ahmad: *Tabaqat*, vol. 3, pp. 470–72; Badauni: *Muntakhab*, vol. 2, pp. 200–204; Rezavi: 'Religious.'
18 Badauni: *Muntakhab*, vol. 2, pp. 260–61. C.f., Ahmad: *Tabaqat*, vol. 3, pp. 511–12; Qandhari: *Tarikh*, p. 272.
19 Iqtidar Alam Khan: 'Akbar's'; O'Hanlon: 'Kingdom.'
20 Ahmad: *Tabaqat*, vol. 3, pp. 520–21; Abu-l-Fazl: *Akbar*, vol. 3, pp. 395–6.
21 Wright: *Catalogue*, Plate IV, no. 318.
22 Badauni: *Muntakhab*, vol. 2, pp. 276–7.
23 Ahmad: *Tabaqat*, vol. 3, pp. 523–4; Badauni: *Muntakhab*, vol. 2, pp. 279–80.
24 Blockmann, in Abul al-Fazl: *Ain*, vol. 1, pp. 168–87.
25 Ibn Hasan: *Central*; S. Nurul Hasan: *Religion*; Moin: *Millennial*.
26 Athar Ali: *Apparatus*; Naqvi: *Urbanisation*, Appendices A–B.
27 Mehta: 'Akbar'; Pollock: 'New'; Pushpa Prasad: 'Akbar.'
28 Abu al-Fazl: *Ain*, vol. 3, pp. 394–6; Iqtidar Alam Khan: 'Mughal.'
29 Richards: *Mughal Empire*, p. 47.
30 Alam and Subrahmanyam: 'Frank,' p. 463; Maclagan: *Jesuits*, p. 24; Monserrate: *Commentary*, p. 2.
31 Monserrate: *Commentary*, p. 28.
32 Koch: 'Symbolic'; Monserrate: *Commentary*, p. 126.
33 Abu al-Fazl: *Ain*, vol. 3, p. 42.
34 Carvalho: *Mir'at*.
35 Abu'l Fazl: *Makatabat*, pp. 8–11; Maclagan: *Jesuits*, p. 37; Monserrate: *Commentary*, pp. 159, 163–4.
36 Digby: 'Bayazid'; Farooqi: 'Moguls'; Monserrate: *Commentary*, pp. 166–90.
37 Abu al-Fazl: *Ain*, vol. 3, p. 394; Badauni: *Muntakhab*, vol. 2, p. 296.
38 Anooshahr: 'Dialogism'; Moin: *Millennial*, pp. 493–526.
39 Abu'l-Fazl: *Makatabat*, pp. 33–6; Badauni: *Muntakhab*, vol. 2, p. 319.
40 Bilgrami: 'Mughal'; Zaidi: 'Akbar's.'
41 Asher: *Architecture*; Bailey: 'Lahore'; Latif: *Lahore*.
42 Bailey: 'Indian'; Seyller: 'Workshop.'
43 Truschke: 'Mughal.'
44 Badauni: *Muntakhab*, vol. 2, pp. 413–14.
45 Kalhana: *Rajatarangini*.
46 Ernst: 'Muslim,' pp. 180–82.
47 Busch: 'Hidden.'
48 Chandra et al: 'Akbar.'
49 Badauni: *Muntakhab*, vol. 2, pp. 335–6.
50 Steingass: *Comprehensive*, s.v. Tauhid.
51 Iqtidar Alam Khan: 'Akbar's'; O'Hanlon: 'Kingdom.'
52 Badauni: *Muntakhab*, vol. 2, p. 336; Richards: *Mughal Empire*, p. 48; Rizvi: *Religious*.
53 Badauni: *Muntakhab*, vol. 2, p. 299.
54 Ibid., vol. 2, p. 375.
55 Ibid., vol. 2, p. 336.
56 Alvi: *Perspectives*, p. 13.
57 Moosvi: *Economy*, pp. 214–19; Athar Ali: *Apparatus*, p. xiii.

58 Moosvi: 'Estimate.'
59 Alam and Subrahmanyam: 'Deccan'; M. Siraj Anwar: *Mughals*; Firishta: *History*, vol. 1, p. 385.
60 Eaton: *Social*, pp. 231–81; Shyam: *Life*; Tamaskar: *Life*.
61 Banarsidasa: *Ardhakathanaka*, pp. 38–40.

Chapter 7: Emperor Jahangir and the Efflorescence of the Imperial Court, 1605–27

1   Jahangir: *Tuzuk*, vol. 1, p. 68.
2   Badauni: *Muntakhab*, vol. 2, p. 391.
3   Banarsidasa: *Ardhakathanaka*, pp. 18–21.
4   Badauni: *Muntakhab*, vol. 2, p. 390.
5   Beveridge: 'Sultan'; Faruqui: *Princes*, pp. 30–31.
6   Beach: *Mughal*, pp. 70–78; Faruqui: *Princes*, pp. 158–62; Seyller: 'Workshop'; Verma: *Aspects*, vol. 1, pp. 49–50.
7   Jahangir: *Tuzuk*, vol. 1, pp. 24–5.
8   Ibid., pp. 65ff.
9   Urwick: *Indian*, p. 166.
10 Fenech: 'Martyrdom.'
11 Jahangir: *Tuzuk*, vol. 1, p. 22.
12 Moosvi: *Economy*, pp. 195–200.
13 Athar Ali: *Apparatus*, p. xiv.
14 Shivram: *Jagirdars*, p. 15.
15 Siddiqi: *Land*.
16 Lefevre: 'Recovering.'
17 Jahangir: *Tuzuk*, vol. 2, pp. 6–7.
18 Wright: *Catalogue*, Plate VI, 1618–23 CE.
19 Ibid., vol. 1, 306–10.
20 Mukhia: *Mughals*, pp. 72–111; Najm-i Saini: *Advice*.
21 Lefevre: 'Recovering,' p. 461.
22 Jahangir: *Tuzuk*, vol. 1, pp. 306–10.
23 Beach: *Mughal*, pp. 78–110.
24 Seyller: 'Workshop,' p. 24.
25 Jahangir: *Tuzuk*, vol. 2, pp. 20–21.
26 Roe: *Embassy*, vol. 1, pp. 224–6.
27 Seyller: 'Mughal.'
28 Lefevre: '*Majalis*,' p. 274.
29 Jahangir: *Tuzuk*, vol. 2, pp. 98–9.
30 Lefevre: '*Majalis*.'
31 Asher: *Architecture*, p. 126.
32 Jahangir: *Tuzuk*, vol. 2, pp. 91–2; S. Nurul Hasan: *Religion*.
33 Jahangir: *Tuzuk*, vol. 1, pp. 267–8, 279.
34 Nathan: *Baharistan*, vol. 1, p. 25.
35 Moosvi: 'Mughal.'
36 Gokhale: 'Tobacco.'
37 Jahangir: *Tuzuk*, vol. 2, p. 369.
38 Nathan: *Baharistan*. See also Bhadra: 'Two.'
39 Jahangir: *Tuzuk*, vol. 1, p. 236.

40 Ibid., vol. 1, pp. 137–8, 144–5.
41 Findly: *Nur*; Lal: *Nur*.
42 Jahangir: *Tuzuk*, vol. 2, pp. 348ff.
43 Athar Ali: *Apparatus*.
44 Jahangir: *Tuzuk*, vol. 2, p. 351.
45 S. Nurul Hasan: *Religion*.
46 Athar Ali: *Apparatus*, p. xx.
47 Courtesy Gopal Aggarwal, http://gopal1035.blogspot.com
48 Asher: *Architecture*, pp. 127–33; Begley: 'Four.'
49 Wright: *Catalogue*, Plate VIII, 1625–8 CE.
50 Jahangir: *Tuzuk*, vol. 1, pp. 435–6.
51 Inayat Khan: *Shah*, pp. 333–4.
52 Jahangir: *Tuzuk*, vol. 2, p. 234.
53 Ibid., vol. 2, p. 236.
54 Monshi: *History*, vol. 1, pp. 1237, 1290–93.
55 Alam and Subrahmanyam: 'Envisioning.'
56 Chandra: *Medieval*, vol. 2, pp. 244–5; Richards: *Mughal*, p. 115; Faruqui: *Princes*.
57 Asher: *Architecture*, pp. 127–33.
58 (Exterior) Vincent Smith: *History*, fig. 241, p. 438; (Interior) Courtesy American Institute of Indian Studies.

Chapter 8: Emperor Shah Jahan and Building Up the Mughal Empire, 1628–58/66

1   Elliot: *History*, vol. 7, p. 45.
2   Chann: 'Lord'; Moin: *Millennial*.
3   Murray: *Handbook*, Plate I, facing p. 15.
4   Asher: *Architecture*, pp. 175–8.
5   Beach and Koch: *King*, p. 135.
6   Inayat Khan: *Shah*, p. 203.
7   Ibid.; Beach and Koch: *King*.
8   Beach and Koch: *King*.
9   Athar Ali: *Apparatus*, p. xvi.
10 Haider: 'Prices'; Moosvi, 'Expenditure.'
11 Inayat Khan: *Shah*, pp. 84–7, 117.
12 Ibid., p. 570.
13 Asher: *Architecture*, pp. 209–15; Begley and Desai: *Taj*; Koch: *Complete*.
14 Murray: *Handbook*, facing p. 172.
15 Asher: *Architecture*, pp. 191–204; Blake: *Shahjahanabad*.
16 Ibid., p. 196.
17 Urwick: *Indian*, p. 176.
18 Firdos Anwar: *Nobility*, pp. 188–9; Beach and Koch: *King*, p. 11.
19 Inayat Khan: *Shah*, pp. 278–89.
20 Athar Ali: *Apparatus*; Inayat Khan: *Shah*, pp. 221–32.
21 Foltz: 'Central,' 'Mughal.'
22 Inayat Khan: *Shah*, p. 335; Foltz: 'Mughal.'
23 Moosavi: 'Expenditure.'
24 Athar Ali: *Apparatus*, pp. xvi, xx; Firdos Anwar: *Nobility*; Inayat Khan: *Shah*, pp. 339–40; Richards: *Mughal*, pp. 143–5.

25 Moosavi: 'Estimate.'
26 Inayat Khan: *Shah*, pp. 510ff.
27 Athar Ali: *Apparatus*, p. 322; Hasrat: *Dara*; Inayat Khan: *Shah*, pp. 297, 505–6.
28 Begam: *Princess*.
29 Inayat Khan: *Shah*, pp. 309–14.
30 Ernst: 'Muslim'; Hasrat: *Dara*; Kinra: 'Infantilizing.'

Chapter 9: Expanding the Frontiers and Facing Challenges under Emperor 'Alamgir, 1658–1707

1 Saqi Mustaid Khan: *Maasir*, p. 169.
2 Ibid., p. 11.
3 Ibid., p. 155.
4 Ibid., p. 17.
5 Ibid., e.g., p. 78.
6 Ibid., p. 144.
7 Jadunath Sarkar: *Studies*, pp. 118–52.
8 'Alamgir: *Rukaat*, pp. 14–19; Jadunath Sarkar: *Studies*, p. 107.
9 Bokhari: *Imperial*.
10 Saqi Mustaid Khan: *Maasir*, p. 66.
11 Jadunath Sarkar: *History*, vol. 1, Introduction.
12 'Alamgir: *Rukaat*, pp. 14–19.
13 Brown: 'Did'; Schofield: 'Courtesan,' 'Reviving'; Saqi Mustaid Khan: *Maasir*, p. 45.
14 Caine: *Picturesque*, p. 124.
15 Asher: *Architecture*, pp. 257–9.
16 Murray: *Handbook*, facing p. 234.
17 Parodi: 'Bibi.'
18 Saqi Mustaid Khan: *Maasir*, p. 62.
19 Ibid., pp. 71–2.
20 Syan: *Sikh*.
21 Saqi Mustaid Khan: *Maasir*, pp. 36–7; Pearson: 'Shivaji.'
22 'Alamgir: *Rukaat*, pp. 166–8.
23 Saqi Mustaid Khan: *Maasir*, p. 53.
24 Athar Ali: *Apparatus*, p. 96.
25 Athar Ali: *Mughal*, pp. 17–25.
26 'Alamgir: *Rukaat*, p. 23.
27 Hallissey: *Rajput*.
28 Jadunath Sarkar: *History*, vol. 3, pp. 156–7, *Studies*, pp. 91–110.
29 Caine: *Picturesque*, p. 460.
30 Richards: *Mughal Administration*, 'Imperial.'
31 Richards and Rao: 'Banditry.'
32 Richards: 'Norms,' p. 286; Bhimsen: *Tarikh*.
33 Bhimsen: *Tarikh*, p. 233.
34 Farooqi: 'Moguls,' p. 198.
35 E.g., Harihar Das: *Norris*.
36 'Alamgir: *Rukaat*, pp. 73–4; Faruqui: *Princes*, pp. 281–308.
37 Jadunath Sarkar: *Short*, pp. 366–8.

Chapter 10: The Thinning of the Empire, 1707–1857

1 Cited in Dalrymple: *Last*, p. 300.
2 Alavi: *Eighteenth*; Pearson: 'Shivaji'; Richards: 'Imperial'; Jagdish Narayan Sarkar: *Study*; Subrahmanyam: 'Making.'
3 Calkins: 'Formation.'
4 Alam: *Crisis.*
5 Bhargava: *Decline*; Cheema: *Forgotten*; Irvine: *Later.*
6 Sangwan: *Jodhpur.*
7 Lakhnawi: *Shahnama*, pp. 5–6.
8 Nayeem: 'Working.'
9 Chatterji: 'Mughal'; Malik: 'Financial.'
10 Lakhnawi: *Shahnama*; Malik: *Mughal.*
11 Malik: *Reign.*
12 Alam and Subrahmanyam: 'Envisioning'; 'Witnesses.'
13 Bayly: *Indian*; Chandra: *Eighteenth*; Indrani Chatterjee: 'Slave's'; Datta: *Dutch*, *Survey*; Prakash: 'Dutch.'
14 Neamet Ullah: *History*; Ganda Singh: *Ahmad.*
15 Nur Muhammad: *Jang.*
16 Datta: *Shah*; Polier: *Shah.*
17 Hodges: *Travels*, facing p. 30.
18 Shah Alam II: 'Letter.' C.f., Buckler: *Legitimacy*; Fisher: *Counterflows*, pp. 86–90.
19 I'tesamuddin: *Wonders*; Gulfishan Khan: *Indian*, pp. 72–8.
20 National Archives of India: *Calendar*, vol. 3, pp. 84–5, 271.
21 Pernau and Jaffe: *Information.*
22 *Illustrated London News* (5 September 1857), p. 251.
23 Alam and Subrahmanyam: 'Envisioning.'
24 Fisher: *Counterflows*, pp. 250–59.
25 Fisher: 'Imperial.'
26 Fisher: *Inordinately*, p. 61.
27 Urwick: *Indian*, p. 174.

Chapter 11: Contested Meanings of the Mughal Empire into the 21st Century

1 Marx: 'East.'
2 For bibliographies, see Kamal Kishore Das: *Economic*; Elliot: *History*; D.N. Marshall: *Mughals*; Robinson: *Mughal.*
3 Mukhia: 'Time.'
4 E.g., Nathan: *Baharistan.*
5 Abu al-Fazl: *Ain*; Abu-l-Fazl: *Akbar*; Badauni: *Muntakhab.*
6 Carvalho: *Mir'at.*
7 Banarsidasa: *Ardhakathanaka.*
8 E.g., Alam and Subrahmanyam: *Indo-Persian*; Kumkum Chatterjee: *Cultures*; Curley: *Poetry*; Gordon: *Marathas*; Guha: 'Serving'; Wink: *Land.*
9 E.g., Alam and Subrahmanyam: 'Deccan'; Jadu Nath Sarkar: *Bengal.*
10 See Narayana Rao et al.: *Textures.*
11 Busch: 'Hidden'; Pauwels: 'Saint'; Talbot: 'Justifying'; Ziegler: 'Marvari.'
12 Alam and Subrahmanyam: *Indo-Persian*; Reis: *Travels.*

13 Correia-Alfonso: *Jesuit, Letters*; Guerreiro: *Jahangir*; Jarric: *Akbar*; Maclagan: *Jesuits*.
14 Bernier: *Travels*.
15 Manucci: *Memoirs*.
16 Pelsaert: *Jahangir's*; Roe: *Embassy*; Tavernier: *Travels*.
17 Hakluyt: *Hakluyt's*; Purchas: *Hakluytus*.
18 Mukhlis: *Mir'at*.
19 Rizvi: *Shah*; Syros: 'Early.'
20 Naim: 'Syed.'
21 E.g., Jadu Nath Sarkar: *Bengal*.
22 E.g., Sayid Ghulam Husain Khan: *Seir*.
23 E.g., Abu Talib Khan: *History*.
24 Fisher: 'From.'
25 Abu Talib Khan: *Masir*; 'Vindication.'
26 Francklin: *History*.
27 Mill: *History*.
28 Marx: 'East.'
29 Erskine: *History*, vol. 1, p. vii.
30 Savarkar: *Indian*.
31 Cohn: *Colonialism*.
32 E.g., Beveridge: 'Sultan'; Irvine: *Army, Later*; Moreland: *Agrarian, From*; Vincent Smith, *Akbar*, 'Death,' *History*; Williams: *Empire*.
33 Elliot: *History*.
34 Erskine: *History*, vol. 1, p. vii.
35 E.g., Siddiqi: *Land*.
36 E.g., Saran: *Provincial*; Tripathi: *Some*; Ibn Hasan: *Central*.
37 E.g., Qureshi: *Administration*.
38 E.g., Arshad: *Advanced*, pp. 132–7.
39 Devika Singh: 'Approaching.'
40 Kavuri-Bauer: *Monumental*.
41 Habib: *Agrarian, Atlas*.
42 For thoughtful historiographies see Alam and Subrahmanyam: *Mughal*; Iqtidar Alam Khan: 'State'; Subrahmanyam: 'Mughal.'
43 Iqtidar Alam Khan: 'State'; Pearson: 'Shivaji'; Richards: 'Imperial.'
44 Sri Ram Sharma: *Mughal, Religious*.
45 Alam: 'Mughals'; Dalrymple: *Last*; Eaton: *Rise*; Gilmartin and Lawrence: *Beyond*.
46 Haider: 'Norms'; Kinra: 'Master'; Scholfield: 'Courtesan,' 'Reviving.'
47 Alam: *Crisis*; Barnett: *North*; Das Gupta: *Indian*; Flores: 'Sea'; Farhat Hasan: *State*; Mukhia: 'Illegal'; Pearson: 'Political'; Rana: 'Dominant'; Shah: 'Political'; G.N. Sharma: *Mewar*; Chetan Singh: *Region*.
48 Busch: 'Hidden'; Mayaram: 'Mughal'; Pauwels: 'Saint'; Phukan: '"Through"'; Talbot: 'Justifying'; Ziegler: 'Marvari.'
49 Bhadra: 'Two'.
50 E.g., Anooshahr: 'Mughal'; Zutshi: *Kashmir's*, Chapter 2.
51 Alavi: *Eighteenth*; Bayly: *Indian, Rulers*; Chandra: *Eighteenth*; Leonard: '"Great"'; P.J. Marshall: *Eighteenth*; Stein: 'Eighteenth'; Washbrook: 'South.'
52 Subrahmanyam: *Explorations*.
53 Eaton: *Social*; Richards, *Mughal Empire*; Streusand: *Formation*.

Bibliography

Abu al-Fazl, *Ain-i Akbari*, tr. H. Blochmann, H.S. Jarrett, 3 vols (Calcutta: Asiatic Society of Bengal, 1873–94).

—— *Akbar Nama*, tr. H. Beveridge, 3 vols (Calcutta: Asiatic Society of Bengal, 1907–39).

—— *Makatabat-i Allami*, tr. Mansura Haidar (Delhi: Munshiram Manoharlal, 1998).

Aftabachi, Jawar, *Tazkiratul-Waqiat*, in *Three Memoirs of Humayun*, tr. W.M. Thackston (Costa Mesa: Mazda, 2009), pp. 71–175.

Ahmad, Khwaja Nizamuddin, *Tabaqat-i Akbari*, tr. Bajendranath De, ed. Bani Prasad, 3 vols (Delhi: Low Price, 1992).

Alam, Muzaffar, *Languages of Political Islam* (Chicago: University of Chicago Press, 2004).

—— 'Mughals, the Sufi Shaikhs and the Formation of the Akbari Dispensation,' *Modern Asian Studies*, 43/1 (2009): 135–74.

—— *Crisis of Empire in Mughal North India* (Delhi: Oxford University Press, 2013).

—— and Sanjay Subrahmanyam, 'Deccan Frontier and Mughal Expansion, c. 1600,' *Journal of the Economic and Social History of the Orient*, 47/3 (2004): 357–89.

—— 'Envisioning power,' *Indian Economic and Social History Review*, 43/2 (2006): 131–61.

—— *Indo-Persian Travels in the Age of Discovery* (Cambridge: Cambridge University Press, 2007).

—— 'Frank Disputations,' *Indian Economic and Social History Review*, 46/4 (2009): 457–511.

—— 'Witnesses and Agents of Empire,' *Journal of the Economic and Social History of the Orient*, 53/1 (2010): 393–423.

—— and Sanjay Subrahmanyam, eds, *Mughal State, 1526–1750* (Delhi: Oxford University Press, 1998).

'Alamgir, *Rukaat-i-'Alamgiri*, tr. Jamshid H. Bilimoria (London: Luzac, 1908).

Alavi, Seema, *Eighteenth Century in India* (Delhi: Oxford University Press, 2002).

Alvi, Sajida Sultana, *Perspectives on Mughal India Rulers, Historians, 'Ulama and Sufis* (New York: Oxford University Press, 2012).

Anooshahr, Ali, 'Mughal Historians and the Memory of the Islamic Conquest of India,' *Indian Economic and Social History Review*, 43/3 (2006): 275–300.

—— '"King Who Would Be Man",' *Journal of the Royal Asiatic Society*, 18 (2008): 327–40.

—— 'Author of One's Fate,' *Journal of the Economic and Social History of the Orient*, 49/2 (2012): 197–224.

—— 'Dialogism and Territoriality in a Mughal History of the Islamic Millennium,' *Journal of the Economic and Social History of the Orient*, 55/2–3 (2012): 220–54.

Ansari, Muhammad Azhar, *Social Life of the Mughal Emperors, 1526–1707* (Allahabad: Shanti Prakashan, 1974).

Anwar, Firdos, *Nobility under the Mughals (1628–1658)* (Delhi: Manohar, 2001).

Anwar, M. Siraj, *Mughals and the Deccan* (Delhi: BR, 2007).

Arshad, Mohammad, *Advanced History of Muslim Rule in Indo-Pakistan* (Dacca: Ideal, 1967).

Asher, Catherine, *Architecture of Mughal India* (Cambridge: Cambridge University Press, 1992).

—— 'Architecture of Raja Man Singh,' in *Powers of Art*, ed. Barbara Stoler Miller (Delhi: Oxford University Press, 2002), pp. 389–94.

Athar Ali, M., *Apparatus of Empire* (Delhi: Oxford University Press, 1985).

—— *Mughal Nobility under Aurangzeb* (New York: Oxford University Press, 2001).

Babur, *Baburnama*, tr. W.M. Thackston (New York: Modern Library, 2002).

Badauni, *Muntakhabu-t-Tawarikh*, 3 vols, tr. George S.A. Ranking, et al. (Delhi: Atlantic, 1990).

Bailey, Gauvin, 'Lahore *Mirat al-Quds* and the Impact of Jesuit Theatre on Mughal Painting,' *South Asian Studies*, 13/1 (1997): 31–44.

—— 'Indian Conquest of Catholic Art,' *Art Journal*, 57/1 (1998): 24–30.

Balabanlilar, Lisa, 'Begims of the Mystic Feast,' *Journal of Asian Studies*, 69/1 (2010): 123–47.

Banarsidasa, *Ardhakathanaka, Half a Tale*, tr. Mukund Lath (Jaipur: Rajasthan Prakrit Bharati Sansthan, 1981).

Barnett, Richard, *North India between Empires* (Berkeley: University of California Press, 1980).

Bayat, Bayazid, *Tarikh-i Humayun*, in *Three Memoirs of Humayun*, vol. 2. tr. W.M. Thackston (Costa Mesa: Mazda, 2009).

Bayly, C.A., *Indian Society and the Making of the British Empire* (Cambridge: Cambridge University Press, 1987).

—— *Rulers, Townsmen and Bazaars* (Cambridge: Cambridge University Press, 1988).

—— *Empire and Information* (Cambridge: Cambridge University Press, 1996).

Beach, Milo, *Early Mughal Paintings* (Cambridge: Harvard University Press, 1987).

—— *Mughal and Rajput* (Cambridge: Cambridge University Press, 1992).

—— and Ebba Koch, eds, tr. Wheeler Thackston, *King of the World* (London: Azimuth Editions, 1997).

Begam, Q.J., *Princess Jahan Ara Begam* (Karachi: S.M. Hamid Ali, 1991).

Begley, Wayne, 'Four Mughal Caravanserais Built during the Reigns of Jahangir and Shāh Jahan,' *Muqarnas*, 1 (1983):167–79.

—— and Z.A. Desai, *Taj Mahal, the Illuminated Tomb* (Seattle: University of Washington Press, 1989).

Bernier, François, *Travels in the Mogul Empire*, tr. Archibald Constable (New York: Oxford University Press, 1914–16).

Beveridge, Henry, 'Sultan Khusrau,' *Journal of the Royal Asiatic Society* (July 1907): 597–609.

Bhadra, Gautam, 'Two Frontier Uprisings in Mughal India,' in *Subaltern Studies II*, ed. Ranajit Guha (Delhi: Oxford University Press, 1983), pp. 43–59.

Bhargava, Meena, ed., *Decline of the Mughal Empire* (Delhi: Oxford University Press, 2014).

Bhimsen, *Tarikh-i-Dilkasha*, tr. Jadunath Sarkar (Bombay: Department of Archives, 1972).

Bilgrami, Fatima Zehra, 'Mughal Annexation of Sind,' in *Akbar and His India*, ed. Irfan Habib (Delhi: Oxford University Press, 2000), pp. 33–54.

Blake, Stephen, 'Patrimonial-Bureaucratic Empire of the Mughals,' *Journal of Asian Studies*, 39/1 (1979): 77–94.

——— *Shahjahanabad* (Cambridge: Cambridge University Press, 1993).

Bokhari, Afshan, *Imperial Women in Mughal India* (London: I.B. Tauris, forthcoming).

Brand, Michael and Glenn Lowry, eds, *Fatehpur-Sikri* (Bombay: Marg Publications, 1987).

Brown, Katherine, 'Did Aurangzeb Ban Music?,' *Modern Asian Studies*, 41/1 (2007): 77–120.

Buckler, W.F., *Legitimacy and Symbols*, ed. M.N. Pearson (Ann Arbor: University of Michigan Press, 1985).

Busch, Allison, 'Hidden in Plain View,' *Modern Asian Studies*, 44/2 (2010): 267–309.

——— 'Portrait of a Raja in a Badshah's World,' *Journal of the Economic and Social History of the Orient*, 55/2–3 (2012): 287–328.

Caine, W.S., *Picturesque India* (London: Routledge, 1890).

Calkins, Philip, 'Formation of a Regionally Oriented Ruling Group in Bengal, 1700–1740,' *Journal of Asian Studies*, 29/4 (1970): 799–806.

Carvalho, Pedro Moura, *Mir'at al-quds (Mirror of Holiness)*, tr. Wheeler M. Thackston (Leiden: Brill, 2012).

Chandra, Satish, 'Some Aspects of the Growth of a Money Economy in India during the Seventeenth Century,' *Indian Economic and Social History Review*, 3/4 (1966): 321–31.

——— *Eighteenth Century in India* (Calcutta: K.P. Bagchi, 1986).

——— *Medieval India from Sultanate to the Mughals*, 2 vols (Delhi: Har Anand, 2009).

——— et al., 'Akbar and His Age,' *Social Scientist*, 20/9–10 (1992): 61–72.

Chann, Naindeep Singh, 'Lord of the Auspicious Conjunction,' *Iran and the Caucasus*, 13/1 (2009): 93–110.

Chatterjee, Indrani, 'Slave's Quest for Selfhood in Eighteenth-century Hindustan,' *Indian Economic and Social History Review*, 37/1 (2000): 53–86.

Chatterjee, Kumkum, *Cultures of History in Early Modern India* (Delhi: Oxford University Press, 2009).

Chatterji, A.K., 'Mughal Administration under Siyar, Farrukh,' *Journal of Historical Research*, 24/1 (1989): 9–39.

Cheema, G.S., *Forgotten Mughals* (Delhi: Manohar, 2002).

Cohn, Bernard, *Colonialism and its Forms of Knowledge* (Princeton: Princeton University Press, 1996).

Correia-Alfonso, John, *Jesuit Letters and Indian History, 1542–1773* (Bombay: Oxford University Press, 1969).

——— *Letters from the Mughal Court* (Bombay: Heras Institute, 1980).

Curley, David, *Poetry and History* (Delhi: Chronicle, 2008).

Dale, Stephen, 'Steppe Humanism,' *International Journal of Middle East Studies*, 22/1 (1990): 37–58.

——— 'Poetry and Autobiography of the *Babur-nama*,' *Journal of Asian Studies*, 55/3 (1996): 635–64.

——— *Garden of the Eight Paradises* (Leiden: Brill, 2004).

—— *Muslim Empires of the Ottomans, Safavids, and Mughals* (Cambridge: Cambridge University Press 2010).

—— and Alam Paynd, 'Ahrari Waqf in Kabul in the Year 1546 and the Mughul Naqshbandiyyah,' *Journal of the American Oriental Society*, 119/2 (1999): 218–33.

Dalrymple, William, *Last Mughal* (London: Bloomsbury, 2006).

Das, Harihar, *Norris Embassy to Aurangzeb (1699–1702)*, ed. S.C. Sarkar (Calcutta: Firma K. L. Mukhopadhyay, 1959).

Das, Kamal Kishore, *Economic History of Moghul India* (Calcutta: Shantiniketan, 1991).

Das, Kumudrajan, *Raja Todar Mal* (Calcutta: Saraswat, 1979).

Das Gupta, Ashin, *Indian Merchants and the Decline of Surat (c. 1700–1750)* (Delhi: Manohar, 1994).

Datta, Kalikinkar, *Shah Alam II and the East India Company* (Calcutta: World Press, 1965).

—— *Dutch in Bengal and Bihar, 1740–1825* (Delhi: Motilal Banarsidas, 1968).

—— *Survey of India's Social Life and Economic Condition in the Eighteenth Century* (Delhi: Munshiram Manoharlal, 1978).

Delvoye, François, 'Image of Akbar as a Patron of Music in Indo-Persian and Vernacular Sources,' in *Akbar and His India*, ed. Irfan Habib (Delhi: Oxford University Press, 2000), pp. 188–214.

Desoulières, Alain, 'Mughal Diplomacy in Gujarat (1533–1534),' *Modern Asian Studies*, 22/3 (1988): 433–54.

Digby, Simon, 'Bayazid Beg Turkman's Pilgrimage to Makka and Return to Gujarat,' *Iran*, 42 (2004): 159–77.

Dughlat, Mirza Muhammad Haidar, *Tarikh-i Rashidi*, tr. W.M. Thackson (Cambridge: Harvard University Press, 1996).

Eaton, Richard, *Rise of Islam and the Bengal Frontier, 1204–1760* (Berkeley: University of California Press, 1996).

—— *Social History of the Deccan, 1300–1761* (Cambridge: Cambridge University Press, 2005).

—— '"Kiss My Foot," Said the King,' *Modern Asian Studies*, 43/1 (2009): 289–313.

Elliot, H.M., *History of India As Told by Its Own Historians*, ed. John Dowson, vols 4–8 (London: Trubner, 1873–7).

Ernst, Carl, 'Muslim Studies of Hinduism?,' *Iranian Studies*, 36/2 (2003): 173–95.

Erskine, William, *History of India under the Two First Sovereigns of the House of Taimur*, 2 vols (London: Longman, Brown, Green, and Longmans, 1854).

Farooqi, Naim, 'Moguls, Ottomans, and Pilgrims,' *International History Review*, 10/2 (1988): 198–220.

—— 'Six Ottoman Documents on Mughal-Ottoman Relations during the Reign of Akbar,' *Journal of Islamic Studies*, 7/1 (1996): 32–48.

Faruqui, Munis, 'Forgotten Prince,' *Journal of the Economic and Social History of the Orient*, 48/4 (2005): 487–523.

—— *Princes of the Mughal Empire, 1504–1719* (Cambridge: Cambridge University Press, 2012).

Fenech, Louis, 'Martyrdom and the Execution of Guru Arjan in Early Sikh Sources,' *Journal of the American Oriental Society*, 121/1 (2001): 20–31.

Findly, Ellison, *Nur Jahan* (New York: Oxford University Press, 1993).

Firishta, *History of Deccan*, 2 vols, tr. Jonathan Scott (London: John Stockdale, 1794).

Fisher, Michael, 'Imperial Coronation of 1819,' *Modern Asian Studies*, 19/2 (1985): 113–51.

—— *Counterflows to Colonialism* (Delhi: Permanent Black, 2004).

—— 'From India to England and Back,' *Huntington Library Quarterly*, 70/1 (2007): 153–72.

—— *Inordinately Strange Life of Dyce Sombre* (New York: Oxford University Press, 2013).

Flores, Jorge, 'Sea and the World of the Mutasaddi,' *Journal of the Royal Asiatic Society*, 21 (2011): 55–71.

Foltz, Richard, 'Central Asian Naqshbandi Connections of the Mughal Emperors,' *Journal of Islamic Studies*, 7/2 (1996): 229–39.

—— 'Mughal Occupation of Balkh, 1646–1647,' *Journal of Islamic Studies*, 7/1 (1996): 49–61.

Fox, Richard, *Kin, Clan, Raja, and Rule* (Berkeley: University of California Press, 1971).

Francklin, W., *History of the Reign of Shah-Aulum* (London: The Author, 1798).

Gilmartin, David, and Bruce Lawrence, eds, *Beyond Turk and Hindu* (Gainesville: University Press of Florida, 2000).

Gokhale, B.G., 'Tobacco in Seventeenth-Century India,' *Agricultural History*, 48/4 (1974): 484–92.

Gordon, Stewart, *Marathas, 1600–1818* (Cambridge: Cambridge University Press, 1993).

—— ed., *Robes and Honor* (New York: Palgrave, 2001).

—— ed., *Robes of Honour* (Delhi: Oxford University Press, 2003).

Grover, B.R., *Collected Works*, vols 4–5, eds Amrita Grover, et al. (Delhi: D.K., 2005).

Guerreiro, Father Fernao, *Jahangir and the Jesuits*, tr. C. H. Payne (Delhi: Munshiram Manoharlal, 1997).

Guha, Sumit, 'Serving the Barbarian to Preserve the *Dharma*,' *Indian Economic and Social History Review*, 47/4 (2010): 497–525.

Gulbadan, *History of Humayun (Humayun-nama)*, tr. Annette Beveridge (London: Royal Asiatic Society, 1902).

Habib, Irfan, *Atlas of the Mughal Empire* (Delhi: Oxford University Press, 1982).

—— *Agrarian System of Mughal India* (Delhi: Oxford University Press, 1999).

Haider, Najaf, 'Prices and Wages in India (1200–1800),' in *Towards a Global History of Prices and Wages* (Utrecht: International Institute of Social History, 2004), pp. 52–9.

—— 'Norms of Professional Excellence and Good Conduct in Accountancy Manuals of the Mughal Empire,' *International Review of Social History*, 56 (2011): 263–74.

Hakluyt, Richard, *Hakluyt's Voyages* (New York: Viking Press, 1965).

Hallissey, Robert, *Rajput Rebellion Against Aurangzeb* (Columbia: University of Missouri Press, 1977).

Hasan, Farhat, *State and Locality in Mughal India* (Cambridge: Cambridge University Press, 2004).

Hasan, Ibn, *Central Structure of the Mughal Empire* (Oxford: Oxford University Press, 1936).

Hasan, Mohibbul, *Babur* (Delhi: Manohar, 1985).

Hasan, S. Nurul, 'Position of the Zamindars in the Mughal Empire,' *Indian Economic and Social History Review*, 1/4 (1964): 107–19.

—— *Religion, State, and Society in Medieval India*, ed. Satish Chandra (Delhi: Oxford University Press, 2005).

Hasrat, Bikrama Jit, *Dara Shikuh* (Delhi: Munshiram Manoharlal, 1982).

Havell, E.B., *Handbook to Agra and the Taj, Sikandra, Fatehpur-Sikri* (London: Longmans, Green, 1904).

Hodges, William, *Travels in India* (London: The Author, 1793).

Husain, Afzal, *Nobility under Akbar and Jahangir* (Delhi: Manohar, 1999).

Illustrated London News.

Irvine, William, *Army of the Indian Mughals* (Delhi: Eurasia, 1962).

—— *Later Mughals*, ed. Jadunath Sarkar (Delhi: Oriental, 1971).

I'tesamuddin, Mirza Sheikh, *Wonders of Vilayet*, tr. Kaisar Haq (Leeds: Peepal Tree, 2002).

Jahangir, *Tuzuk-i-Jahangiri*, 2 vols, tr. Alexander Rogers, ed. Henry Beveridge (London: Royal Asiatic Society, 1914).

Jarric, Pierre du, *Akbar and the Jesuits*, tr. C.H. Payne (London: George Routledge, 1926).

Kalhana, *Rajatarangini*, 4 vols, tr. M.A. Stein (Delhi: Motilal Banarsidas, 1989).

Kavuri-Bauer, Santhi, *Monumental Matters* (Durham: Duke University Press, 2011).

Khan, Abbas, *Tarikh-i Sher Shahi*, in H.M. Elliott, *History of India As Told by Its Own Historians* (London: Trubner, 1873–7), vol. 4, pp. 301–433.

Khan, Abu Talib, 'Vindication of the Liberties of Asiatic Women,' *Asiatic Annual Register* (1801): 100–107.

—— 'Masir-i Talibi' (1804), Persian Add. 8145–47, British Library, London.

—— *History of Asafu'd Daula, Nawab Wazir of Oudh*, tr. W. Hoey (Lucknow: Pustak Kendra, 1971).

Khan, Ahsan Raza, *Chieftains in the Mughal Empire During the Reign of Akbar* (Simla: Indian Institute of Advanced Study, 1977).

Khan, Gulfishan, *Indian Muslim Perceptions of the West during the Eighteenth Century* (Karachi: Oxford University Press, 1998).

Khan, Inayat, *Shah Jahan Nama*, tr. A.R. Fuller, eds W.E. Begley and Z.A. Desai (Delhi: Oxford University Press, 1990).

Khan, Iqtidar Alam, 'Nobility under Akbar and the Development of His Religious Policy, 1560–80,' *Journal of the Royal Asiatic Society*, 1–2 (1968): 29–36.

—— 'Akbar's Personality Traits and World Outlook,' *Social Scientist*, 20/9–10 (1992): 16–30.

—— 'Mughal Assignment System during Akbar's Early Years, 1556–1575,' in *Medieval India*, ed. Irfan Habib (Delhi: Oxford University Press, 1992), vol. 1, pp. 62–128.

—— 'State in Mughal India,' *Social Scientist*, 30/1–2 (2001): 16–45.

Khan, Saqi Mustaid, *Maasir-i 'Alamgiri*, tr. Jadunath Sarkar (Calcutta: Royal Asiatic Society of Bengal, 1947).

Khan, Sayid Ghulam Husain, *Seir Mutaqherin*, 4 vols., tr. M. Raymond (Calcutta: T.D. Chatterjee, 1902).

Khwandamir, *Qanun-i Humayuni*, tr. M. Hidayat Hosain (Calcutta: Royal Asiatic Society of Bengal, 1940).

Kinra, Rajeev, 'Infantilizing Baba Dara,' *Journal of Persianate Studies*, 2/2 (2009): 165–93.

—— 'Master and Munshi,' *Indian Economic and Social History Review*, 47/4 (2010): 527–61.

Koch, Ebba, *Complete Taj Mahal* (London: Thames and Hudson, 2006).

—— 'Symbolic Possession of the World,' *Journal of the Economic and Social History of the Orient*, 55/2–3 (2012): 547–80.

Kolff, D.H.A., *Naukar, Rajput, and Sepoy* (Cambridge: Cambridge University Press, 1990).

Lakhnawi, Shiv Das, *Shahnama Munawwar Kalam*, tr. Syed Hasan Askari (Patna: Janaki Prakashan, 1980).

Lal, Ruby, 'Historicizing the Harem,' *Feminist Studies*, 30/3 (2004): 590–616.

—— *Domesticity and Power in the Early Mughal World* (Cambridge: Cambridge University Press, 2005).

—— *Nur Nama* (New York: Random House, forthcoming).

Latif, Syad Muhammad, *Lahore* (Lahore: New Imperial Press, 1892).

Lefevre, Corinne, 'Recovering a Missing Voice from Mughal India,' *Journal of the Economic and Social History of the Orient*, 50/4 (2007): 452–89.

—— '*Majalis-i Jahangiri* (1608–11),' *Journal of the Economic and Social History of the Orient*, 55/2–3 (2012): 255–86.

Leonard, Karen, '"Great Firm" Theory of the Decline of the Mughal Empire,' *Comparative Studies in Society and History*, 21/2 (1979): 151–67.

Los Angeles County Museum of Art, www.LACMA.org (accessed 1 September 2014).

Maclagan, Edward, *Jesuits and the Great Mogul* (Gurgaon: Vintage, 1990).

Maddison, Angus, *Contours of the World Economy* (Oxford: Oxford University Press, 2007).

Malik, Zahir Uddin, 'Financial Problems of the Mughal Government During Farrukh Siyar's Reign,' *Indian Economic and Social History Review*, 4/3 (1967): 265–75.

—— *Mughal Statesman of the Eighteenth Century, Khan-i Dauran, Mir Bakhshi of Muhammad Shah, 1719–1739* (Aligarh: Aligarh Muslim University, 1973).

—— *Reign of Muhammad Shah, 1719–1748* (Delhi: Icon, 2006).

Manucci, Niccolao, *Memoirs of the Mogul Court, Storia do Mogor*, 4 vols, tr. William Irvine (London: John Murray, 1907–8).

Marshall, D.N., *Mughals in India* (Bombay: Asia, 1967).

Marshall, P.J., ed., *Eighteenth Century in Indian History* (Delhi: Oxford University Press, 2003).

Marx, Karl, 'East India Question,' *New York Daily Tribune* (25 July 1853).

Masson, Charles, *Narrative of Various Journeys in Belochistan, Afghanistan, the Panjab and Kabul*, 4 vols (London: Richard Bentley, 1844).

Mayaram, Shail, 'Mughal State Formation and Indian History,' *Indian Economic and Social History Review*, 34/2 (1997): 169–97.

Mehta, Shirin, 'Akbar as Reflected in the Contemporary Jain Literature in Gujarat,' *Social Scientist*, 20/9–10 (1992): 54–60.

Mill, James, *History of British India* (London: Baldwin, Cradock and Joy, 1818).

Moin, Ahmed Azfar, *Millennial Sovereign* (New York: Columbia University Press, 2012).

—— 'Peering through the cracks in the *Baburnama*,' *Indian Economic and Social History Review*, 49/4 (2012): 493–526.

Monserrate, Antonio, *Commentary*, tr. J.S. Hoyland, ed. S.N. Banerjee (Delhi: Asian Educational Services, 1992).

Monshi, Estakdar Beg, *History of Shah Abbas the Great*, 2 vols, tr. Roger M. Savory (Boulder: Westview, 1978).

Moosvi, Shireen, 'Zamindars' Share in the Peasant Surplus in the Mughal Empire,' *Indian Economic and Social History Review*, 15/3 (1978): 359–73.

—— 'Share of the Nobility in the Revenues of Akbar's Empire, 1595–96,' *Indian Economic and Social History Review*, 17/3 (1980): 329–41.

—— 'Expenditure on Buildings under Shahjahan,' *Proceedings of Indian History Congress* (1985): 285–99.

———— *Economy of the Mughal Empire, c. 1595* (Delhi: Oxford University Press, 1987).

———— 'Estimate of Revenues of the Deccan Kingdoms, 1591,' in *Akbar and His India*, ed. Irfan Habib (Delhi: Oxford University Press, 1997), pp. 288–93.

———— 'Mughal Encounter with Vedanta,' *Social Scientist*, 30/7–8 (2002): 13–23.

Moreland, W.H., *From Akbar to Aurangzeb* (London: Macmillan, 1923).

———— *Agrarian System of Moslem India* (London: W. Heffer and Sons, 1929).

Mukhia, Harbans, 'Illegal Extortions from Peasants, Artisans and Menials in Eighteenth Century Eastern Rajasthan,' *Indian Economic and Social History Review*, 14/2 (1977): 231–45.

———— *Mughals of India* (Oxford: Blackwell, 2004).

———— 'Time in Abu'l Fazl's Historiography,' *Studies in History*, 25 (2009): 1–12.

Mukhlis, Anand Ram. *Mir'atu-l Istilah*, tr. Tasneem Ahmad (Delhi: Sundeep Prakashan, 1993).

Murray, John, *Handbook for Travellers in India, Burma and Ceylon*, 6th ed. (London: John Murray, 1908).

Mushtaqi, Shaikh Rizqullah, *Waq'iat-i Mushtaqi*, in *Mughal Relations with the Indian Ruling Elite*, ed. Iqtidar Siddiqui (Delhi: Munshiram Manoharlal, 1983).

Naim, C.M., 'Syed Ahmad and His Two Books Called "Asar-al-Sanadid",' *Modern Asian Studies*, 45/3 (2011): 669–708.

Najm-i Saini, Muhammad Baqir, *Advice on the Art of Governance, An Indo-Islamic Mirror for Princes*, tr. Sajida Sultana Alvi (Albany: State University of New York Press, 1989).

Naqvi, H.K., *Urbanisation and Urban Centers under the Great Mughals* (Shimla: Indian Institute of Advanced Study, 1972).

Narayana Rao, Velcheru, et al., *Textures of Time* (Delhi: Permanent Black, 2001).

Nath, Ram, *Fatehpur Sikri and Its Monuments* (Agra: Historical Research Documentation Programme, 2000).

Nathan, Mirza, *Baharistan-i-Ghaibi*, 2 vols, tr. M.I. Borah (Gauhati: Narayani Handiqui Historical Institute, 1936).

National Archives of India, *Calendar of Persian Correspondence*, 5 vols (Delhi: Government of India, 2013).

Nayeem, M.A., 'Working of the Chauth and Sardeshmukhi System in the Mughal Provinces of the Deccan (1707–1803 A.D.),' *Indian Economic and Social History Review*, 14/2 (1977): 153–91.

Neamet Ullah, *History of the Afghans*, tr. Bernhard Dorn (Delhi: Bhavana, 2000).

Nizami, Khaliq Ahmad, *Akbar and Religion* (Delhi: IAD Oriental, 1989).

Nur Muhammad, Qazi, *Jang Namah*, tr. Ganda Singh (Amritsar: Khalsa College, 1939).

Oberoi, Harjot Singh, *Construction of Religious Boundaries* (Chicago: University of Chicago Press, 1994).

O'Hanlon, Rosalind, 'Manliness and Imperial Service in Mughal North India,' *Journal of the Economic and Social History of the Orient*, 42/1 (1999): 47–93.

———— 'Kingdom, Household, and Body,' *Modern Asian Studies*, 41/5 (2007): 889–923.

Pandian, A.S., 'Predatory Care,' *Journal of Historical Sociology*, 14/1 (2001): 79–107.

Parodi, Laura, 'Bibi-ka Maqbara in Aurangabad,' *East and West*, 48/3–4 (1998): 349–83.

Pauwels, Heidi, 'Saint, the Warlord, and the Emperor,' *Journal of the Economic and Social History of the Orient*, 52/2 (2009): 187–228.

Pearson, M.N., 'Political Participation in Mughal India,' *Indian Economic and Social History Review*, 9/2 (1972): 113–31.

—— 'Shivaji and the Decline of the Mughal Empire,' *Journal of Asian Studies*, 35/2 (1976): 221–35.

Pelsaert, Francisco, *Jahangir's India*, tr. W.H. Moreland and Peter Geyl (Cambridge: W. Heffer and Sons, 1925).

Pernau, Margrit, and Yunus Jaffe, eds, *Information and the Public Sphere* (Oxford: Oxford University Press, 2009).

Phukan, Shantanu, '"Through Throats Where Many Rivers Meet",' *Indian Economic and Social History Review*, 38/1 (2001): 33–58.

Polier, Antoine Louis Henri, *Shah Alam II and His Court*, ed. Pratul C. Gupta (Calcutta: S.C. Sarcar, 1947).

Pollock, Sheldon, 'New Intellectuals in Seventeenth-century India,' *Indian Economic and Social History Review*, 38/1 (2001): 3–31.

Prakash, Om, 'Dutch East India Company in Bengal,' *Indian Economic and Social History Review*, 9/3 (1972): 258–87.

Prasad, Ishwari, *Life and Times of Humayun* (Allahabad: Central Book Depot, 1976).

Prasad, Pushpa, 'Akbar and the Jains,' in *Akbar and His India*, ed. Irfan Habib (Delhi: Oxford University Press, 2000), pp. 97–108.

Purchas, Samuel, *Hakluytus Posthumus, or, Purchas His Pilgrimes*, 20 vols (New York: AMS, 1965).

Qandhari, Muhammad Arif, *Tarikh-i Akbar*, tr. Tasneem Ahmad (Delhi: Pragati, 1993).

Qureshi, I.H., *Administration of the Mughal Empire* (Karachi: Oxford University Press, 1966).

Rana, R.P., 'Dominant Class in Upheaval,' *Indian Economic and Social History Review*, 24/4 (1987): 395–409.

Raychaudhuri, Tapan, *Bengal under Akbar and Jahangir* (Delhi: Munshiram Manoharlal, 1966).

Reis, Sidi Ali, *Travels and Adventures*, tr. A. Vambery (Leyden: Luzac, 1899).

Rezavi, Syed Ali Nadeem, 'Religious Disputations and Imperial Ideology,' *Studies in History*, 24 (2008): 195–209.

—— ed., *Fatehpur Sikri Revisited* (Delhi: Oxford University Press, 2013).

Richards, John, *Mughal Administration in Golconda* (Oxford: Clarendon, 1975).

—— 'Imperial Crisis in the Deccan,' *Journal of Asian Studies*, 35/2 (1976): 237–56.

—— 'Norms of Comportment for Mughal Officers,' in *Moral Conduct and Authority*, ed. Barbara Metcalf (Berkeley: University of California Press, 1984), pp. 255–89.

—— *Document Forms for Official Orders of Appointment in the Mughal Empire* (Cambridge: F.J.W. Gibb Memorial, 1986).

—— *Mughal Empire* (Cambridge: Cambridge University Press, 1993).

Richards, John, and V.N. Rao, 'Banditry in Mughal India,' *Indian Economic and Social History Review*, 17/1 (1980): 95–120.

Rizvi, Saiyid Athar Abbas, *Fathpur-Sikri* (Bombay: D.B. Taraporevala Sons, 1975).

—— *Religious and Intellectual History of the Muslims in Akbar's Reign* (Delhi: Munshiram Manoharlal, 1975).

—— *Shah Wali-Allah and his Times* (Canberra: Ma'rifat, 1980).

Robinson, Francis, *Mughal Emperors and the Islamic Dynasties of India, Iran and Central Asia, 1206–1925* (New York: Thames and Hudson, 2007).

Roe, Thomas, *Embassy*, 2 vols, ed. William Foster (London: Hakluyt Society, 1899).

Roy, Sukumar, *Humayun in Persia* (Calcutta: Royal Asiatic Society, 1948).

—— *Bairam Khan*, ed. M.H.A. Beg (Karachi: University of Karachi, 1992).

Sangwan, R.S., *Jodhpur and the Later Mughals* (Delhi: Pragati, 2006).

Saran, Paratma, *Provincial Government of the Mughals, 1526–1658* (Allahabad: Central Book Depot, 1941).

Sarkar, Jadu Nath, *Bengal Nawabs* (Calcutta: Asiatic Society, 1952).

Sarkar, Jadunath, *History of Aurangzeb*, 4 vols (Calcutta: M.C. Sarkar, 1912–16).

—— *Studies in Mughal India* (Calcutta: M.C. Sarkar, 1919).

—— *Short History of Aurangzib* (Calcutta: M.C. Sarkar, 1962).

Sarkar, Jagdish Narayan, *Study in Eighteenth Century India* (Calcutta: Saraswat Library, 1976).

Satyal, Amita, *Mughal Empire, Overland Trade, and Merchants of Northern India, 1526–1707*, Ph.D. Thesis (University of California, Berkeley, 2008).

Savarkar, V.D., *Indian War of Independence, 1857* (Bombay: Phoenix, 1947).

Schofield, Katherine, 'Reviving the Golden Age Again: "Classicization", Hindustani Music, and the Mughals,' *Ethnomusicology*, 54/3 (2010): 484–517.

—— 'Courtesan Tale: Female Musicians and Dancers in Mughal Historical Chronicles, *c.*1556–1748.' *Gender and History*, 24/1 (2012): 150–71.

Seyller, John, 'Workshop and Patron in Mughal India,' *Artibus Asiae, Supplement* 42 (1999): 2–344.

—— 'Mughal Code of Connoisseurship,' *Muqarnas*, 17 (2000): 177–202.

Shah, A.M., 'Political System in Eighteenth Century Gujarat,' *Enquiry*, n.s. 1/1 (1964): 83–95.

Shah Alam II, 'Letter to King of Great Britain,' Sutton Court Collection, MSS EUR F.128/111, ff. 100–102, British Library, London.

Sharma, D.V., *Archaeology of Fatehpur Sikri* (Delhi: Aryan, 2008).

Sharma, Gauri, *Prime Ministers under the Mughals (1526–1707)* (Delhi: Kanishka, 2006).

Sharma, G.N., *Mewar and the Mughal Emperors* (Agra: Shiva Lal Agarwala, 1962).

Sharma, Sri Ram, *Mughal Government and Administration* (Bombay: Hind Kitabs, 1951).

—— *Religious Policy of the Mughal Emperors* (London: Asia, 1962).

Shivram, Balkrishan, *Jagirdars in the Mughal Empire during the Reign of Akbar* (Delhi: Manohar, 2008).

Shyam, Radhey, *Life and Times of Malik Ambar* (Delhi: Munshiram Manoharlal, 1968).

Siddiqi, Noman, *Land Revenue Administration Under the Mughals (1700–1750)* (London: Asia, 1930).

—— 'Classification of Villages Under the Mughals,' *Indian Economic and Social History Review*, 1/1 (1964): 73–83.

—— '*Faujdar* and *Faujdari* under the Mughals,' in *Mughal State, 1526–1750*, ed. Muzaffar Alam and Sanjay Subrahmanyam (Delhi: Oxford University Press, 1998), pp. 234–51.

Siddiqui, Iqtidar, *Mughal Relations with the Indian Ruling Elite* (Delhi: Munshiram Manoharlal, 1983).

Singh, Chetan, *Region and Empire* (Delhi: Oxford University Press, 1991).

—— 'Forests, Pastoralists and Agrarian Society in Mughal India,' in *Nature, Culture, Imperialism*, ed. David Arnold and Ramachandra Guha (Delhi: Oxford University Press, 1995), pp. 21–48.

Singh, Devika, 'Approaching the Mughal Past in Indian Art Criticism,' *Modern Asian Studies*, 47/1 (2013): 167–203.

Singh, Ganda, *Ahmad Shah Abdali* (Bombay: Asia, 1959).

Sinha, Parmeshwar Prasad, *Raja Birbal (Life and Times)* (Patna: Janaki Prakashan, 1980).

Smith, Edmund, *Moghul Architecture of Fathpur-Sikri*, Part I (Allahabad: N.-W. P. and Oude Press, 1894).

Smith, Vincent, *History of Fine Art in India and Ceylon* (Oxford: Clarendon, 1911).

―― 'Death of Hemu in 1556, after the Battle of Panipat,' *Journal of the Royal Asiatic Society* (July 1916): 527–35.

―― *Akbar the Great Mogul* (Oxford: Oxford University Press, 1919).

Stein, Burton, 'Eighteenth Century India,' *Studies in History*, 5 (1989): 1–26.

Steingass, Francis, *Comprehensive Persian-English Dictionary* (London: Routledge and Kegan Paul, 1892).

Streusand, Douglas, *Formation of the Mughal Empire* (Delhi: Oxford University Press, 1999).

―― *Islamic Gunpowder Empires* (Boulder: Westview, 2011).

Subrahmanyam, Sanjay, 'Mughal State—Structure or Process?,' *Indian Economic and Social History Review*, 29/3 (1992): 291–321.

―― 'Making Sense of Indian Historiography,' *Indian Economic and Social History Review*, 39/2–3 (2002): 121–30.

―― *Explorations in Connected History*, 2 vols (Delhi: Oxford University Press, 2005).

Subrahmanyam, Sanjay, and C.A. Bayly, 'Portfolio Capitalists and the Political Economy of Early Modern India,' *Indian Economic and Social History Review*, 25/4 (1988): 401–24.

Syan, Hardip Singh, *Sikh Militancy in the Seventeenth Century* (London: I.B. Tauris, 2012).

Syros, Vasileios, 'Early Modern South Asian Thinker on the Rise and Decline of Empires,' *Journal of World History,* 23/4 (2013): 793–840.

Taft, F.H., 'Honor and Alliance,' in *Idea of Rajasthan*, 2 vols, ed. K. Schomer et al. (Delhi: Manohar, 1994), vol. 2, pp. 217–41.

Talbot, Cynthia, 'Becoming Turk the Rajput Way,' *Modern Asian Studies*, 43/1 (2009): 211–43.

―― 'Justifying Defeat,' *Journal of the Economic and Social History of the Orient*, 55/2–3 (2012): 329–68.

Tamaskar, B.G., *Life and Work of Malik Ambar* (Delhi: Idarh-i Adabiyat-i Dilli, 1978).

Tavernier, Jean-Baptiste, *Travels in India*, 2 vols, tr. V. Ball (London: Oxford University Press, 1925).

Tripathi, R.P., *Some Aspects of Mughal Administration* (Allahabad: Central Book Depot, 1936).

Truschke, Audrey, 'Mughal *Book of War*,' *Comparative Studies of South Asia, Africa and the Middle East*, 31 (2011): 506–20.

Urwick, W., *Indian Pictures* (London: Religious Tract Society, 1891).

Vanina, Eugenia, 'Madhavanala-Kamakandala by Alam,' *Indian Historical Review*, 20/1–2 (1993–4): 66–77.

Verma, Som Prakash, *Aspects of Mughal Painters*, 2 vols (Delhi: Abhinav, 2009).

Wade, Bonnie, *Imaging Sound* (Chicago: University of Chicago Press, 1998).

Washbrook, David, 'South Asia,' *Journal of Asian Studies*, 49/3 (1990): 479–508.

Wee, Maarten van der, 'Semi-Imperial Polity and Service Aristocracy,' *Dialectical Anthropology*, 13/3 (1988): 209–25.

Williams, L.F. Rushbrook, *Empire Builder of the Sixteenth Century* (London: Longmans, Green, 1918).

Wink, Andre, *Land and Sovereignty in India* (Cambridge: Cambridge University Press, 1986).

Wright, H. Nelson, *Catalogue of the Coins in the Indian Museum Calcutta*, vol. 3 (Oxford: Clarendon, 1908).

Zaidi, Sunita, 'Akbar's Annexation of Sind,' in *Akbar and His India*, ed. Irfan Habib (Delhi: Oxford University Press, 1997), pp. 25–32.

Ziegler, Norman, 'Marvari Historical Chronicles,' *Indian Economic and Social History Review*, 13/2 (1976): 219–50.

——— 'Some Notes on Rajput Loyalties During the Mughal Period,' in *Kingship and Authority in South Asia*, ed. John Richards (Madison: University of Wisconsin-Madison Press, 1978), pp. 242–84.

Zutshi, Chitralekha, *Kashmir's Contested Pasts* (Delhi: Oxford University Press, 2014).

Index

'Abd-un-Nabi, Shaikh,
115, 124
'Abd-ur-Rahim, 85
'Abu-al-Faiz, 113, 125,
139
'Abu-al-Fazl, 68, 73–4,
86, 96, 113, 134–38,
228
death, 146–7, 172
Abu-al-Hasan (artist),
cover
Abyssinia, 87, 117, 139,
152, 157, 162–3, 188
Adham Khan, 73–4, 83
adivasi, 38–9, 42–4, 114
Afghans, 2–4, 32, 77,
194, 216–8, 229
Afghanistan, 29, 32,
37, 106, 197
Akbar, 74, 77–9, 83,
105–6, 115, 132
'Alamgir, 194, 197
Babur, 15, 23–32, 41,
45–51, 59–63
Dari dialect, 27, 49
Humayun, 6–7, 56,
59–68, 92, 95–6
Shah Jahan, 163, 173,
180
see also Lodi; Pashtun;
Rohilla; Suri;
Yusufzai
Afghan Begum, Bibi
Mubaraka, 27
Afridi Afghans, 194

Afzal Khan, 147
Agra, 60, 75, 212, 215
Akbar, 76, 80–1, 86,
109–17, 138–40,
143, 147
'Alamgir, 190–1, 194–7,
206, 211
Babur, 16, 32–3, 51,
53–4
Humayun, 61–3, 68
Jahangir, 146–7, 155,
157
Shah Jahan, 165–7,
172, 175–6, 184–5,
189–90
ahadis, 97
Ahmad Shah Durrani,
217–8
Ahmadnagar, 46, 189,
206, 210–1
Sultanate, 45–6, 138–9,
152, 157, 162–3,
173–4
Ahmedabad, 118
Ahom, 156, 190
Ahrar, Khwaja
'Ubaidullah,
Naqshbandi, 19, 52
Ain-i Akbari, 138
Ajit Singh Rathor of
Marwar, 213
Ajmer, 75, 168, 189, 206,
211, 213
Akbar, 80, 86–7, 114,
117

Akbar, 7–9, 73–140,
142–8, 155, 227–8,
236
administration, 83–4,
93–107, 181
architecture, 109–12,
117, 121–3, 134,
176
court culture, 27, 107–
13, 122, 129–35,
151–2, 167, 171
diplomacy, 130, 134,
138
ethnic policies, 87–9,
112, 115, 127
Europeans, 108,
128–30
household, 92, 103,
115
political marriage, 78,
81, 84–92, 133–5,
139, 159
prince, 65–6, 68, 75–6
religion, 93, 99, 108,
115–37, 146, 154
warfare, 95, 105–6,
113–20, 130–9,
146, 156–7
Akbar, son of 'Alamgir,
198–9, 205, 215
Akbar II, 222, 224
'Alamgir, 7–9, 186–206,
209–11, 235–6
administration, 193–4,
197, 201–3

court culture, 191–3
diplomacy, 188, 196, 205
ethnic policies, 197–8, 201
household, 182, 190, 194
Prince Aurangzeb, 7–8, 172, 180–2, 184–7
religion, 187–8, 190–1, 195–7, 201–2
warfare, 189–90, 195, 197–9
'Alamgir II, 215
'Alamgirnama, 191
alcoholism, 25, 77, 132, 146, 151, 162, 164, 167
Ali Khan, Raja of Khandesh, 91
Ali Mardan Khan, 180
Aligarh Muslim University, 235, 238
Allahabad, 75, 120, 144, 163, 182, 189, 197, 206, 212
Jahangir, 79, 109, 143–7, 149, 151, 157, 163
Shah 'Alam, 221–2
Amar Singh, Rana of Mewar, 157
Amber, 75, 81, 86, 88, 213
Americas, 5, 98, 129, 153, 155, 240
Amrit Rai, 88
Amu Darya, 16, 22–6, 33, 66
Anup Talao, 122–23
appanage, 49, 76, 94–8, 100, 148, 211
Arabs, 30, 32, 40–1, 117
Arabia, 2, 18, 33, 120
Arabic, 130, 135–6, 228, 232
Arakanese, 114, 156–57, 173, 184, 190
Archaeological Survey of India, 238

Arjumand Banu, Mumtaz Mahal, 159, 168, 175–6, 182–5
army, see horses; individual emperors by name; mansab
artillery, 44, 60–2, 97, 156, 162–3, 200, 216, 219
Babur, 28–31, 48, 50–1, 59–61
Asaf Khan, 159–68, 171, 174
Asirgarh, 139
Askari, Mirza, 7, 27, 48–9, 54, 57, 61, 65–6
Asmat Begum, 165
Assam, 9, 189–90
astrology, 19, 47, 58, 113, 150, 191
atlas, cartographic, 129
Aurangabad, 189, 192, 206
Aurangzeb, see 'Alamgir
Awadh, 184, 189, 206, 216–7, 219–20, 224, 237
Ayisha Sultan Begum, 26
Ayodhya, 237
'Azam, Mirza, 190, 199, 205–6, 209–11, 215
Azim-ush-Shan, 211–2, 215

Babur, 2, 6–7, 15–35, 47–57, 94, 137, 237
administration, 28, 32, 49, 51
architecture, 55, 122
court culture, 16–17, 22, 24–5, 27–8, 52–5, 108
diplomacy, 15, 22–3, 25, 137
ethnic policies, 16–7, 21–4
household, 15, 18, 25–8, 32

political marriage, 22, 26–7, 132
prince, 16, 21
religion, 18–9, 21–5, 47–8, 51–3
warfare, 15–7, 20, 22–4, 28–31, 47–51
Baburnama, 22, 25, 52, 151, 170
Badakhshan, 9, 24, 16, 48, 60, 180
Akbar, 78, 91, 132, 137
Humayun, 27, 29–30, 48, 54, 56–57
Badakhshi, Shah, Qadri, 183
Badauni, 96–7, 104, 125–7, 134–7, 228
Badhchand, Raja of Kangra, 116
Baghela Rajputs, 113–4
Bahadur Nizam Shah, of Ahmadnagar, 139
Bahadur Shah I, 199–200, 205–6, 209–11, 215
Bahadur Shah II, Zafar, 209, 224–5, 234
Bahadur Shah, of Gujarat, 59–60
Bahadur Shah, of Khandesh, 139
Bahmani Sultanate, 45, 138
Bai Indra Kunwar, 213
Bairam Khan, 64–9, 75–85, 95–6, 112–5
bakhshi, 83
Bakhshi Banu Begum, 91
Balkh, 16, 24, 29, 48, 60, 66, 180, 188
Baluch, 30, 32, 49, 65
Banaras, 184
Banarsidas, 97, 106, 140, 229
Banda Bahadur Sikh, 213
Bangladesh, 5, 10, 227, 237
bankers, 43, 98, 106

Basra, 196
Bengal, 9, 35–7, 41, 75,
189–90, 224, 237
Akbar, 77, 114–5,
118–20
'Alamgir, 190, 203, 206
Bahadur Shah I, 211–2
Europeans, 45–6, 114,
128, 219–21
Farrukh-siyar, 212–4
Humayun, 7, 59–63
Jahangir, 147, 156–7,
159
Shah 'Alam, 219–21
Shah Jahan, 163, 173,
176–7, 180, 183–4
Sultanate, 49, 59, 62,
118
Berar, 45–6, 138–9, 189,
206
Bernier, François, 231
Bhadra, Gautam, 239
Bhagavad Gita, 183
Bhagwantdas, Raja of
Amber, 86–7
Bharatiya Janata Party,
237
Bharatpur, 213
Bhat jati, 105
Bhati Rajputs, 114
Bhatta, 114
Bichitr (artist), 170
Bidar, 45–6, 138, 182,
189, 206
Bidar Bakht, 215, 222
Bihar, 60, 63, 163, 212,
214
Akbar, 114, 118–20,
147
'Alamgir, 189, 206
Shah 'Alam, 219–21
Bihari Mal, Raja of
Amber, 81, 86
Bijapur, 45–6, 162, 174,
189
'Alamgir, 195–6, 199–
201, 206
Shah Jahan, 162, 174,
180–2

Sultanate, 45–6, 138,
174, 180–2, 195–6,
199–201
Bikaner, 114
Bir Singh Dev, Raja of
Orchha, 146–7, 172,
194
Birbal, Raja, 105–6, 116,
133
Bombay, 189, 204
Brahmins, 38–40, 81,
105, 116, 154, 200
see also Hindus
Braj Basha, 88, 105, 135,
229
British colonialism, 5, 47,
155, 204–5, 217–22,
224, 231–7
Buddhism, 17
Bukhara, 188
bullocks, 44
Bundela Rajputs, 146
Burhan Nizam Shah II, of
Ahmadnagar, 138–9
Burhanpur, 139, 173–5
Burma, 225
Buxar, battle of, 220

calligraphy, 21–2, 152, 176
canals, 179
cannon, *see* artillery
caravanserai, 53, 153,
160–1
cartaz, 46
see also Portuguese
Empire
caste, 38–41, 99–100, 239
cavalry, *see* horses
Central Asians, 2, 17–20,
54–8, 74–6, 108,
132, 157, 167, 238
Akbar, 74–6, 80, 91,
102–5, 112–4, 127,
132–4
'Alamgir, 203
Babur, 6–7, 15, 22–30,
32, 47–52, 54
culture, 18–20, 37, 51,
167–8, 216

Farrukh-siyar, 212–15
Humayun, 56–66
immigrants from, 2, 4,
39, 229
Jahangir, 155–7, 160–1
Mongols, 2–3, 6–7,
16–8, 21–4, 30–1,
80–8, 101, 128,
227
Mughal heritage, 2–3,
6–9, 76, 144, 155,
164, 206
Nadir Shah, 216–7
Shah Jahan, 167–8,
179–81
Uzbeks, 22–3, 77–8,
137, 171, 229, 231,
238
Chaghatai Mongol, 17,
88
Chaldiran, battle of, 29
Chand Bibi, Regent of
Ahmadnagar, 139
charity, 37, 120–2, 169,
183, 188
Chausa, battle of, 60, 63
chilli peppers, 155
China, 1, 9, 17, 24, 101
Chingiz Khan Mongol, 7,
16–8, 22, 101, 227
Chishti, 32, 52, 87, 193
see also Mu'in-ud-Din;
Salim
Chittagong, 189–90
Chittor, 59–60, 75, 89,
113
Christianity, 40–1, 127–
30, 154–5, 164, 176,
228, 230
see also Europeans;
Portuguese Empire
chronogram, 48, 113
Chunar, 60–3, 75, 83
Churaman, Raja of Jats,
213
Circassian slave, 87
Clive, Robert, 220
see also English East
Indian Company

cloth trade, 43, 114, 204
colonialism, 2, 5, 209,
    217, 232–37, 240
    see also English East
        Indian Company;
        Portuguese Empire
communication system,
    53, 84, 67, 99, 229
concubines, 20, 57, 85,
    158, 162, 206, 212
Constantinople, 50
Cooch Bihar, 120, 156,
    189–90
co-opt enemies, 156–8,
    171, 174, 182, 195,
    200–1
Court of Directors, 219–
    21, 224
    see also English East
        India Company
cow slaughter, ban on,
    116, 127–8
cuisine, 21–2, 37, 40,
    111
currency, 67, 96–8, 126

da Gama, Vasco, 240
dagh, 67, 103–4, 181
Dalai Lama, 190
Daman, 45–6, 60, 155
dance, 22, 122, 191
    see also music
Daniyal, Mirza, 7, 87,
    139, 144–6, 155, 164
Daniyal, Shaikh, Chishti,
    87
Dara Shukoh, Mirza, 7,
    180–5, 195, 197
darshan, 122, 136, 191
Dastur al-'Amal, 100
Daulatabad, 189, 193
Dawar Bakhsh, 7, 164
Deccan, 9, 35–6, 41–2,
    45, 51, 181, 211,
    213–4
    Akbar, 8, 90, 99, 109,
        114, 137–9, 145
    'Alamgir, 9, 186–8,
        195–6, 199–204

Jahangir, 152, 157–8,
    161–4
Shah Jahan, 161–4,
    182, 172–5, 182–4
    see also sultanates by
        name
Delhi, 46–8, 60, 74–5,
    81, 189, 195, 206
    Akbar, 74, 79, 109, 148
    Babur, 6, 15–6, 29,
        32–3, 48, 51
    Humayun, 67–9, 109–10
    Nadir Shah, 217
    Shah 'Alam II, 219
    Shah Jahan, 175–7
    Syed Ahmad Khan, 231
    Timur, 17, 29
    see also New Delhi;
        Shahjahanabad
Delhi sultans, 25, 40–1,
    45–7, 51–2, 67, 115,
    173, 233
    see also Ibrahim Lodi;
        Sher Shah Suri
dharma, 38–9, 81, 88
Dildar, 27
Dilras Banu, 192
Din-i Illahi, 135
Diu, 45–6, 60
diwan (hall), 111, 121–2,
    195–6, 225
diwan (office), 83, 99, 159,
    182, 194, 203, 221
Dravidian languages,
    41–2, 45, 158
Dughlat, Mirza
    Muhammad Haidar,
    56, 61
Durgavati, Rani of
    Garha-Katanga, 114
Dutch, 47, 155, 204–5,
    231
    see also Europeans

economy, 5, 8, 37, 67,
    42–6, 95–8, 150,
    155, 181, 204
economic historians,
    238

    see also Europeans;
        famine, inflation
Egypt, 47
elephants, 30–1, 50, 158,
    162, 191
    Akbar, 80–1, 84, 87,
        111, 114, 122
Elliot, H.M., 235
English East India
    Company, 47, 155,
    204–5, 217, 219–24,
    231–4
environment, 6–8, 34–7,
    41, 45–7, 51–4, 120,
    213, 219, 133, 156,
    188, 240
Erskine, William, 233,
    235
Esän Dawlat Begim, 18
escheat, 104–5
Ethiopians, 87, 117, 139,
    152, 157, 162–3, 188
eunuchs, 92
Europeans, 1–3, 5, 17,
    36, 44, 94, 230
    Akbar, 129, 176, 228
    'Alamgir, 191, 205
    captives, 173–4
    colonialism, 47, 155,
        209, 217, 219–20,
        231–7, 240
    global trade, 98, 114,
        117, 181, 204–5,
        238
    historians, 5, 134, 228,
        230–6
    Jahangir, 153, 155
    mercenaries, 5, 51, 156,
        217, 219
    sea power, 5, 9–10,
        44–7, 205
    Shah Jahan, 171, 177,
        181
    technology, 10, 129–30,
        231
    viewed by Indians, 38,
        221, 231–2
    See also Portuguese
        Empire

Faizi, 'Abu-al-Faiz, 113, 125, 139
Fakhr-un-Nissa Begum, 78
famine, 37, 67, 188, 200
Farrukh-siyar, 212–5
Fatawa-i 'Alamgiri, 191
Fatehpur, 75, 86–7, 109, 117–32, 138, 176
fatwa, 119, 187
faujdar, 99
Fergana, 16, 21, 25, 32
feudalism, 94, 105, 234, 236
First War for Indian Independence, 224, 233–4
forest-dwellers, 38–9, 42–4, 114
French, 47, 204, 219–20, 231
see also Europeans

Ganges macro-region, 35–6, 41, 45–7, 120, 213, 219
Ganges River, 7, 35–7, 45, 59–63, 184, 212, 219
gardens, 20, 122, 153, 175–9, 183
Babur, 22, 28, 32, 53, 117
charbagh style, 22
Garha-Katanga, 114
gender, 3, 38, 107, 111, 131, 213, 230, 240
Akbar, 78, 81, 84–92, 103, 112–16, 133–5, 139, 159
'Alamgir, 182, 190, 194
Babur, 15, 18, 22, 25–8, 32, 53, 132
Central Asian culture, 18, 20
Humayun, 57, 65, 67
hypergamy, 39, 86, 90–1, 229
Jahangir, 91, 145, 148, 160–5

patronage by imperial women, 161, 183
Shah Jahan, 159, 175
see also harem
genealogists, 105
George III, King, 221
ghazi (Islamic warrior), 47–8, 79, 126
Ghazni, 16, 24, 46–8, 60, 75–6
Ghulam Qadr Rohilla, 222
ghusal-khana, 111, 121, 194
globe, cartographic, 10, 129
Goa, 45–6, 128, 130, 153
Gokula, Raja of Jats, 194
gold, 98, 102, 129–30, 150, 155, 183, 191
Golkonda, 189, 206, 211, 214, 216
Sultanate, 45–6, 138, 162–3, 174, 180–2, 196, 199–201
Gonds, 114, 172
Gujarat, 46, 60, 75, 189, 211, 214
Akbar, 91, 117–8, 120, 128, 130, 139, 144
'Alamgir, 190, 205–6
Humayun, 59–61
Shah Jahan, 182, 184
Sultanate, 45–6, 91, 117–8
Gulbadan Begum, 18, 27–8, 54, 57, 120, 137
Gulrukh Begum, 27
gunpowder, *see* artillery
Gwalior, 52, 75, 80, 154, 172
Rajas of, 30, 32, 112

Habib, Irfan, 238
Hada Rajputs, 113
Hadith, 126–7
Hajj, 120–1, 129, 167, 199, 205

Hajji Begum, Empress of Akbar, 120
Hajji Begum, Empress of Humayun, 63
Hakim, Mirza, 7, 68, 77–8, 115, 119, 132, 137, 146
Hakim Beg, 154
hamam, 111, 121
Hamida Banu, 65, 82
Hanafi legal school, 19, 99, 124, 191
harem, 107, 150, 160, 190, 214–6, 230, 233
Akbar, 73, 84–8, 92, 111, 114, 121, 128
Shah Jahan, 175, 183
see also by name of woman; gender
Harkha Bai, 86–7
Hazara Afghans, 32
Hemu, Raja Vikramajit, 79, 81
Herat, 16, 26–7
Hijri calendar, 48, 131, 137, 170, 188
Himalayan mountains, 16, 35–7, 116, 157, 179
see also environment
Hindal, Mirza, 7, 15, 27, 54, 57, 62, 65–6, 76, 85
Hindu Kush mountains, 23
Hindus, 2–4, 38–40, 51–2, 81, 105, 116–7, 200, 212–3, 227, 235–7
Brahminic Hinduism, 3, 6, 34, 37–40, 128, 154, 183, 196
law, 99, 128, 134, 196
nationalism, 235, 237
temples, 89, 116, 168–9, 191, 196
see also by Mughal emperor; Rajputs
Hindustani language, 15, 37, 49, 134, 231–2

Hindutva, 237
Hira Kunwari, 86–7
Hissar Firoza, 182
historiography, 2, 5–6,
    10, 124, 134, 226–38
horses, 17, 44, 129
    Akbar, 84, 97, 103–6
    Babur, 29–31, 50–1
    dagh, 67, 103–4, 181
    sawar, 106, 149, 162,
        171, 181, 194
Hugli, 45–6, 173, 189,
    204
Humayun, 7, 56–69,
    76–7, 109–10, 133,
    137, 144, 235
    administration, 58–9,
        67–8, 94
    court culture, 57
    diplomacy, 65–6, 137
    exile, 62–6
    household, 57, 65, 68
    prince, 27, 29–32,
        47–8, 50, 54
    religion, 64
    warfare, 59–62, 66–8
Humayunnama, 57
hundi, 43, 98, 106
hunting, 28, 44, 180,
    191, 214
    Akbar, 80–1, 109, 124,
        138
    Jahangir, 145, 153,
        155–6, 159, 163
Husain Quli Khan, 116
Hyderabad, 189, 199,
    214, 216
    see also Golkonda
hypergamy, 39, 86, 90–1,
    229

'ibadat-khana, 122–4,
    127
Ibn al-'Arabi, 135
Ibrahim Lodi, Sultan of
    Delhi, 15–7, 29–32,
    41, 51
Ibrahim, son of Rafi-ush-
    Shan, 215

ijaradara, 150, 211, 231
imam, 125–6, 188
inam, 52, 89, 96, 115,
    125, 149, 196
India, Republic, 114,
    227, 234, 236–8
Indian Muslims, 6, 47,
    51, 58, 67, 76, 80,
    105, 127, 146, 160
    see also Afghans;
        Central Asians;
        Iranians
Indian National Archive,
    238
Indian Ocean, 36, 42,
    45–7, 51, 59, 120,
    204
Indians in Europe, 221,
    224, 232
Indo-Afghans, *see*
    Afghans
Indo-Persians, *see*
    Iranians
Indus macro-region,
    35–7, 45
Indus River, 15–6, 29,
    132–3, 217
inflation, silver, 98, 181
iqta, 49, 76, 94–8, 100,
    148, 211
Iranians, 2, 4, 18, 85,
    148–9, 182, 216–7
    Akbar, 76, 80, 96, 109,
        112–4, 127–8, 132
    'Alamgir, 188, 203
    Humayun, 65–6, 76
    Iran, 17, 40, 42, 45,
        83, 216
    Jahangir, 154, 158–60,
        165, 175
    Mughal refugees in,
        65–6, 163, 205
    Parsis, 40, 89, 128
    qizilbash, 23, 25, 29,
        66
    Shah Jahan, 163, 165,
        168
    see also Persian
        language; Safavids

Isfahan, 162
Islam, 2, 17–9, 45, 75–7,
    183, 198, 230–1
    Akbar, 89–93, 99, 104,
        108, 111, 115–37,
        146, 154
    'Alamgir, 187–8, 190–
        4, 196–7, 201–3
    Babur, 18–23, 25, 32,
        47–8, 51–3
    Caliph, 127, 196
    conversion from, 168,
        213
    conversion to, 39, 41,
        47, 67, 85, 112,
        173–4, 194
    Humayun, 64–6
    Jahangir, 153–5, 157
    jihad, 47, 115
    Mahdi, 54, 67, 115,
        132, 137
    Shah Jahan, 167–8,
        172, 175, 178, 183
    Sharia, 19, 99, 168
    Shi'ias, 2, 25–7, 83, 96,
        112, 168, 216
    Sufis, 3, 19, 25, 41, 52,
        64–7, 117, 135,
        183
    Sunnis, 112, 149, 187,
        191, 196, 216, 236
itihasa, 228
I'timad-ud-Daula, Ghiyas
    Beg Tehrani, 148–9,
    154, 158–60, 165,
    175
I'tisam-ud-Din, 232

Jadrup, Gosain, 154
Jagat Singh, Raja of
    Kangra, 179
jagirs
    Akbar, 97, 100, 103–7,
        109, 116, 133
    'Alamgir, 197–98,
        200–5, 211
    Jahangir, 149–50, 154,
        163
    Shah Jahan, 181–82

watan jagirs, 105, 133,
197–8
Jahanara Begum, 182–83,
185, 190
Jahandar Shah, 212, 215
Jahangir, 34, 48, 62, 73,
90, 143–65
administration, 149–
51, 156
architecture, 153
court culture, 151–7
diplomacy, 152, 162
ethnic policies, 157–8
Europeans, 153–5
household, 91, 145,
148, 160–5
Prince Salim, 7, 79, 87,
109, 139–47, 151,
163
religion, 153–5
warfare, 156–7, 162
Jahangir, Mirza, 25
Jaichand, Raja of Kangra,
116
Jains, 39–40, 89, 97,
106, 127–8, 140,
155, 229
Jaisalmir, 114
Jami' Mosque,
Shahjahanabad,
177–8, 225
Jani Beg Tarkhan, of
Sind, 133
janissary, 29
Japan, 94, 98
Jaswant Singh Rathor,
Raja of Marwar, 198
jati, 38–41, 99–100, 239
Jats, 40, 194–5, 213
jauhar, 113
Jaunpur, 60, 68, 75, 80,
114, 119, 140
Jesuits, 40–1, 127–30,
154–5, 164, 228, 230
see also Portuguese
Empire
jharoka, 122, 136, 157,
169
jihad, 47, 115

jizya, 40–1, 89, 116,
196–8, 213
Jodhpur, 113
Jujhar Singh, Raja of
Orchha, 172
Jumna River, 35–6, 109,
146, 175–6, 179

Kabul, 9, 46, 75, 84, 189,
216
Akbar, 75–8, 82, 119,
132
'Alamgir, 194, 205–06
Babur, 15–7, 23–9, 32,
44, 53–5, 84
Humayun, 7, 57, 60,
64–6, 68
Jahangir, 137, 148,
164
Shah Jahan, 180, 184
Kachhwaha, Rajputs, 81,
86–8, 145
Kaki, Shaikh Bakhtiar
Chishti, 32
Kalhana, 134
Kalinjar, 114
Kam Bakhsh, 206, 209,
211, 215
Kamla Devi, of Garha-
Katanga, 114
Kamran, Mirza, 7, 27–9,
54, 57, 64–6
Kamrup, 156, 189–90
Kanauj, 60, 64, 68, 82
Kangra, 116, 157, 161,
179
Karan Singh, Rana of
Mewar, 157
karkhanas, 107, 112, 121
Karnal, 216
Kashmir, 9, 16, 64, 179,
183–4, 217–8
Akbar, 109, 132–4, 137
'Alamgir, 189–190,
197, 206
Jahangir, 157, 162, 164
Kayasthas, 100, 217
Khair Ullah Musawir
(artist), 223

khalisa, 96–7, 149–50,
194, 198, 202, 214
khanazad, 102, 157, 169,
174, 197, 212–3
Khandesh, 46, 75, 146,
189, 206
Sultanate, 90–1, 114,
138–9, 146
Khanua, battle of, 31,
47–8, 81, 117
Khanzada Begum, 22, 54
Khanzada Humayun
Sultana, Regent of
Ahmadnagar, 139
Khatak Afghans, 194
Khatris, 40, 96, 100,
217
khilat, 102, 111, 161,
203, 222, 224, 233
Khuista Akhtar, 215
khutba, 25, 32, 62, 78,
125–6, 146, 217
Khwandamir, 58
Khyber Pass, 6, 198
Kishtwar, 157
Koh-i Nur diamond, 32,
217
Kora, battle of, 220
krori, 96–7
Kshatriya varna, 38–9
see also Rajputs
kufr, 185

Ladakh, 9, 16, 157, 190
Ladli, 159, 162, 165
Lahore, 60, 189, 193
Akbar, 109, 131–8
'Alamgir, 192–3, 205
Babur, 15, 29
Humayun, 67–8, 109
Jahangir, 148, 153,
155, 165, 175
Shah Jahan, 169, 175,
179, 182
Lahori, Shaikh 'Abd-al-
Hamid, 166
Lakshmi, Hindu goddess,
88
Lal Kunwar, 212

land revenues, 43, 67, 89, 92, 107, 109, 156, 179, 204
   Akbar, 86, 93–6, 102–3, 105, 115
   'Alamgir, 190, 200–1, 204
   Babur, 17, 33, 38–9, 41–4
   Humayun, 59, 65
   see also iqta; zabt; zamindars
Little Tibet, 9, 16, 157, 190
Lodi Afghans, 6–7, 15–6, 29–32, 34, 41, 51, 173
   see also Delhi Sultanate
London, 219, 221, 224
   see also English East India Company

ma'jun, 22, 53
macro-regions, 35–6, 45
Madras, 189, 204
   see also English East India Company
Mah Chuchak Begum, 77–8
Mahabat Khan, 163–64, 174
Mahabharata, 134
Maham Anaga, 74, 82–3
Maham Begum, 27
Mahdi, 54, 67, 115, 132, 137
Mahmud of Ghazni, 48
mahzar, 126–7
maize, 155
Majma'-al-Bahrayn, 183
Malik Ambar, 139, 152, 157, 162–3
Maliki legal school, 124
Malwa, 60, 75, 77, 83, 144, 173, 184, 206, 214
Man Singh, Raja of Amber, 86–9, 120, 132–3, 136, 145, 147, 158

Manbhawati Bai, 87, 145, 147
Mandu, 60, 68, 162
mansab
   Akbar, 100–9, 112–3, 116, 133, 139, 144–7
   'Alamgir, 195, 197–8, 200–1
   Jahangir, 149, 156–7, 159, 161–3, 165
   sawar, 106, 149, 162, 171, 181, 194
   Shah Jahan, 167, 172–4, 179–84
   zat, 106, 162, 171, 194
Manucci, Niccolao, 231
Marathas, 158, 204, 214–9, 222, 229, 235, 237
   'Alamgir, 195–206
   Shah Jahan, 174, 182
Mariam-uz-Zamani, 86
Marwar, 39, 46–7, 75, 81, 113, 168, 189, 198, 213
Marx, Karl, 226, 233, 235, 238–9
Mashhad, 83
Masuma Sultan Begum, 26
Mathura, 154, 194, 213
Mawarannahr, 16–7, 22–6, 33, 66
Mecca, 33, 47, 64, 147, 167
   Akbar, 78, 82, 91, 120–1, 129
   'Alamgir, 188, 196, 199, 204–5
Medini Rai, Charo Raja, 189–90
mehr, 87
Merv, 16, 22
Mewar, 39, 46–7, 75, 157, 189, 198, 213
   Akbar, 81, 89–90, 113
Mewat, 46, 48, 60, 67–8, 81, 105

military-fiscalist state, 75, 93
military history, 240
military labor market, 43, 51, 59, 67, 95, 156
Mill, James, 232
millenarian movements, 54, 67, 115, 132, 137
millennial sovereign, 3, 58, 127, 136, 167
mint, 98, 125, 137, 146, 150, 229
mir bakhshi (official), 83
Mir Jumla, 182
Mir Muhammad Mahdi, Khwaja, 54
Miran Mubarak Shah II, Sultan of Khandesh, 90
Mirza Nathan, 156
modernity, 240
moneylenders, 43, 98, 106
Mongols, 2–3, 6–7, 16–8, 21–4, 30–1, 80–8, 101, 128, 227
Monserrate, Fr. Antonio, S.J., 108, 129
monsoon, 36–7, 51, 54, 62, 188
   see also environment
Moscow, 33
mosque, see Islam
Moti Mosque, 192
Mu'azzam, see Bahadur Shah I
Mu'in-ud-Din Chishti, Khwaja, 86–7, 117, 154, 168, 183
Mu'nis-al-Arwah, 183
Mubarak, Shaikh, 113, 126
Muhammad, Prophet, 40, 126–7, 130, 137, 227
Muhammad 'Adil Suri, Sultan, 67
Muhammad Nasir al-Munshi (artist), 145

Muhammad Shah,
  Rangila, 215–8
Muhammad Sultan, 184
Muhammadi Raj, 198
Muhtasib (official), 187
Multan, 189
Mumtaz Mahal, 159,
  168, 175–6, 182–5
Munim Khan, 77, 83
Murad, Mirza, son of
  Akbar, 7, 87, 130,
  139, 144–6
Murad Bakhsh, son of
  Shah Jahan, 7, 184
Murad IV, Ottoman
  Sultan, 180
Murshid Quli Khan, 203,
  211
music, 21–2, 28, 112,
  122, 129, 191–2
Muslim nationalism,
  235
mut'ah, 124
Muzaffar Husain Khan,
  Mirza, of Gujarat, 91
Muzaffar Khan Turbati,
  Khwaja, 85, 96, 119
Mysore, 189, 214

Nadir Shah, 216–7
Naqshbandi, 19, 52, 77,
  115–7, 168, 180,
  187, 191
  see also Ahrar; Sirhindi
Nasir, Mirza, 7, 25
National Museum, India,
  238
naubat, 192
Navanagar, Gujarat, 190
navy, 5, 9, 45–7, 59, 114,
  117, 156, 205
Nawab-Wazir of Awadh,
  184, 216–7, 219–20,
  224
nazr, 102, 111, 203, 224,
  233
Nehru, Jawaharlal, 236,
  238
Neku-siyar, 215

New Delhi, 234
  see also Delhi
newswriter, 84, 99, 227,
  229
nikah, 84, 87, 91, 123–4
Nizam-al-Mulk, 213–14,
  216–17
Nizam-ud-Din Aulia,
  Shaikh, Chishti, 32
Nuno da Cuna, Viceroy,
  60
Nur Jahan, 159–65, 175

opium, 62, 64, 111, 151
Orchha, 146–7, 172, 194
Oriental despotism, 230
Orientalism, 232
Orissa, 114, 120, 163,
  183, 189, 206, 214
Ottomans, 2, 9, 25, 47,
  50–1, 59, 216, 229
  Akbar, 76, 117, 120, 127
  'Alamgir, 196
  Babur, 28–9
  Caliphate, 127, 196
  Jahangir, 149, 152, 156
  Shah Jahan, 171, 180

padshah (title), 25, 54,
  56, 64, 76, 79, 107,
  126, 146
Padshahi Mosque,
  Lahore, 192–3
Padshahnama, 170
Pakistan, 5, 10, 227,
  236–7
panchayats, 99
Panipat
  battle of 1526, 15–7,
    29–32, 56, 75, 81,
    216
  battle of 1760, 218–9
pargana, 96, 99
Parliament, British, 221
Parsis, 40, 89, 128
Parvez, Mirza, 7, 157,
  161, 163–4
Pashtun Afghans, 24,
  27, 29

pastoralists, 21–2, 39,
  43–4
Patna, 118
Peacock Throne, 166–7,
  171, 176, 187, 217,
  223
Persian language, 27, 42,
  65, 183, 191, 227–9,
  231–2
  Akbar, 88–9, 100, 113,
    128–30, 134–5
  Babur, 49
  culture, 8, 20, 22–3,
    188, 221–2, 235,
    238
  Jahangir, 151–2
Persian water wheel, 179
peshkash, 102
Peshwa, 214
Philip II, king of Spain
  and Portugal, 130
plague, 67, 200
Plassey, battle of, 220
poetry, 22, 28, 53, 88,
  105, 192, 214
Portuguese Empire, 41,
  45–7, 51, 204, 228,
  230
  Akbar, 114, 117–8,
    120, 127–30, 134
  'Alamgir, 190
  Humayun, 59–60
  Jahangir, 153–6, 164
  Portugal, 130
  Shah Jahan, 173
Punjab, 16, 35–7, 40, 60,
  68, 75–8, 195, 206,
  211–4, 216–8
  Akbar, 76–8, 116, 119,
    132–3
  'Alamgir, 184, 189,
    194–5, 206
  Babur, 29
  Humayun, 57, 64, 67–8
  Jahangir, 148, 159–60,
    164

Qadri, 183
qalandar, 64

qamargha, 80, 124
Qandahar, 9, 16, 57,
   159
   Akbar, 80, 109, 132–3,
      137
   Babur, 24, 29, 65–6
   Jahangir, 162–4
   Shah Jahan, 180–1
Qanun-i Humayuni, 58
Qaqshal Afghans, 77
qasba, 43, 98, 100, 114
qazi, 87, 99, 119, 187
qizilbash, 23, 25, 29, 66,
   216
Qur'an, 40, 47, 126–7,
   176, 188, 194
Qutb-al-Mulk, Sultan of
   Golkonda, 182
Qutluq Nigar Khanum,
   21

Rafi-ud-Darjat, 214–5
Rafi-ush-Shan, 215
Raigarh, 201
Rajaram Bhonsle
   Maratha, 201, 206
Rajasthan, 35–6, 39, 47,
   60, 64, 75, 89, 114,
   184, 211, 213–4
   Rajasthani language,
      88, 229
   see also Rajputs
Rajatarangini, 134
Rajputs, 39, 42, 44–5,
   67, 211, 213, 229,
   239
   Akbar, 76, 79–91, 94,
      103–5, 112–6, 128,
      145–6
   'Alamgir, 191, 197–9,
      201, 203
   Jahangir, 157–8, 160
   Shah Jahan, 168, 180
   see also Baghela; Bhati;
      Bundela; Hada;
      Kachhwaha;
      Rathor; Sisodia
Ram, Hindu deity, 237
Ramayana, 134

Rammohun Roy, 224
Ramnagar, Gujarat, 190
Rana Sanga of Mewar,
   47–8, 81
Ranthambhor, 113
Rashtriya Swayamsevak
   Sangh, 237
Rasila-i Mubin, 28
Rathor Rajputs, 39, 113–
   4, 168, 198, 213
Razmnama, 134
Red Fort, 176–9, 192,
   218–9, 225, 237–8
Risala-i Sahabiyya, 183
Risala-i Walidiyya, 52
Roe, Sir Thomas, 152
Rohilla Afghans, 216,
   222
Rohtas, Bihar, 120
Rohtas, Punjab, 132
Roman Catholicism, 40–
   1, 127–30, 154–5,
   164, 228, 230
   see also Portuguese
      Empire
Roshanara Begum, 190
Roshaniyya movement,
   132
Rumi Khan, title, 50,
   59–61
Ruqaiya Sultana Begum,
   84–5, 167

Sa'adat Khan, of Awadh,
   216–7
sadr, 80, 99, 115, 125
Safavids, 216, 229, 231,
   238–9
   Akbar, 77, 80, 120,
      127, 132–3, 137,
      199
   Babur, 22–25, 29, 47
   Humayun, 65–6
   Jahangir, 152, 158–9,
      162–3
   Shah Jahan, 171, 174,
      180, 185, 188
salatin, 215, 222
Saliha Sultan Begum, 26

Salim, Mirza, *see*
   Jahangir
Salim, Shaikh, Chishti,
   86–7, 117–18, 132,
   154
Salima Sultan Begum,
   Makhfi, 26, 68, 85
Salima Sultana Begum,
   120
saltpeter, 204
Samarkand, 16, 20–22,
   25, 48, 180
Sambhaji Bhonsle
   Maratha, 195, 198,
   200–1
Sangaram Sanga Singh,
   Rana of Mewar,
   47–8, 81
Sanskrit, 38–9, 41–2, 88,
   196, 228–9, 232
   Akbar, 105–6, 122,
      128, 134
Sanskritize, 39
Sarkar, Sir Jadunath, 235
sarkars, 99
Satgaon, 45–6
sati, 99, 230
Satnami movement, 194,
   195
sawar mansab, 106, 149,
   162, 171, 181, 194
   see also horses
Sayyid brothers, Hasan
   and Husain Ali Khan,
   212–5
Sayyids of Barha, 105,
   212
sepoy, 219–20, 224
Sepoy Mutiny, 224,
   233–4
Shah Abbas II, Safavid,
   188
Shah Abdul Ma'ali, 77–8
Shah 'Alam II, 218–24
Shah Ismail Safavid, 23–5
Shah Jahan, 7–8, 163–87,
   190, 196
   administration, 167,
      171, 179, 181, 194

Index

architecture, 165, 168, 174–9
court culture, 161, 167–71
diplomacy, 171
ethnic policies, 168, 182, 198
household, 159, 175
Prince Khurram, 7, 85, 145–9, 153, 157–67
religion, 167–8
warfare, 162–4, 171–4, 179–82
Shah Jahan II, 215
Shah Jahan III, 215, 219
Shah Safi Safavid, 180
Shah Shuja', 7, 174, 183
Shah Tahmasp Safavid, 65–6
Shah Wali Ullah, 231
Shahjahanabad, 177, 189, 192, 197, 211
India, Republic, 237–8
later Mughal emperors, 214–9, 222–5, 231, 233–4
Shah Jahan, 166, 176–9, 183
Shahr ashob, 231
Shahriyar, 7, 158, 162–4
Shahrukh, Mirza, of Badakhshan, 78, 91
Shahuji Bhonsle Maratha, 174, 201
Shaibani Khan Uzbek, 22–3
Shaikh Gadai Kamboh, 67, 80
Shaikh I'tisam-ud-Din, Mirza, 221
Shakr-un-Nissa Begum, 91
Shams-ud-Din Ataka Khan, 64, 73, 82–3
Sharaf-ud-Din Husain, Mirza, 91
Sharia, 19, 99, 168
Shattari, 52, 58, 168

Sher Afgan Khan, 159
Sher Shah Suri, Sultan, 61–4, 66–8, 92, 95–6
Shigrifnama-i Wilayat, 221
Shi'ias, *see* Islam
Shivaji Bhonsle Maratha, Chatrapati, 195–7, 237
Shudra varna, 38
Shuja'-ud-Daula, Nawab-Wazir of Awadh, 184, 219–20
Sidi Ali Rais, 76
sijdah, 169
Sikandara, 148
Sikhs, 40, 148, 195, 211, 213, 229
Sikri, 75, 86–7, 109, 117–32, 138, 176
Silk Road, 24, 44
silver, 98, 150, 155, 181
Sind, 29, 35–6, 60, 75, 163, 189
Akbar, 65, 74–5, 83, 90, 109, 132–3, 137
'Alamgir, 184–5
Humayun, 64–5
sipahsalar, 163, 173
Sirhind, 60, 67–8, 75, 79
Sirhindi, Shaikh Ahmad, Naqshbandi, 137, 153–4
Sirr-i Akbar, 183
Sisodia Rajputs, 39, 47, 89–90, 113, 157, 198
size of Mughal Empire, 1, 5, 8–9, 34–6, 58, 100, 156, 230
slaves, 25, 32, 57, 139, 174, 217
Akbar, 83, 87, 91, 117, 139
Babur, 28, 44, 57
Malik Ambar, 139, 152, 157, 162–3
sovereignty, 1–4, 8–10, 20, 41, 209, 224, 227–8

Akbar, 76–80, 86, 94, 113–20, 125–7, 130–31, 135–6
'Alamgir, 187–8
Babur, 25, 32, 47, 54, 57–8
Hindu, 79, 86, 88, 195–7, 237
Humayun, 57–9, 61–6, 76
Jahangir, 146, 164
Muhammad Shah, 217
Shah 'Alam II, 221–2
Shah Jahan, 167, 174, 187
Spain, 130
Srinagar, 16, 133
subadar, 99, 101, 116, 203
Subaltern Studies historiographic school, 239
succession, imperial, 4, 20, 48, 142–4
Akbar, 73, 75–9, 88, 107, 139–40, 142–8
'Alamgir, 182–8, 190, 193, 197–9, 203, 205–6, 209–11
Babur, 25–6, 54
Humayun, 57, 67–8, 76–7, 109–10, 133, 137
Jahangir, 140, 147, 158, 161–4, 175
later Mughal Emperors, 209, 219, 222, 224
Shah Jahan, 171–3, 180, 182–7, 190, 196
Sufis, 3, 19, 25, 41, 52, 64–7, 80, 117, 135, 183
see also Chishti; Naqshbandi; name of saint
Suhrawardi, 52, 67, 80
Sulaiman, Mirza, of Badakhshan, 57, 78

Sulaiman Shikoh, 185
sulh-i kul, 130
Sunnis, see Islam
Surat, 128, 130, 155, 195–6, 204–5
Suri Afghans, 61–4, 66–8, 92, 95–6
Swat, 16, 132
Swinton, Captain Archibald, 221
Syed Ahmad Khan, Sir, 231, 235
Syr Darya, 16, 22–6, 33, 66

Taj Mahal, 166, 175–6, 190
Tanjavur, 189, 201, 214
tanka, copper coin, 96, 98
Tansen, Mian, 112–3
Tardi Beg Khan, 79
tarikh genre, 227
Tarikh-i Alfi, 137
Tarikh-i Ilahi, 131
Tauhid-i Ilahi, 135
Telugu, 158, 200
Thatta, 75, 90, 133, 189, 206
Tibet, 9, 16, 157, 190
Timur, 7, 15–20, 52, 78, 90, 117, 127
  conquests, 15–7, 20, 29, 31–2, 48, 54, 217
  legacy, 16, 20, 24–7, 34, 40, 64, 132–3
  political economy, 19, 76, 84–5, 158, 167, 180, 227
  religion, 19, 52, 91, 109–11, 167

tobacco, 155
Todar Mal, Raja, 96, 106, 118
tomatoes, 155
Transoxiana, 16–7, 22–6, 33, 66
tulughma, 17, 31
Tura, 17
Turanis, see Central Asians
Turkey, see Ottomans
Turki language, 17, 20, 22, 26–8, 42, 49, 151
Turks, 3, 6, 15–24, 30, 39, 45, 64, 77, 116, 216
Tuzuk-i Jahangiri, 151, 170

Udaipuri Mahal, 190, 206
'ulama, 19, 77, 99, 115–16, 123–27, 146, 149, 168, 187, 191
'Umar Shaikh Mirza, of Fergana, 21
Uzbeks, 22–3, 77–8, 137, 171, 229, 231, 238

Vaishya varna, 38
varna, 38–41, 99–100, 239
Vedanta, 154
vegetarianism, 40, 128
Venice, 231
viceroy, 60, 128, 234
Victoria, Queen-Empress, 234
Vijayanagar, 45–6
Vikramajit, Raja of Gwalior, 30, 32

Vishnu, Hindu god, 88
Vishva Hindu Parishad, 237
Vrindavan, 89

wahdat al-wujud, 135
wakil, 79, 83
waqai', 227
watan jagirs, 105, 133, 197–8
wazir, 83, 148, 159–60
Weber, Max, 235
Western Ghats, 36
wine, 22, 28, 47, 52–3, 150–1, 165

Yasa, 17
Yemen, 120
Yusufzai Afghans, 27, 106, 132–3, 194

zabt, 96–8, 104, 118
Zain-ud-Din, Shaikh, Chishti, 193
zamin-bos, 169
zamindars, 42–3, 95–6, 98–100, 103–5, 115, 156, 171, 190, 200, 204
  see also land revenue
zat mansab, 106, 162, 171, 194
Zaynab Sultan Begum, 26
Zeb-un-Nissa Begum, 190, 192, 198
zimmi, 40
Zinat-un-Nissa Begum, 190
Zinda-fil, Shaikh Ahmad, 27, 65
Zoroastrians, 40, 89, 128